Mr. Fiske's Historical Works.

THE DISCOVERY OF AMERICA, with some account of Ancient America and the Spanish Conquest. With Maps. 2 vols. crown 8vo, $4.00.

OLD VIRGINIA AND HER NEIGHBOURS. 2 vols. crown 8vo, $4.00.

Illustrated Edition. Containing Portraits, Maps, Facsimiles, Contemporary Views, Prints, and other Historic Materials. 2 vols. 8vo, $8.00, *net*.

THE BEGINNINGS OF NEW ENGLAND, or the Puritan Theocracy in its Relations to Civil and Religious Liberty. Crown 8vo, $2.00.

Illustrated Edition. Containing Portraits, Maps, Facsimiles, Contemporary Views, Prints, and other Historic Materials. 8vo, $4.00, *net*.

THE DUTCH AND QUAKER COLONIES IN AMERICA. With 8 Maps. 2 vols. crown 8vo, $4.00.

Illustrated Edition. Containing Portraits, Maps, Facsimiles, Contemporary Views, Prints, and other Historic Materials. 2 vols. 8vo, $8.00, *net*.

NEW FRANCE AND NEW ENGLAND. With Maps. Crown 8vo, $2.00.

THE AMERICAN REVOLUTION. 2 vols. crown 8vo, $4.00.

Illustrated Edition. Containing Portraits, Maps, Facsimiles, Contemporary Views, Prints, and other Historic Materials. 2 vols. 8vo, $8.00, *net*.

THE CRITICAL PERIOD OF AMERICAN HISTORY. 1783–1789. Crown 8vo, $2.00.

Illustrated Edition. Containing Portraits, Maps, Facsimiles, Contemporary Views, Prints, and other Historic Materials. 8vo, $4.00, *net*.

THE MISSISSIPPI VALLEY IN THE CIVIL WAR. With 23 Maps and Plans. Crown 8vo, $2.00.

THE WAR OF INDEPENDENCE. In Riverside Library for Young People. 16mo, 75 cents.

HISTORY OF THE UNITED STATES FOR SCHOOLS. With Topical Analysis, Suggestive Questions, and Directions for Teachers, by FRANK A. HILL. 12mo, $1.00, *net*.

CIVIL GOVERNMENT IN THE UNITED STATES. CONSIDERED WITH SOME REFERENCE TO ITS ORIGINS. Crown 8vo, $1.00, *net*.

For Mr. Fiske's Historical and Philosophical Works and Essays see pages at the back of Volume II.

HOUGHTON MIFFLIN CO., BOSTON.

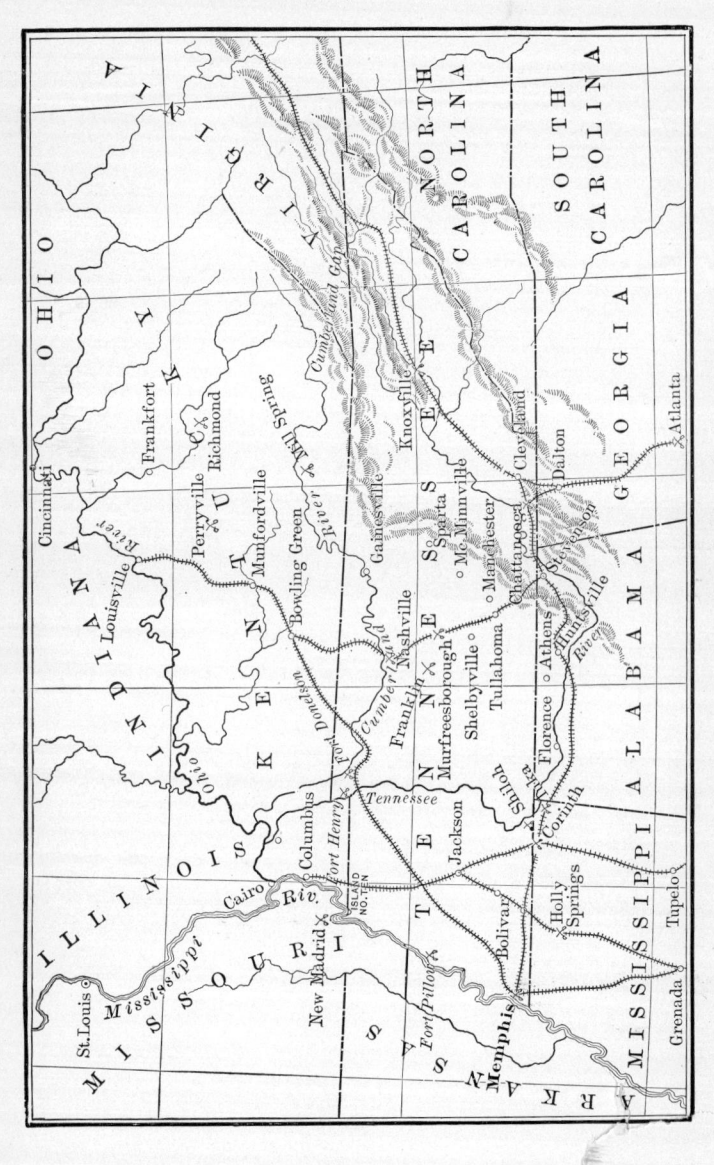

THE CAMPAIGNS IN TENNESSEE AND KENTUCKY

THE MISSISSIPPI VALLEY
IN THE CIVIL WAR

BY

JOHN FISKE

Bellum atrox, multiplex, immane, pertinax
cui simile nulla usquam narrat antiquitas
  JORNANDES, *De Rebus Geticis,* **xl.**

BOSTON AND NEW YORK
HOUGHTON MIFFLIN COMPANY
The Riverside Press, Cambridge

COPYRIGHT, 1900, BY JOHN FISKE
ALL RIGHTS RESERVED

TO
MY OLD FRIEND AND COLLEAGUE
MARSHALL SOLOMON SNOW
PROFESSOR OF HISTORY IN THE
WASHINGTON UNIVERSITY AT ST. LOUIS
THIS BOOK IS AFFECTIONATELY
INSCRIBED

PREFACE

IN the course of my annual visit to St. Louis, in the spring of 1886, I gave four lectures in the great theatre of the Exposition Building, in aid of the fund for erecting a monument to General Grant. These lectures touched upon many of the points treated in chapters i.–viii. of the present work, ending with the battle of Chattanooga. It is pleasant to remember the warm interest shown in the lectures by General Sherman, who "presided" on each occasion, and enlivened the suppers which followed with his abounding good-fellowship and his flashes of quaint wit. Those were evenings not to be forgotten.

The lectures — illustrated with maps, diagrams, views of towns and fortresses, landscapes and portraits, with the aid of the stereopticon — were given during two years in many cities north of Mason and Dixon's line, from Lewiston in Maine to Portland in Oregon. For illustrating battles a stereopticon is most useful, enabling a lecturer to throw upon the screen his diagrams and his landscapes by turns, so that each helps to elucidate the other. It is desirable, however, to keep a sharp lookout for accidents; as I was once rudely reminded in Buffalo, when my operator's hydrogen unexpectedly gave out, leaving me to expound the battle of Shiloh with nothing but a blackboard and piece of chalk!

After an interval of some years there was a renewed call for these lectures, and in the autumn of 1895 they were given in Sanders Theatre at Harvard University. The interest thus freshly aroused led me to prepare the present volume. It contains a great deal of material that I never put into the lectures, some of it written before 1886, some of it after. The ninth chapter, on the "crowning mercy" of Nashville, has been added quite lately.

The present volume does not belong to the series in which I have for several years been dealing with the history of the United States. Should I ever, in the course of that work, arrive at the Civil War, it will of course be treated on a very different plan from that of this book, which is a purely military narrative, restricted in its scope, and detached from the multitude of incidents which in a general history would form its context.

In preparing this narrative I have had due recourse to the abundant printed sources of information, and owe much besides to personal association with many of the actors. While the war was going on it was, to me as to others, a subject of most intense moment, and its incidents were burnt into the tablets of memory. I kept large maps, and marked the movements of the Union and Confederate forces, as reported from day to day, with blue-headed and red-headed pins. Among the friends of my childhood who gave up their lives for their country, one in the army and another in the navy — General Mansfield and Commander Renshaw — stand before me with especial vividness. In later years I valued highly the friendship of Sherman, McDowell, and Ericsson; and I had more or less acquaintance — sometimes slight, but unfailingly fruitful in suggestions — with Sheridan, Meade, McClellan, Rosecrans, Garfield, Gibbon, Pope, Geary, Francis Walker, "Baldy" Smith, Hazen, Hancock, Beauregard, Preston Johnston, and one of the noblest Romans of all, Joseph Johnston, whose hand-grip at eighty years of age was like that of a college athlete, and whose shrewd and kindly talk was as delightful as his presence was imposing.

Among those to whom specific thanks are due for valuable counsel must be mentioned Colonel Snead, chief of staff to Sterling Price and member of the Confederate congress, author of that excellent book, "The Fight for Missouri;" Major Hutchinson, chief of staff to General Bowen, whose heroic resistance to Grant is mentioned on page 230; Colonel Samuel Simmons, first on Lyon's staff and later on that of Rosecrans; Colonel Henry Hitchcock, of Sherman's staff; Colonel Henry Stone, of Thomas's staff; General Fullerton, chief of staff to Gordon Granger; General Fry, chief of staff to Buell; General Cullum, chief of staff to Halleck; and especially my dear friends, now passed away, Dr. Eliot, chancellor of Washington University, and Colonel Gantt, sometime of McClellan's staff, whose hospitable house was for many years my home during my visits to St. Louis.

To that profound student of military history, the late John Codman Ropes, my obligations are greater than I can express, not so much for any specific suggestions intended for this book, as for the liberal education which came from knowing him. During a peculiarly intimate friendship of thirty years, the cosy midnight hours that we spent in discussing his favourite themes were many and full of profit.

It may be observed that this book sometimes alludes to the Confederates as "rebels." I have been surprised to find how generally people seem to think that some sort of stigma is implied by that word. For my own part, I have sympathized with so many of the great rebellions in history, from the revolt of the Ionian cities against Darius Hystaspes down to the uprising of Cuba against the Spaniards, that I am quite unable to conceive of "rebel" as a term of reproach. In the present case, it enables one to avoid the excessive iteration of the word "Confederate," while it simply gives expression to the undeniable fact that our Southern friends were trying to cast off an established government. In England, to this day, Cromwell's admirers do not hesitate to speak with pride of the Great Rebellion. While my own sympathies have always been intensely Northern, as befits a Connecticut Yankee, I could still in all sincerity take off my hat to the statue of Lee when I passed it in New Orleans. His devotion to the self-government which seemed to him in mortal peril was no more reprehensible than the loyalty of Falkland to the prerogative of Charles I., though in both cases the sentiments were evoked under circumstances which made them dangerous to the nation's welfare.

In treating such a subject as the present one, the difficulties in ensuring complete accuracy of statement and perfect soundness of judgment are manifold. If my opinions are sometimes strongly expressed, they are always held subject to revision.

CAMBRIDGE, *February* 24, 1900.

CONTENTS

CHAPTER I

FROM ST. LOUIS TO BELMONT

Scope of the present narrative	1
Importance of the border states in 1861	2
Of Virginia	3, 4
Of Maryland	4, 5
Of Kentucky and Missouri	5, 6
Position of Missouri in the causal sequence of events	6, 7
Some account of Francis Preston Blair and his family	8, 9
Claiborne Jackson and his schemes	10
Nathaniel Lyon, and Blair's "Home Guards"	10
Plots and counter-plots; "rebellion against Missouri"	11
President Lincoln, through General Scott, authorizes certain gentlemen to act as a Committee of Safety	12
Lyon removes the arms from the arsenal and guards the neighbouring hills	13
The state troops select a camping-ground on Lindell's Meadow and enclose it	13
Camp Jackson, its avenues and its denizens	14
Why Blair and Lyon deemed prompt action necessary	14
Arrival of arms from Baton Rouge	15
Hospitalities at Camp Jackson; a visitor in bombazine	15, 16
A lady with spurs	16
Lyon summons the Committee of Safety	17
Replevin *vs.* capture	18
Camp Jackson surrenders to Lyon	19
A secessionist flag in Pine Street is hauled down	20
Colloquy on a street-car	20

Contents

The governor appoints Sterling Price to command his secessionist militia	21
Lyon and Blair have a conference with Jackson and Price at the Planters' Hotel	22
Lyon takes possession of Jefferson City	22
And routs the secessionists at Booneville	23
Sigel's fight at Carthage	24, 25
Appointment of Fremont to command the Department of the West	25
Battle of Wilson's Creek, and death of Lyon	26, 27
His great qualities	28
Causes of Fremont's popularity	28, 29
His "emancipation proclamation"	29
His military incapacity	30
Fate of Mulligan's detachment at Lexington	31, 32
Fremont is superseded by Hunter	33
Who in turn is superseded by Halleck	34
Halleck's incapacity	34
Curtis defeats Van Dorn at Pea Ridge	35–37
Importance of these early campaigns	38
Affairs in Kentucky; attempt to preserve an attitude of neutrality	39, 40
Previous career of Leonidas Polk; he enters Kentucky and fortifies the bluffs at Columbus	41
Zollicoffer advances through Cumberland Gap	41
Kentucky declares for the Union	42
Previous career of Ulysses Simpson Grant	43
He is made brigadier-general of volunteers	44
He seizes Paducah; importance of the movement	45
Oglesby goes in pursuit of guerrillas	46
Grant defeats Pillow on the flats of Belmont	47
His troops disperse for pillage, but are with difficulty set in order	48
The Confederates attempt unsuccessfully to cut off their retreat	48, 49

Comments on the Belmont affair 49-51
Grant's own comment 51

CHAPTER II
FORT DONELSON AND SHILOH

The first Confederate line of defence 52
Albert Sidney Johnston 53
George Henry Thomas 54
He destroys Zollicoffer's force at Mill Spring . . . 55
Grant captures Fort Henry 56
Position of Fort Donelson 57
Its commanders, — Floyd, Pillow, and Buckner . . . 58
Grant moves upon Fort Donelson and invests it . . 58, 59
Artillery battle between fort and gunboats 60
Sortie of the Confederate garrison 61
Ferguson Smith storms the Confederate entrenchments . 62
While Lew Wallace seizes the Charlotte road and cuts off
  their retreat 62, 63
Escape of Floyd and Pillow 63
Grant's only terms: "Unconditional surrender" . . . 63
Importance of the victory 64
It completely shattered the first Confederate line of defence 65
Halleck's injustice toward Grant 66-69
Strategic importance of Corinth 69
The assembling of forces at Corinth 70
Arrival of Braxton Bragg 70, 71
Importance of Pittsburg Landing 71
Opinion of the Count of Paris 72
The position at Pittsburg Landing 72-74
Arrangement of the Federal forces at Shiloh . . . 73
The open front between Owl and Lick creeks . . . 74
The eve of battle; difference of opinion between Johnston
  and Beauregard 75
How far were the Federals surprised at Shiloh? . . . 76

Contents

Grant was not expecting any attack on Sunday morning, nor was Sherman	77
The Federals were surprised	78
The opening attack on Prentiss's division	78, 79
Grant hastens up from Savannah Landing and meets Lew Wallace at Crump's Landing	79
How Wallace's march was delayed	80
Grant's order should have been more specific	81
Johnston's plan of attack	81
The slow pushing back of Prentiss	82
And of McClernand and Sherman	82, 83
Glorious stand of Prentiss in the "Hornet's Nest," supported by Hurlbut and William Wallace	84
Death of Johnston	84
Victory was not within his grasp; grave mistake in his tactics	85
The long stoppage at the Hornet's Nest was fatal to the Confederates	85, 86
Prentiss is captured and William Wallace mortally wounded	86
Failure of the Confederates to take Pittsburg Landing	87
Difference of opinion between Bragg and Beauregard	88
The fundamental facts in the case	89
Arrival of Nelson and Lew Wallace	90
Buell's arrival at Savannah on Saturday evening	91
Nelson's report of Grant's expectations on that evening	91
Grant's letter to Buell written Sunday noon	92
How Buell and Grant spent the remainder of the day	92
A cold bivouac in the rain	93
Arrival of Crittenden and McCook	94
The opposing forces on Monday	94, 95
Conditions of Monday's battle; defeat of the Confederates	96
Why was there no pursuit after Shiloh?	97, 98
Sherman's humorous explanation	99
Terrible slaughter	99
Significance of the battle	100

CHAPTER III

THE CAPTURE OF NEW ORLEANS

The second Confederate line of defence	101
Island Number Ten	101
Pope captures New Madrid	102
How the Federal army sawed out a channel through the submerged forest	103
How the Carondelet ran past the batteries	104, 105
Surrender of the garrison; results of the victory	106
Importance of rivers and of the river fleets in the Civil War	107, 108
The Titanic work done by the navy	108–110
Naval inferiority of the South	110, 111
Military importance of New Orleans	112
Need for prompt action	113
Views of President Lincoln and Commander Porter	114
Benjamin Franklin Butler, his military qualifications	115
Previous career of David Farragut; he is appointed to command the fleet	115, 116
Character of the fleet	117
Forts Jackson and St. Philip	118
The chain of anchored schooners, and the Confederate rams	119
A difficult task for wooden vessels	120
Porter bombards Fort Jackson	121
Difference of opinion between Farragut and Porter	121, 122
The gunboat Itasca breaks the chain of schooners	122, 123
The fleet advances up the Mississippi river	123, 124
Farragut's flag-ship in danger	125
Destruction of the Confederate fleet; fate of the ram Manassas	126
Farragut's arrival at New Orleans	127, 128
Surrender of Forts Jackson and St. Philip	128, 129
Arrival of Butler; the selection of such a man to govern New Orleans was an insult to the people of the city	129

Opinion of the Count of Paris as to the execution of Mumford 130
The notorious " woman order ; " " Beast Butler " . 131, 132
Value of prompt action in warfare 132

CHAPTER IV

FROM CORINTH TO STONE RIVER.

Halleck takes the armies of Pope, Grant, and Buell, and advances against Corinth 133
Which Beauregard forthwith evacuates 134
Much cry and little wool 135
Breaking of the second Confederate line of defence . . 136
Naval battle at Memphis 137
Van Dorn begins to fortify Vicksburg 138
The Confederate ram Arkansas 139
Destruction of the Arkansas; Van Dorn fortifies Port Hudson 140
A melancholy tale of lost opportunities 141
Military and political importance of Chattanooga . 142, 143
Mitchel's brilliant raid in Alabama 143
Why Buell was "slow;" because he had an Old Man of the Sea, yclept Halleck, bestriding his shoulders . . 144
Halleck's innocent hope that the enemy would do what he desired him to do 145
Beauregard is superseded by Braxton Bragg, who leaves Van Dorn to cover Vicksburg, while he himself seizes Chattanooga 145
How Halleck frittered away a golden opportunity . . 146
How the said Halleck was called to Washington as general-in-chief, because of Grant's victory at Fort Donelson, Grant's and Buell's at Shiloh, and other western successes 147
How he forthwith proceeded to do as the enemy wished by removing McClellan's army from the James river, and thus exposing the northern states to invasion 148

Contents

Bragg is emulous of Lee, and prepares the way by great cavalry raids 149
Meanwhile Buell is "slow" because the government will give him no help in getting cavalry, but expects him to chase cavalry with infantry 149
Kirby Smith defeats Nelson at Richmond, in Kentucky . 149
Bragg invades Kentucky 150
Panic throughout the northern states 151
Defect in the Confederate strategy; Kirby Smith's movements should have been distinctly controlled by Bragg; too many cooks 152
Battle of Perryville 153
Battle of Iuka 154
Rosecrans defeats Van Dorn at Corinth 155
Van Dorn is unwisely superseded by Pemberton . . 155
Buell is made a scapegoat for Halleck 156
How Buell incurred the enmity of Oliver Morton and Andrew Johnson 157, 158
Buell is superseded by Rosecrans 159, 160
The battlefield of Stone river or Murfreesboro, and the arrangement of the Confederate troops . . . 161
The arrangement of the Union troops at Stone river . 162
Rosecrans's plan of attack 163
Bragg's plan of attack 164
Faulty position of the Union right wing . . . 165, 166
McCook's want of vigilance 167
The Confederate attack, and rout of two Union divisions 167, 168
The Union army thrown upon the defensive . . . 169
Sheridan's magnificent fighting 170
Thomas stands invincible, while Rosecrans forms a new battle-front 171
Failure of Bragg's original plan 172
Terrific but fruitless attacks upon Palmer, who holds the Round Forest 173
The Confederates baffled **174**

Results of the day's fighting 175
Renewal of the battle; retreat of the Confederates . . 176
Comments 177, 178

CHAPTER V

THE VICKSBURG PROBLEM

Physical characteristics of the Mississippi river . . . 179
The bayous 180
The bluffs 181
Mutual relations of Vicksburg and Port Hudson . 182, 183
Unapproachableness of Vicksburg from the South . . 184
And from the north 185
How Halleck lost the opportunity in 1862 . . . 186
Grant's position and forces at Corinth 187
Grant's first movement against Vicksburg by way of the Mississippi Central railroad 188, 189
The outflanking strategy 189, 190
The task of supplying an army; difficulties and dangers attendant upon lengthening the line of communications 191, 192
Rivers more secure than lines of railroad . . . 193, 194
Insecurity of Grant's position at Oxford . . . 194, 195
Sherman moves down the Mississippi river against Vicksburg 196
Mr. Davis's mistake in reinforcing Vicksburg from Tennessee, rather than from Arkansas 197
Forrest's raid upon the railroads and telegraph lines in Tennessee 198
Van Dorn captures Holly Springs, and Grant is thus compelled to retreat upon Grand Junction . . . 199
Sherman is defeated at Chickasaw bayou . . . 200–202
McClernand's ambitious schemes 202–205
Capture of Arkansas Post 205
McClernand and his "star" 206
Evils of amateur generalship 207

Contents

Why Grant moved to the west bank of the Mississippi	208
His first plan, thus abandoned, was the correct one, had he been properly supported by the government	209
The situation in front of Vicksburg; various alternatives	210, 211
"Grant's big ditch"	212
The Lake Providence experiment	213, 214
The Yazoo Pass experiment	214–217
Fort Pemberton proves an insuperable obstacle	217, 218
The Big Sunflower experiment	218–220

CHAPTER VI

THE FALL OF VICKSBURG

The armoured gunboats Queen of the West and Indianola	221, 222
Moral effect of a dummy monitor	222
Farragut's fleet runs past the batteries of Port Hudson	224
Complaints against Grant; a gloomy outlook	224, 225
Grant's dogged determination	225
Fresh alternatives	226
The great southward movement to Bruinsburg	227, 228
Grant crosses to the east bank of the Mississippi	228, 229
First victory; at Port Gibson	229, 230
The Confederates evacuate Grand Gulf	230
The critical moment in a great career	231
A situation bristling with difficulties	232
Grant's sublime audacity; he cuts loose from his communications	233, 234
Grierson's extensive cavalry raid	234
Grant moves eastward toward the city of Jackson	235
Second victory; at Raymond	236
Third victory; at Jackson	236
Pemberton completely hoodwinked; Grant turns westward	237
Fourth victory; at Champion's Hill; decisive	238
Fifth victory; at Big Black river	239
Fall of Haines Bluff	240

A marvellous campaign 241
Vicksburg is invested 242
Two unsuccessful assaults; why the second one was made 243
Dismissal of McClernand for insubordination . . . 244
The siege of Vicksburg; mule meat in demand . . 245
Surrender of Vicksburg 246
The turning point of the Civil War 247

CHAPTER VII

CHICKAMAUGA

Importance of Chattanooga 248
The loyal mountaineers of the Alleghanies . . . 249
The upper Tennessee river not a good line of communications 250
How the opportunity was lost in 1862 251
The cavalry raids of 1863 252
Their diligence in the destruction of railroads . . . 253
Why Rosecrans was so long in starting 254
How Halleck tried to hasten matters, and how Rosecrans snubbed him 254, 255
Comparative "slowness" of Rosecrans and Buell . . . 255
Rosecrans decides to move 256
By skilful manœuvres he drives Bragg back upon Chattanooga 256, 257
Description of the difficult mountainous approaches to Chattanooga 258-260
In moving over the mountains Rosecrans greatly extends his front 261
Bragg evacuates Chattanooga and moves to Lafayette . 262
Seeds of disaster in the extension of the Union lines . . 262
Two alternatives presented to Rosecrans . . . 263
He chooses the wrong one 263, 264
An appalling situation 264
Bragg loses the golden opportunity 265

Rosecrans slowly concentrates his forces; McCook's delay, and its evil results	266
Arrival of Longstreet with his corps	267
The problem at Chickamauga	268
First day of the battle	269
Morning of the second day; the fatal order	270
The dire catastrophe; rout of the Federal right wing	271, 272
An appalling crisis	272
Thomas, with the left wing, retreats to Horseshoe Ridge	273
Some of the most desperate fighting recorded in history	274
The "Rock of Chickamauga"	275
Rosecrans and Garfield misinformed	276
A brave man stunned by sudden calamity	277
The battle was lost, but Thomas saved the army	278
Awful slaughter	279, 280

CHAPTER VIII

CHATTANOOGA

Bragg seizes Lookout Mountain and Missionary Ridge, and lays siege to Rosecrans in Chattanooga	281, 282
Joseph Wheeler attacks the supply trains, and the rain proves even a worse enemy	283
Hooker arrives upon the scene with two corps	284
Grant is placed in command of all the forces west of the Alleghanies, and supersedes Rosecrans by Thomas	285
Jefferson Davis utters a prophecy from Pulpit Rock	286
Grant arrives at Chattanooga	287
A happy thought occurs to "Baldy" Smith	287
The scheme for opening a new line of communications through Brown's Ferry	288, 289
Its complete success	290
Hooker occupies Lookout valley and repels a midnight attack by Longstreet	291
The siege of Chattanooga was thus raised	292

Contents

Bragg sends Longstreet into eastern Tennessee to crush Burnside	293
What could have induced him thus to weaken his army?	294
A possible explanation	295
Sherman starts from Vicksburg for Chattanooga, and shows that, while weighted with Halleck, he can move as slowly as Buell	296
But a despatch from Grant frees him, and he arrives	297
Importance of Chickamauga station	298
Sherman's stealthy advance toward it	298, 299
Thomas captures Orchard Knob and the adjacent hills	300
Breaking of the bridge at Brown's Ferry	301
Sherman reaches the north end of Missionary Ridge	301, 302
His disappointment	302, 303
Effect of the broken bridge upon Hooker's movements	303, 304
Geary leads the way up Lookout Mountain	305
Hooker follows; storming of the mountain; the "battle above the clouds"	306
The stars and stripes hoisted over Pulpit Rock	307
Absurdity of the notion that the battle of Chattanooga was fought as Grant originally planned it	307, 308
Progress of Sherman's attack upon Bragg's right	308
Hooker moves against Bragg's left by way of Rossville	309
Bragg weakens his centre to strengthen his right	310
Grant decides to threaten Bragg's centre, in order to aid Sherman's attack	310
The orders to the storming line	311
Magnificent bayonet charge of Thomas's four divisions	311
Without orders they continue the charge up the slope of Missionary Ridge	312
A moment of anxiety for Grant and Thomas	312
The four divisions reach the crest of the ridge and crush Bragg's centre	313
While Hooker routs his left wing; total defeat of the Confederates	313, 314

Contents

Greatness of the Union victory 314
Grand scenery of the battlefield 315
The Mississippi valley recovered 316

CHAPTER IX

NASHVILLE

At the beginning of 1864 each of the four cardinal victories
   in the West had been won under the leadership of Grant . 317
But Lee, in the East, still maintained as bold a front as ever 317
Need for unity of operations 318
Grant is made lieutenant-general and placed in command of
   all the armies of the United States . . . 318, 319
In his first Virginia campaign he was outgeneralled by Lee 320
The popular notion that Grant was averse to manœuvring . 321
In fact his manœuvres were frequent and skilful . 321, 322
After three months of alternate hammering and manœu-
   vring, Grant's problem was reduced to detaining Lee at Pe-
   tersburg until the whole Confederacy should be knocked
   away from behind him 323
The latter part of the work was done by the army with
   which Sherman started from Chattanooga for Atlanta . 323
Sherman, having succeeded Grant in the chief command
   of the West, unites its three armies under McPherson,
   Thomas, and Schofield 324
Bragg is superseded by Joseph Johnston . . . 324
Sherman's object is secondarily to take Atlanta, but pri-
   marily to destroy Johnston's army 325
How the golden opportunity was lost at Resaca . 325, 326
Johnston, having been slowly pushed back upon Atlanta, is
   superseded by Hood 327
Hood's previous career 328
What the Union generals thought of his appointment . . 329
Finding it impossible, after hard fighting, to save Atlanta,

Hood evacuates it, and thus creates a difficult situation for
  Sherman 330
Hood assumes the offensive and strikes at Sherman's com-
  munications 331
He makes up his mind to invade Tennessee . . . 332
His dreams of glory, and his fatal delay at Tuscumbia . 333
Sherman marches to the sea-coast, leaving Thomas to dispose
  of Hood 334
Ought not Sherman to have left more men with Thomas? . 335
Thomas's forces, present and prospective . . . 336, 337
Hood crosses the Tennessee river at Florence, and marches
  northward 337
Schofield's retreat through Spring Hill to Franklin . . 338
Hood loses an opportunity 339
Position of the Federal army at Franklin 340
Further retreat upon Nashville ordered by Thomas . . 341
Furious charge of the Confederates upon the Federal lines at
  Franklin 341, 342
They are defeated with terrible slaughter . . . 343, 344
Wilson defeats the Confederate cavalry 343
Schofield effects a junction with Thomas at Nashville . . 344
Hood follows and entrenches himself close by . . 344, 345
Why Thomas was not ready to attack Hood . . . 345, 346
Grant's impatience 347
He sends Logan on a needless journey to Louisville, and
  going himself to Washington, is barely saved from com-
  mitting a gross act of injustice 348
Grant's unsatisfactory account of this affair in his "Memoirs" 349
Position of Thomas's army at Nashville 350
Position of Hood's army 351
Hood's imminent peril 352
Splendid tactics of Thomas 353, 354
Advance of the Federal right wing . . . 354, 355
Outposts taken; Hood's left wing broken 355
Hood's new position next day; the salient at Shy Hill . 356

Contents

The assault upon Overton Hill	357
The assaults upon Shy Hill; total rout of the Confederates	358
A pursuit of ten days, and annihilation of Hood's army	359
Results of Thomas's great victory	359, 360

MAPS

(All from sketches by the author)

The Campaigns in Tennessee and Kentucky	*Frontispiece*
The Strategic Position of Missouri	*Facing page* 24
Fort Donelson, February 13–16, 1862	56
Shiloh, April 6, 1862, morning	74
Shiloh, April 6, 1862, evening	86
Shiloh, April 7, 1862, morning	94
New Madrid and Island Number Ten, March 3–April 7, 1862	102
Stone River, December 31, 1862, morning	162
Stone River, December 31, 1862, evening	172
Grant's First Movement against Vicksburg, November 24, 1862–January 10, 1863	188
The Lake Providence Experiment, February and March, 1863	214
The Yazoo Pass and Big Sunflower Experiments, February and March, 1863	216
Vicksburg and its Approaches, May, 1863	226
Chattanooga and its Approaches, September, 1863	260
Chickamauga, September 19, 1863	266
Chickamauga, September 20, 1863, morning	268
Chickamauga, the fatal order	270
Chickamauga, September 20, 1863, evening	274
Environs of Chattanooga, October–November, 1863	288
Campaigns of Sherman and Thomas in 1864	326
Franklin, November 30, 1864	340
Nashville, December 15, 1864	350
Nashville, December 16, 1864	356

THE MISSISSIPPI VALLEY IN THE CIVIL WAR

CHAPTER I

FROM ST. LOUIS TO BELMONT

MY object in the present narrative is to exhibit an outline of the military events which brought about the overthrow of the Southern Confederacy by turning its left flank. In this mighty work the successive conquests of Vicksburg and Chattanooga were cardinal events of no less importance than the final conquest of Richmond. We have here to follow, from their first small beginnings in the state of Missouri, the military transactions, growing ever vaster in dimensions, which culminated in the course of the year 1863 in the capture of the two great strongholds that dominated the lower waters of the Mississippi and the upper reaches of the Tennessee. After the close of this continuous story, a crowning episode will claim our attention, in the decisive victory at Nashville, which left Sherman's army free to advance upon the rear of Vir-

<small>Scope of the present narrative.</small>

ginia, thus sealing the doom of the exhausted Confederacy. Our story may best begin by calling attention to the circumstances which made Kentucky and Missouri supremely important in the spring of 1861.

While all the Gulf states were prompt in following the lead of South Carolina and passing ordinances of secession, the action of their neighbours to the northward was slow and vacillating. The people of the border states did not in general wish to secede, but many of them believed in the constitutional right of secession, and held that if the Gulf states wished to leave the Union the Federal government had no right to retain them by force. Accordingly there was no decisive action until after the fall of Fort Sumter and President Lincoln's proclamation calling upon the loyal states for 75,000 men to aid in restoring the authority of the government. Then the southern zone of border states — North Carolina, Tennessee, and Arkansas — at once seceded from the Union and joined the Confederacy. Enormous political consequences now depended upon the action of the four remaining border states, — Maryland, Virginia, Kentucky, and Missouri. The most powerful of the four, — the state which had given birth to Washington and Jefferson and Marshall; the state which had once been ar-

Importance of the border states.

rayed in sympathy with Massachusetts and in opposition to South Carolina in its attitude toward negro slavery, — the great state of Virginia, was won over to the side of the Confederacy, yet not without a bitter struggle. So irreconcilable was the diversity of interests and sentiments that the state was torn in twain, the doctrine of secession received an unexpected and unwelcome illustration, and the sturdy Virginians west of the Alleghanies straightway formed a new commonwealth pledged to the defence of the Union. But even as thus curtailed, the accession of Virginia to the southern cause was an event of the first importance. When once her hand had found this thing to do, she did it with all her might, and for lavish expenditure of blood and treasure Virginia was foremost in the War of Secession. It was not simply, however, in the physical strength which she added to the Confederacy that the accession of Virginia was so important. There was the moral prestige of the grand historic associations which clustered about the home of Washington; there was the military advantage of a position which threatened the Federal capital and exposed the soil of the northern states to invasion; there was the spell which these things cast upon the imagination of European statesmen, tempting them to interfere in the struggle; and moreover, Virginia was still.

Virginia.

as in the Revolutionary period, a country fertile in leaders of men. But for her secession it would doubtless have been Robert Lee, with Stonewall Jackson as his right arm, that would have led the Union soldiers to speedy victory. Take away from the history of the southern army these names with those of Joseph Johnston, Ambrose Hill, Ewell, Stuart, Early, and Pickett, and how different that history would have been! It is not too much to say that, except for Virginia, the summer of 1862 might have seen the rebellion completely suppressed. Was it not Virginia that, stubborn and defiant to the last, held even the indomitable conqueror of the southwest at bay until his great lieutenant, sweeping from the mountains to the sea and turning northward straight toward Richmond, had cut away from her all the rest of the Confederacy, leaving her to fall alone, vanquished but not humiliated?

The task of suppressing so great a rebellion was herculean. All the world except the Americans of the northern states — and some even of these — believed it to be impossible. If the remaining border states had followed the lead of Virginia, it might have proved to be impossible.

Maryland. The attitude of Maryland in April, 1861, was very dangerous. Endless gratitude is due to the unwavering loyalty of Governor Hicks, and to the promptness with which John Andrew hurried the forces of Massachusetts to the front. But for these men the first task of the Federal army might have been to win back the Federal capital.

As the action of Maryland was thus important by virtue of her position, so the action of Kentucky and Missouri was important by virtue of their sheer magnitude. Not that the strategic position was not here, too, of vast importance. The panic along the right bank of the Ohio, upon General Bragg's approach in the summer of 1862, may serve to remind us how unpleasant it would have been for the North had the area and the forces of Kentucky been added to the Confederacy; and the mischief that might have been wrought by a seceding Missouri, controlling the Father of Waters as far as Burlington and taking the state of Illinois in flank, would perhaps have been still more serious. But the magnitude of these two states was alone enough to make their action of critical importance. South Carolina, with her six attendant states upon the Gulf, contained a population of about 5,000,000 souls; the secession of the southern zone of border states immediately added 2,500,000 to this; the secession of Virginia added another million. It was high time for this to stop.

Missouri and Kentucky, if they had left the Union, would have carried over yet another 2,500,000 souls to the Confederacy, besides adding to it an area nearly as large as Italy. Once saved to the Union, the military aid rendered by Kentucky in putting down the rebellion was at least two thirds as great as that rendered by Michigan; and gallant Missouri, with 25,000 fewer white men of military age than Massachusetts, had a death-roll in the Union army of 13,887, while that of Massachusetts was 13,942.

It would be difficult, therefore, to overrate the services of the heroic men who at the first outbreak of rebellion succeeded in crushing out the nascent secessionist tendencies in those two powerful states. Especial praise is due to the men who acted thus decisively and promptly in Missouri. If they had failed, it would have fared ill with the Union cause in Kentucky also. Flanked on the right by so powerful a state as Missouri, the friends of the Federal government in Kentucky would have found it hard to put forth their full strength. But as the campaigns of McClellan and Rosecrans in West Virginia freed Kentucky from lateral pressure on the east, so the prompt action of a few high-minded and resolute men in Missouri freed her from lateral pressure on the west, and made it possible for Grant to

Missouri.

strike that great blow at Fort Donelson which first carried the Union forces into the interior of the Confederacy. It was in Missouri that the long series of events was set in motion which terminated in the suppression of the rebellion. From the seizure of Camp Jackson in 1861 down to the appearance of Sherman's army in the rear of Virginia in 1865, there may be traced an unbroken chain of causation. As we look along this line we can see something like a steady progression of events toward the final goal. In spite of occasional reverses here and there, we see the Union arms steadily gaining ground, and the forces of the Confederacy steadily weakening, from the beginning to the end of the struggle. A different impression is obtained if we confine our attention to Virginia. There we see the formidable Lee defeating or baffling one Union general after another, remaining unconquered and apparently unconquerable, until at last with his swift and sudden overthrow the rebellion seems all at once to collapse like a bubble. The obstinate resistance of Lee served for a long time to mask the desperate condition into which the fortunes of the Confederacy were sinking; and the student of that history cannot obtain an adequate view without carefully following the sequence of events in the Mississippi Valley. Bearing this in mind, we shall the better appreciate the significance of the stirring scenes which the streets of St. Louis witnessed in the spring and summer of 1861.

Among the staunch defenders of the Union at that most anxious and critical moment, the foremost name was that of the younger Francis Preston Blair. He was of the family of that redoubtable Scottish parson, Dr. James Blair, first president of William and Mary College, in conflict with whom three royal governors of Virginia had one after another come to grief.[1] His father, the elder Francis Preston Blair, long time editor of the "Globe," was one of the ablest exponents of Jacksonian Democracy, and deserved high honour for the energy with which he fought against the doctrine of nullification. His courage and weight of sense gave him great influence with President Lincoln, of whose cabinet his eldest son, Montgomery Blair, was a member. The younger Francis Preston Blair had lived in St. Louis since 1842, and for several years had been recognized as one of the leaders of the Benton wing of the Democratic party. While he had approved of the annexation of Texas, and had served with credit in the ensuing war against Mexico, he was always consistently opposed to the extension of slavery into the territories, and during the

Francis Preston Blair.

[1] See my *Old Virginia and Her Neighbours*, ii. 118, 123, 389.

stormy administrations of Pierce and Buchanan he set his face unflinchingly against every measure that hinted even remotely at secession. Few men of that day were so highly endowed with political sagacity, or realized, as he did, the tendency of public events and the tremendous nature of the struggle into which we were drifting. Along with this rare foresight he was endowed with a lofty and unselfish public spirit, a weight of character that impressed itself upon every one, and a courage that nothing could daunt. Such a man is a power in any state. I have heard thoughtful people in Missouri say that if Virginia, during the ten years which preceded the Civil War, had possessed one such citizen as Francis Blair maintaining such a political attitude as he maintained in Missouri, she might have been found in 1861 devoting all her mighty energies to the preservation of the Union. I have heard this said repeatedly by men accustomed to weigh their words, and — whatever may be thought of the implication as to Virginia — it serves to show the esteem in which Blair was held by those who knew him.

The most interesting moment in the career of this man was the spring of 1861. It had been largely due to him and the able men whom he directly influenced that the Union sentiment in Missouri was so strong at the beginning of the war.

It needed all the strength it could summon, for the friends of secession were busy and shrewd. Among them was counted the governor, Claiborne Jackson, who sought to veil his purpose with fair professions of loyalty. The governor was secretly helped by a considerable party in the legislature. Secrecy was forced upon them by the action of the state convention in February in declaring itself emphatically opposed to secession. The efforts of the conspirators were directed toward the gathering of a secessionist state militia and the seizure of the United States arsenal at St. Louis, which contained some 60,000 stand of arms with a great store of other munitions of war.[1]

But Blair was beforehand with them. He sent intelligence to Washington which led General Scott to despatch a small force of regular troops for the protection of the arsenal under command of Nathaniel Lyon, of Connecticut, a captain of the Second United States Infantry, a man of boundless energy and untiring vigilance. Lyon soon succeeded in getting together some 500 men; and when in April the governor refused to call for troops in answer to President Lincoln's proclamation, Blair took the matter in hand, and on his own responsibility raised several regiments of loyal militia, known as "Home

Nathaniel Lyon.

[1] Snead, *The Fight for Missouri*, p. 100.

Guards." Blair and Lyon were kindred spirits; a warm friendship sprang up between them, and they worked zealously and efficiently together. Governor Jackson solicited a supply of arms and ammunition from the Confederate government, and began recruiting volunteers for the defence of the state. The enemy against whom such defence was deemed necessary was the United States. The governor's outward show of loyalty was such that it was difficult to offer any opposition to his proceedings at this early stage; but to wait for an overt act which should publish to the world his true intentions would be the height of folly. It would be simply giving him the initiative, and Blair was not the man to commit such a blunder. He could thwart a plot by a counterplot, if necessary; and for some time his actions wore the semblance of rebellion against the legally constituted government of Missouri. What he represented in that state was the authority of the United States, which the state government could not be trusted to support. Under such abnormal circumstances a certain amount of irregularity, distressing to the souls of those dear old parchment worthies, John Doe and Richard Roe, was unavoidable.

Plots and counterplots; "rebellion against Missouri."

On the last day of April the following remarkable order was addressed by the War Department at Washington to "Captain Nathaniel Lyon, commanding Department of the West:" —

"The President of the United States directs that you enroll in the military service of the United States loyal citizens of St. Louis and vicinity, not exceeding, with those heretofore enlisted, ten thousand in number, for the purpose of maintaining the authority of the United States and for the protection of the peaceable inhabitants of Missouri, and you will if deemed necessary for that purpose by yourself and Messrs. Oliver D. Filley, John How, James O. Broadhead, Samuel T. Glover, J. J. Witzig, and Francis P. Blair, Jr., proclaim martial law in the city of St. Louis."

On the back of this document was written by General Scott, general-in-chief of the United States Army, "It is revolutionary times, and therefore I do not object to the irregularity of this. — W. S.;" and the whole was confirmed by the terse endorsement: " Approved April 30, 1861. — A. Lincoln." [1]

A few days before the arrival of this order — which virtually constituted Blair and Lyon and the other five gentlemen named into a revolutionary Committee of Safety — Lyon had taken the precaution of moving the greater portion of the

[1] Snead, *The Fight for Missouri*, p. 165.

arms stored in the arsenal into the state of Illinois for safe-keeping. This sudden removal checkmated a neat little scheme of Governor Jackson. In accordance with a statute of 1858 it was the custom for the commander of each militia district in Missouri to assemble his men on the 3d of May every year at some convenient place within his district, and there go into encampment for one week. It was Jackson's intention to have the camp for the First District assembled on the hills near the arsenal, in a position favourable for a *coup de main* upon that coveted place. But before April was over Lyon had not only removed the arms, but had occupied the hills with batteries guarded by infantry. The commander of the district, therefore, — Daniel Frost, a gentleman whose loyalty to the state government could be counted on, — selected another place for his encampment. It was a charming spot known as Lindell's Meadow, just southeast of the intersection of Grand Avenue and Olive Street, which were then mere plank roads. This camping-ground was entirely enclosed by a strong fence. It was baptized Camp Jackson, in honour of the governor; and in spite of that gentleman's professions of loyalty, its true proclivities were betrayed by the names "Beauregard" and "Jeff Davis" applied to its two chief avenues.[1] In this pleasant field of May were gathered about 700 men, by no means all secessionists, but all bound to serve the legally constituted government of the state of Missouri. It would not do to let them stay there, and on May 7 Blair and Lyon made up their minds to capture Camp Jackson.

But why was such a step necessary? The legal existence of Camp Jackson would terminate within four days; why, then, such haste? Because General William Selby Harney, who was expected to return from Washington within a few days, was commander of the Department of the West, and Captain Lyon was only acting commander during his absence. Upon Harney's return the activity of Lyon would, for a while at least, be held in abeyance. Harney was a brave and loyal soldier, but did not comprehend the political situation. He was no match in chicanery for Jackson and his friends, who would be sure to find reasons for keeping Camp Jackson in existence as long as suited their purposes. On the 7th of May, therefore, it was high time for Lyon

General Harney.

[1] This was denied by General Frost in an open letter to me in *The Republican*, St. Louis, April 22, 1886; at least the general remembered nothing of the sort. On the other hand, Colonel Samuel Simmons, in some personal reminiscences, declares that these names were marked upon sign-boards. See *Globe Democrat*, St. Louis, May 10, 1881.

and Blair to strike, and the next day furnished them with an excellent occasion.

It will be remembered that Governor Jackson had solicited from the Confederate government at Montgomery a supply of warlike material. On the night of May 8 the siege guns and howitzers sent in response by Jefferson Davis arrived on a steamer from Baton Rouge, packed in boxes marked "Marble," shipped as merchandise, and consigned to persons well known for their Union sentiments. Despite these elaborate blinds, the boxes were met at the wharf by the persons for whom they were really intended, and no time was lost in hauling them out to Camp Jackson. *Arms for Camp Jackson.*

A fine cordial hospitality was dispensed at the camp in those balmy days of early May. The surgeon of Blair's regiment had dined there on the 8th, and he could have told anybody, says General Frost, "that it was a very attractive place, because he saw it filled with the fairest of Missouri's daughters, who 'from morn to dewy eve' threaded its mazes in company with their sons, brothers, and lovers. He could also have described the beautiful United States flag which waved its folds in the breeze from the flagstaff over my tent."[1] One of the visitors next day

[1] Open letter from General Frost to Professor Fiske, *The Republican*, St. Louis, April 22, 1886.

came in a light open carriage then known as a
"Jenny Lind," and was leisurely
driven by a coloured servant up and
down the avenues "Jeff Davis," "Beauregard,"
and "Sumter," and the rest. This visitor,
dressed in a black bombazine gown and closely
veiled, was a familiar sight on the streets of St.
Louis, as she took the air daily in her light carriage. Everybody recognized her as Mrs. Alexander, the mother of Mrs. Blair, but nobody accosted
her or expected recognition from her because she
was known to be blind. What should have
brought this elderly lady to Camp Jackson? was
it simply the negro coachman gratifying some
curiosity of his own?

A visitor in bombazine.

A couple of hours later, as Blair was sitting in
the porch of the southern house of the arsenal,
chatting with Colonel Simmons and a few other
friends, the Jenny Lind carriage drove up, and the
familiar figure, in its black gown and veil, alighted
and came up the steps. It was natural enough
that Blair should greet his wife's mother and escort
her into the house. But as they stepped upon the
threshold, a slight uplifting of the bombazine skirt
disclosed a sturdy pair of cavalry boots
to the eyes of Colonel Simmons and
another gentleman, who glanced at each other significantly but said never a word.

A lady with spurs.

From St. Louis to Belmont 17

Had the close veil been lifted, it would have revealed the short red beard and piercing blue eyes of Nathaniel Lyon, the "little Connecticut abolitionist," as some called him.[1] His Committee of Safety was promptly summoned to the arsenal, to hear him tell how he had "satisfied himself by personal inspection that the men [at Camp Jackson] had in their possession arms and ammunition which had been taken from the United States Arsenal at Baton Rouge, and which, therefore, rightfully belonged, in his opinion, to the Federal government." It was necessary, he said, to seize Camp Jackson and hold its men as prisoners of war. In this opinion Blair, Broadhead, Witzig, and Filley con-

[1] In my opening lecture at St. Louis, April 15, 1886, I mentioned the fact of Lyon's visiting Camp Jackson disguised in woman's clothes. For this statement I was taken to task in some of the newspapers, which derided it as an "old woman's story," too absurd for belief. I was thereupon assured by several members of the Blair family, friends of mine, that the story, although an old woman's, was literally true. In proof thereof General Blair's son, Francis Preston Blair the third, took me to call upon his grandmother, Mrs. Alexander, a fine old lady of eighty-three. From her lips I heard the story, just as I have above given it, and she showed me the bombazine gown and close veil which she had lent to Lyon. As to the Simmons incident, it was told me by Colonel Simmons himself, who was soon afterward on Lyon's staff, and at a later date on the staff of General Rosecrans at Stone river.

Mrs. Alexander was Myra Madison, only daughter of George Madison, governor of Kentucky, and niece of James Madison, bishop of Virginia and president of William and Mary College.

curred, but Glover and How deprecated any rash action. They urged that inasmuch as Camp Jackson kept the stars and stripes flying and had not been concerned in any breach of the peace, it would be best to allow its brief term of existence to expire quietly; if it contained stolen property of the United States, the best way to get it was to send the United States marshal with a writ of replevin, supported if necessary by Lyon's troops. Lyon replied that the camp was a mere "nest of traitors," that the legislature, which had just been convened at Jefferson City, might indefinitely prolong its term of existence, and that as for Harney, there was no counting upon him. To these arguments How and Glover yielded, but were still disposed to insist upon the writ of replevin, which to Blair and Lyon seemed not only a subterfuge, but a lame one.

Replevin vs. capture.

Nevertheless, at a meeting of Glover with two or three confidential friends that night, a writ was duly prepared, in case it should be wanted; and early next morning my dear old friend, Colonel Thomas Tasker Gantt, armed with the precious document, set out on horseback to find Blair. Gantt himself was far from convinced of the efficacy of the replevin method, but he was willing to submit the case once more to Blair's master mind. A few miles

Surrender of Camp Jackson.

below the city, on the bank of the Mississippi, the solitary horseman met his friend marching up with 1000 men from Jefferson Barracks. "Well, Frank," said Gantt, "I have the writ of replevin here in my pocket." Blair's reply was more forcible than elegant; but like Cambronne's famous exclamation at Waterloo, it was forever final, and a sense of relief lightened Colonel Gantt's mind as he reined his horse about. The march ended in a rendezvous with Lyon's forces, and by two o'clock in the afternoon that vigorous commander had invested Camp Jackson, planted his batteries, and sent in to General Frost a summons to surrender. No alternative was possible. The capture was effected without firing a shot, but it was followed by an unfortunate affray between some of Lyon's troops and the street mob, in the course of which about thirty lives were lost. Next day all the prisoners but one were released on parole.

This capture of Camp Jackson was the first really aggressive blow at secession that was struck anywhere within the United States. In the city of St. Louis the immediate effect seemed magical. Secessionists were cowed, and Union men jubilant. On Pine Street, near Fifth, there was a building in which enemies of the Union were wont to assemble, and for some time it had flaunted from one of its windows some kind of a rebel flag. As the startling news from Camp Jackson came down Pine Street, an authoritative shout ordered the emblem of secession to be taken down, and down it came, nevermore to be hoisted in St. Louis. The scene was witnessed by a quiet and modest-looking man, who forthwith stepped upon a street-car headed toward the arsenal, whither he was going to congratulate Lyon and Blair. A dapper youth, voluble with rage and scorn, and craving sympathy, came on board and addressed this quiet person : " Things have come to a d—d pretty pass when a free people can't choose their own flag. Where I came from, if a man dares to say a word in favour of the Union, we hang him to a limb of the first tree we come to." The quiet man replied, " After all, we are not so intolerant in St. Louis as we might be ; I have not seen a single rebel hung yet, nor heard of one ; there are plenty of them who ought to be, however." At this unexpected retort the dapper young man collapsed. The modest person who uttered it was a middle-aged man quite unknown to fame, a leather-dealer named Ulysses Simpson Grant.[1] On that same day, among the bystanders who witnessed some of its stirring scenes was William Tecumseh Sherman, president of the Fifth Street railroad.[2] The

Rebel flag hauled down.

Colloquy on a street-car.

---

[1] Grant's *Memoirs*, i. 236, 237.
[2] Sherman's *Memoirs*, i. 172–174.

next day Grant had crossed the river to muster in the 21st regiment of Illinois infantry, of which he was soon afterward appointed colonel; and three days later Sherman was called to Washington to the colonelcy of the 13th Regular infantry.

On the memorable afternoon when Camp Jackson surrendered, the governor was sitting in the state-house at Jefferson City, plotting secession with his legislature. At the news of Lyon's stroke, flashed over the telegraph wires, many cheeks turned pale with chagrin. Fearing that he might even then be marching on the capital, the governor took the precaution to have a railroad bridge burned, while the legislature remained in session all night to consider what had best be done. Shortly afterward a military bill was passed, clothing the governor with quasi-dictatorial powers, in virtue of which he went on diligently organizing a secessionist militia, and appointed to command it General Sterling Price, an active and enterprising officer, born in Virginia, who had served in the Mexican War, and had been governor of Missouri. For a fortnight Price seemed to be having everything as he wished. After Harney's return, on May 11, Price inveigled him into an arrangement by which he secured for himself the initiative in all the work of calling out the military force of the state, while Harney's at-

<small>Sterling Price.</small>

titude was reduced to that of a bystander. Under these favourable circumstances Price worked vigorously in organizing rebellion, and secretly invited the government of Arkansas to send an armed force to assist him. But his scheme was fathomed by the ever watchful Blair, who sent such reports to Washington that on the 18th of May President Lincoln privately authorized Blair to remove General Harney from the chief command of the department whenever he should deem such a step required by the public safety. In pursuance of this order Harney was removed on the 30th, and Lyon was appointed in his place, with the rank of brigadier-general.

This act brought things to a crisis. Jackson and Price understood that they were now dealing with men who could not be hoodwinked, but before taking extreme measures they sought an interview with Lyon and Blair. A safe-conduct was granted them, and on the 11th of June the conference was held at the Planters' Hotel at St. Louis; but it came to nothing. The governor insisted that the Home Guards should be disbanded and all Federal troops sent out of the state. Blair would not listen to this, but insisted that the governor should disband his own militia. So they parted. Jackson and Price returned the same night to Jefferson City, and next day, throwing off

The crisis.

the mask which could no longer be worn, the governor issued a proclamation calling for 50,000 men to protect the state against the Federal "invaders." But Lyon was ready to strike. He embarked his forces on three swift steamboats and ascended the Missouri river, landing at Jefferson City on the 15th. Once more the stars and stripes were hoisted over the state-house.[1] The governor, carrying

[1] In my lecture for the Grant monument fund, April 15, 1886, I said that Governor Jackson, on his return to Jefferson City, hoisted a secession flag over the state-house, and that Lyon, on the 15th, hauled down this flag before raising the stars and stripes. As these statements were called in question, I inquired of Hon. P. T. Miller, of the state treasury, who lived in Jefferson City in 1861. After due verification of his recollections, his reply was, "No flag ever floated over the state capitol other than the stars and stripes." Accepting this as conclusive, and looking about for the source of my error, I found it in my too hasty reading of two despatches printed in the St. Louis *Daily Democrat*, June, 1861. The two are as follows: —

"Our patriotic governor, with his no less patriotic commander-in-chief of that band of traitors, the Missouri State Guard, has returned to the capital and issued *a proclamation which* casts aside all pretences of loyalty, and *raises boldly the secession flag*, under which he has been fraudulently organizing ever since the Harney indulgence." — *Letter from Jefferson City*, June 13, 1861, signed H.

"[General Lyon and his troops] marched in good order through the city, cheered at several points, and finally occupied Capitol Hill amid tremendous applause. W. H. Lusk was the happy individual selected to raise again the stars and stripes over the cupola, which he did, while the Jefferson band played the 'Star-Spangled Banner.' . . . Old ladies wept, and every one seemed overjoyed at the sight once more of the old flag." — *Despatch from Jefferson City*, June 15, 1861.

with him the great seal of the state, fled fifty miles up the river to Booneville, while Price kept on still farther to Lexington. Both these towns were places of rendezvous for the secessionist militia, but Lyon understood the value of time and did not leave them to assemble unmolested. He left the capital on the 16th, arrived at Booneville next morning, and in a short, sharp action routed the secessionists, taking their guns and many prisoners. Jackson fled toward the southwestern part of the state, with Lyon in hot pursuit, and Price, with the forces gathered at Lexington, set out by a converging route to join the governor. Meanwhile Blair had despatched Colonel Franz Sigel, a veteran of the German revolution of 1849, from St. Louis, with 1500 men, to intercept Jackson and attack him before Price could come to the rescue. On the 5th of July Sigel met Jackson with 4000 men not far from Carthage. A fight ensued in which Sigel

Skirmish at Booneville.

On reading these two paragraphs carefully, with especial reference to the words which I have italicized, it appears that it is not the governor but the proclamation that raises the secession flag; and that, therefore, the phrase is metaphorical. The sense would have been made clearer by omitting the superfluous comma after "loyalty." I dare say it was this comma that turned my mind back to "governor" as the subject of "raises."

According to Mr. Miller, the State Guard, when commanded by Sterling Price, carried the flag of Missouri, containing the state arms on a blue field with yellow fringe.

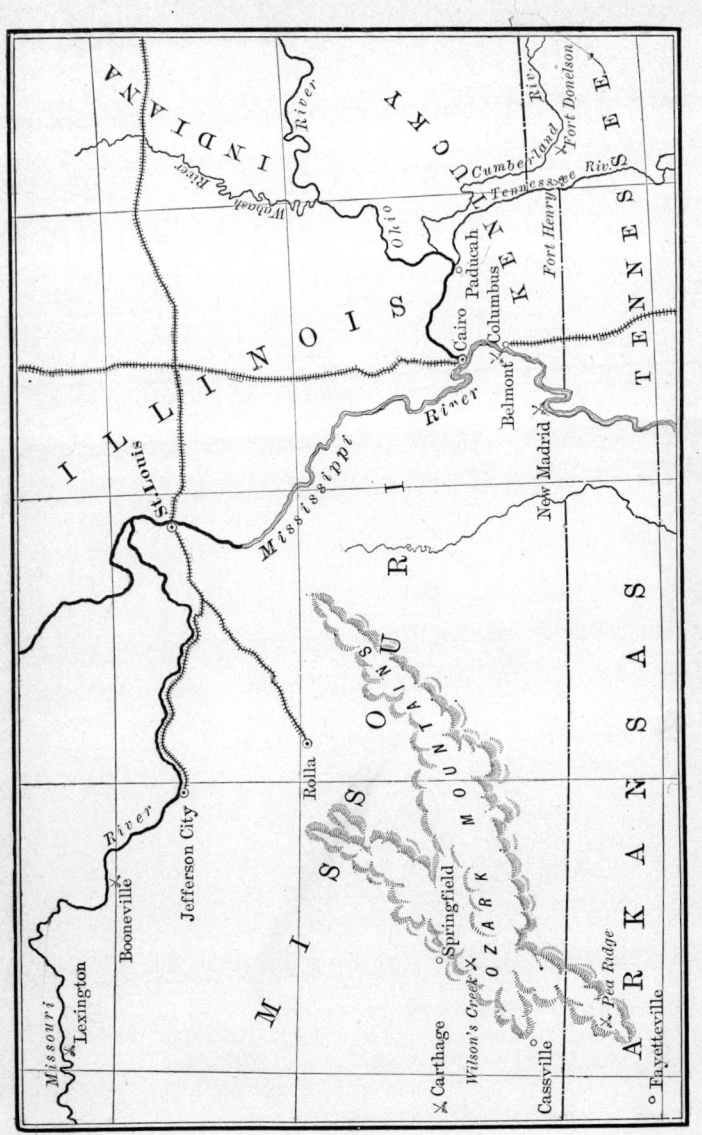

THE STRATEGIC POSITION OF MISSOURI

for some hours had the advantage, but Jackson's superiority in cavalry enabled him to threaten Sigel's baggage-train in his rear and thus compel him to retreat. During the night Jackson was reinforced not only by Price, but also by several thousand troops from Arkansas, Texas, and Louisiana under the noted Texan ranger, McCulloch. Sigel's position thus became perilous, but he effected his escape in a skilful retreat which won him higher encomiums than his subsequent career ever justified; henceforth to "fight mit Sigel" became a favourite war-cry of enthusiastic Germans throughout the country. *Sigel's fight at Carthage.*

On July 9 the incapable Fremont was appointed to command the Department of the West, with disastrous results, the first of which fell upon the devoted Lyon and his little army. When on the 13th Lyon arrived at Springfield and joined his forces to those of Sigel, it was found that their united strength was unequal to maintaining that position. The enemy, in retreating into the southwestern corner of the state, had retreated upon reinforcements, and was now growing stronger daily. Presently the news of Bull Run emboldened the secessionists all over Missouri, and the rebel army, commanded by Benjamin McCulloch, increased till it numbered 12,000 men. Lyon had barely 6000 to oppose to this force, and in face of such odds it was difficult either to attack or to retreat. After waiting in vain for reinforcements which ought to have been sent him by General Fremont, he made up his mind to strike such a blow as would cripple the enemy, and thus secure for himself an unmolested retreat upon Rolla, the terminus of the railroad from St. Louis.[1] On the morning of the 10th of August he accordingly attacked McCulloch in his position at Wilson's Creek, near Springfield. Lyon's plan was bold, even to rashness. He sent Sigel, with 1200 men and a battery of six pieces, to turn the enemy's right flank, while he himself, with 3700 men and ten guns, attacked in front. The nature of the ground was such as to favour this audacious movement. Sigel's march was successfully accomplished, and his assault was admirably begun, but his force was inadequate to

Battle of Wilson's Creek; death of Lyon.

---

[1] The night before the battle Lyon sent a letter to Fremont explaining his situation. I cannot forbear quoting Colonel Snead's remarks on this occasion, in his *The Fight for Missouri*, p. 266. Colonel Snead, a most gallant Confederate officer, thus writes of his noble foe: "Not one word about the desperate battle he was to fight on the morrow, not one fault-finding utterance, not a breath of complaint! But, true to his convictions, true to his flag, true to the Union men of Missouri who confided in and followed him, true to himself, and true to duty, he went out to battle against a force twice as great as his own, with a calmness that was as pathetic as his courage was sublime."

This is the best thing I have ever read about Lyon.

the task assigned it. He was soon overwhelmed by numbers, and repulsed with the loss of five of his guns. The fight in front was kept up for six hours with desperate gallantry, and neither side was able to prevail. After being twice wounded, the brave Lyon was slain while leading a charge. By noon both armies were tired out and ceased fighting, and while the Confederates busied themselves in strengthening their defences, the Union forces retired in good order, and after five days of marching reached Rolla unmolested. The Confederate loss in killed and wounded was 1095, or rather less than one tenth of the number engaged; the Federal loss was 1236, or about one fifth of the number engaged. In its dimensions, therefore, the battle of Wilson's Creek resembled the battles of the Revolutionary War. The dimensions were small, but the losses showed staunch fighting; and the indecisiveness of the result was like that of many another and far bloodier conflict during the next four years, in which Americans, arrayed against one another, gave repeated proof of that wonderful staying power in which we have always resembled our British forefathers, and which seldom can be made to understand that it is beaten.

The one thing really lamentable in the battle of Wilson's Creek was the death of the noble Lyon. Like the death of Joseph Warren at Bunker Hill, it was a loss that could not be made good. In his brief career Lyon had shown extraordinary qualities. He was sagacious and dauntless, quick and sure, and always ready to assume responsibility. If his plan of attack at Wilson's Creek is perhaps liable to the charge of rashness, it should be borne in mind that after all it achieved a drawn battle against overwhelming odds. All our best generals on either side — Grant and Lee as well as the rest — had something to learn from hard experience; and if Lyon had lived to see the end of the war, he would very likely have taken place in the front rank of our great commanders. With the vigour and skill which had characterized his movements down to the day of his death, it is instructive to contrast the incapacity and sloth which ensued thereupon.

<small>Lyon's great qualities.</small>

On the 9th of July General Fremont had been, as we have seen, appointed to command the Western Department, which now comprised the states of Illinois, Kentucky, Missouri, and Kansas, with the adjacent territories. Fremont's work in connection with the exploration of the Rocky Mountains and the conquest of California had made him a favourite with many of the western people; and moreover, having so lately been the first candidate of the Republican party for the presidency, he was at that time an impor-

<small>General Fremont.</small>

From St. Louis to Belmont 29

tant personage whom it seemed quite natural to select for high positions. But neither from a military nor from a political point of view was his career in the Civil War such as to justify the expectations which his admirers had fondly cherished. He gave no proof of military insight, or political acumen. His most memorable act at St. Louis was a proclamation on the 30th of August which declared all slaves belonging to parties in arms against the United States to be free, and threatened instant death to all persons bearing arms within a district which he arbitrarily assigned. By such a decree Fremont not only assumed dictatorial powers which did not belong to him, but he showed a lamentable incapacity for comprehending the political situation. Important as the slavery question was, the question of national sovereignty was far more important, and at this critical moment with such slave states as Missouri and Kentucky, where there was such a struggle between conflicting motives, it was in the highest degree imprudent to hint at the forcible emancipation of negro slaves. Such a hint was calculated to alarm many a loyal slave-holder and array him, against his better judgment, on the side of the Confederates. President Lincoln's unfailing political sagacity was quick to disavow this rash act, and to remind General

His "emancipation proclamation."

Fremont that his powers as military commander were strictly limited.

Soon after Governor Jackson had taken the field in behalf of the Confederacy, the state convention of Missouri met at Jefferson City, declared all the state offices vacant, and inaugurated a new provisional government, with its headquarters at St. Louis. After the battle of Wilson's Creek, McCulloch withdrew his troops to Arkansas, but the indefatigable Price made his presence felt more keenly than ever in the western counties of Missouri. Fremont had forces enough to prevent his doing any serious mischief, if they had only been properly concentrated. He had in all 56,000 men, but they were scattered in small detachments in thirteen different places. To a certain extent this scattering was unavoidable, as there was a vast area to be protected; but Fremont showed himself singularly deficient in handling the elementary problem of moving troops from places where they were idle to places where they were needed. His failure to relieve Lyon was an instance in point, and a still more flagrant one was forthcoming.

At Lexington, on the Missouri river, Fremont had stationed Colonel Mulligan, with 2800 men and eight field-pieces, and ordered him to stay there until relieved. Price made up his mind to overwhelm this detachment, and accordingly on the 11th of September he appeared before Lexington with a force of 14,000 men, which daily reinforcements soon swelled to more than 20,000. On his approach Colonel Mulligan entrenched himself on an elevated plateau some fifteen acres in surface, a little east of the city and close to the broad river. He had a good steamer at his disposal, upon which he might have withdrawn his force to the opposite bank, but in the absence of further orders he deemed it his duty to remain. He sent word to Fremont that he should defend the place to the last extremity, and begged for speedy reinforcements. It would not have been difficult from the garrisons at St. Louis and Jefferson City, and from General Pope's detachment in the northwest, to assemble 20,000 men for the protection of Lexington. Some time was afforded for such a movement, inasmuch as the Confederates, worn out with forced marches and short of ammunition, contented themselves for the moment with investing Mulligan's position, and allowed six days to elapse before making a general attack. But although not only the city of St. Louis but every town in the loyal states was alive with anxiety over Mulligan's situation, Fremont could not make up his mind what to do. He sent no

Fate of Mulligan's detachment.

instructions whatever and no reinforcements until too late, so that the gallant Mulligan was left to contend with a foe that outnumbered him sevenfold. On the 18th the Confederates seized the steamer, and carried by storm a large building used as a hospital, which overlooked Mulligan's works. A desperate struggle ensued about this building. The Federals recaptured it and drove out the enemy, but presently numbers prevailed; the Confederates won it again and held it, cutting off Mulligan's approaches to the river. There was neither spring nor cistern on the plateau, the weather was intolerably hot, and the devoted garrison soon began to suffer the torments of thirst. Next day a scanty reinforcement, tardily sent, arrived on the opposite bank of the river, but was unable to cross. Nevertheless, all that day and night, and through the forenoon of the 20th, a stout resistance was kept up, while the besiegers steadily pounded away with artillery. At length a general assault was made, the Confederates rolling large bales of hemp in front of them as a movable entrenchment, under cover of which they pushed close to the works on every side. Mulligan then surrendered, to avoid useless bloodshed.

The horse being thus stolen, Fremont at last set out to lock the stable door. A cry of indignation went up throughout the northern states. In

Missouri the Union party was despondent, and loud complaints were visited upon the commanding general. On the 27th he started for Lexington with 20,000 men and 86 guns, but Price had no mind to await him in that neighbourhood. Having dealt his blow, he knew how to get out of the way. He crossed the great state by forced marches, and was soon in his southwest corner near the friendly borders of Arkansas. By the middle of October Fremont had increased his army to nearly 40,000. With this force he felt sure of overwhelming Price, and even talked of a triumphant progress of a thousand miles down the Mississippi valley to New Orleans. The absurdity of such a dream was not so apparent then as now, for few people at the North could realize how tremendous the task of crushing the Confederacy was going to be. On the 1st of November, having reached Springfield, Fremont made up his mind that Price must be close by Wilson's Creek, and he prepared to attack him there. In point of fact the Confederate general was at Cassville, about sixty miles distant; but before this had been ascertained, and while the preparations were going on, there came an order from the President removing Fremont and appointing General Hunter in his place.

Fremont's movements.

With all his military incapacity, Fremont had

engaging personal qualities which endeared him to his soldiers, and his departure was regretted by many. Hunter retained his command but a single week. On the 1st of November the aged General Scott had retired from the position of general-in-chief of the Federal armies, and General McClellan had succeeded him. In remodelling the military arrangements, McClellan appointed General Halleck to command the new Department of the Missouri, including the part of Kentucky west of the Cumberland river, and Hunter was thus superseded. The good fortune of Halleck in this western command — vouchsafed him by an inscrutable Providence — was soon to carry him to Washington and to the supreme position in the army, yet he was a worse than mediocre man. He had, or was supposed to have, a thorough knowledge of the art of war as it exists in books; he was familiar with military law; he could sit in his study and plan campaigns with amazing profundity and precision; and he looked so owlishly wise that the soldiers commonly called him "Old Brains;" but with all this he had little power of grappling with practical difficulties, he accomplished nothing in the field, and after he had become general-in-chief his incapacity was responsible for some of the most terrible disasters of the war. His beginnings in the West, however, were auspicious.

General Halleck.

During the month of December Generals Pope and Prentiss, with vigorous marching and skirmishing, but without any serious engagement, restored the Federal authority in all the northern and central portions of Missouri. Price maintained himself for a while at Springfield, but late in January, 1862, General Samuel Curtis moved against him with 12,000 men and 50 pieces of artillery. On the approach of this force the Confederate general retreated into Arkansas, where he was once more joined by McCulloch, and both were placed under the command of the able and enterprising General Van Dorn. Curtis, an excellent officer, pursued cautiously until he reached an eminence known as Pea Ridge, in the Ozark Mountains. Here he waited in a strong position, contenting himself with observing the enemy, for his line of communications was already very long, and he could not safely penetrate farther into a hostile country. He had left small detachments *en echelon* to protect his communications along the main post-road from Missouri which led to Fayetteville in Arkansas, and which was his only available line of retreat. This left him just 10,250 men and 48 guns with which to meet the enemy. Van Dorn, having collected more than 20,000 men, besides 5000 civilized Choctaws and Cherokees

Battle of Pea Ridge.

from the Indian Territory under the lead of an adventurer from Massachusetts named Albert Pike, thought himself strong enough to destroy or capture the Union army. A bold and well-planned march brought him into Curtis's rear, so that by seizing and holding the post-road he could cut off that general's retreat and compel him to surrender. Such movements, however, are often fraught with danger to the attacking party. The nature of the ground was such that in executing the manœuvre the two wings of the Confederate army became separated, and on the first day of the battle, while Van Dorn with his left wing succeeded in defeating the Union right and establishing himself upon the post-road, on the other hand his right wing was completely crushed, and McCulloch, its commander, was slain.

Curtis's situation at the close of that day, the 7th of March, was critical. He had routed and scattered half of the rebel army, but the other half still outnumbered him and cut off his retreat. It was an anxious night, but the next day, with great skill, Curtis so extended his line of battle as to envelop both of Van Dorn's flanks and subject him to a murderous cross-fire, which soon drove him in confusion from the field. The Confederate army had lost in killed, wounded, and missing, not less than

Total defeat of the Confederates.

From St. Louis to Belmont

5000 men, and was completely shattered. The Union loss was 1351. Among the contests of the Civil War this well-fought battle, out on the distant borders of western Arkansas, was peculiar by reason of the presence of Indian auxiliaries. These red men were of small use to the Confederates. Amid the roar of artillery and the obstinate fighting of a stronger race, they quite lost their heads, and only added to the confusion of defeat. So far as the state of Missouri was concerned, the victory at Pea Ridge went far toward ending the serious business of the war. There was more or less cruel and vexatious guerrilla fighting after this, but the rebels never again succeeded in invading the state in force. Van Dorn was called away to Corinth, where the Confederacy was massing its strength for the coming struggle of Titans at Shiloh; and Curtis was thus enabled to march at leisure through Arkansas, until he came out at Helena on the bank of the Mississippi river in the midsummer following.

The interest of these early campaigns is somewhat meagre as compared with the mighty struggles which were to come. But their place in the line of causal sequence which ended in the overthrow of the rebellion is profoundly interesting. Already they begin to reveal the prodigious value of the initia-

Importance of these early campaigns.

tive that was taken by Lyon and Blair. The scene of our story is now to shift to eastward of the Mississippi river, into central regions, where it is no longer a question of saving a single state, but of aiming a blow at the heart of the rebellion. The events which now come crowding upon our attention are conceived upon a grander scale, and their glory and terror are such as to absorb the attention and make it easy to forget the significance of these earlier and more restricted movements. But without the work which we have just passed in review, the history of these grander operations would have been very different. Until the great state of Missouri had been secured, it would have been impossible for a Federal army, without dangerously exposing its right flank and its line of communications, to have advanced upon the first Confederate line of defence in Kentucky. That line of defence, as we shall see, ran through the southern portion of Kentucky, making at one place a slight bend into Tennessee.

If Kentucky could have been persuaded to cast in her lot with the Confederacy, the first defensive line would have been formed by the Ohio river, and no pains were spared by Jefferson Davis to secure so desirable an object. But the Union sentiment in Kentucky was strong. Party feeling ran very high there, as it did in Missouri and all along the border, and many a house was divided against itself. Of the sons of the venerable Crittenden, who had lately sought to avert the irrepressible conflict by crying Peace! when there was no peace, one rose to the rank of corps commander in the Union army, while his brother became almost equally conspicuous among Confederate generals; and this instance was but typical of hundreds. The governor, Beriah Magoffin, was a secessionist, and refused to obey President Lincoln's requisition for troops. The legislature resolved "that this state and the citizens thereof should take no part in the Civil War now being waged, except as mediators and friends of the belligerent parties; and that Kentucky should during the contest occupy the position of strict neutrality."

Affairs in Kentucky.

For a few weeks a sincere attempt was made to preserve this attitude of neutrality, but events made it daily more manifest that this was impossible. The State Guard, numbering some 15,000 men, and possessing nearly all the serviceable arms owned by the commonwealth, was largely commanded by secessionist officers; its inspector-general, Simon Bolivar Buckner, we shall soon see in high command under the Confederacy. Humphrey Marshall began collecting and drilling a rebel force within thirty miles of the capital,

Attempt at neutrality.

while William Nelson showed equal zeal in forming a camp of Union men. Thousands of secessionists left their homes to enlist with the Confederates in Tennessee, while in like manner great numbers went north into Ohio and Indiana and enrolled themselves in the Union ranks. As it became evident that neutrality could not long be preserved, the aversion to secession increased. The leaders of the Confederacy assumed a bullying tone, hinting that Kentucky belonged to them and knew it, but was afraid to take the responsibility of leaving the Union. This sort of talk gave great offence, and in the August election the secessionist party barely obtained a third of the members in either house. On the 3d of September the Confederates, laughing to scorn this attempted neutrality, invaded the soil of Kentucky and took up a strong position.

It was General Leonidas Polk who thus opened the war in this part of the world. This very able commander was one of the picturesque figures of that time. A nephew of President Polk, he had been educated at West Point, but had soon left the army and turned his attention to theology. He became a clergyman in the Episcopal Church, and had now for twenty years been Bishop of Louisiana. His martial spirit reviving at the outbreak of hostilities, he

Leonidas Polk.

exchanged his surplice for the uniform of a major-general, and was at once placed in command of the forces gathering on the eastern bank of the Mississippi. There was a curious flavour of mediævalism in the appearance of this bishop at the head of an army in the middle of the nineteenth century. The latest instance of a fighting divine before the Right Reverend Dr. Polk would seem to have been the Bishop of Derry, who was slain at the battle of the Boyne in 1690. A characteristic touch of ecclesiasticism appeared in the first general order, which declared that " the invasion of the South by the Federal armies had brought with it a contempt for constitutional liberty and the withering influences of the infidelity of New England and of Germany combined ! " With sound military instinct, Polk saw the importance of the town of Cairo, situated at the junction of the Ohio river with the Mississippi, and advancing toward this goal he entered Kentucky and fortified himself at Columbus, on a bold bluff completely commanding the Mississippi river, about twenty miles below Cairo. At the same time General Zollicoffer, coming from eastern Tennessee, invaded Kentucky by way of Cumberland Gap, and threatened the eastern portion of the state.

This simultaneous invasion at points three hundred miles apart revealed the deliberate purpose of the Confederates to seize the state by force, and at once all thought of neutrality was at an end. The stars and stripes were defiantly hoisted over the capitol at Frankfort, and the legislature resolved that Governor Magoffin should "inform those concerned that Kentucky expects the Confederate troops to be withdrawn from her soil unconditionally." The governor vetoed this resolution, and it was instantly passed over the veto. As soon as it was known that Polk had occupied Columbus, a Federal detachment crossed the Ohio and occupied Paducah. A motion in the legislature that the governor should request the removal of these troops also was defeated by a vote of more than two thirds. A few days later it was voted to raise an armed force and drive the Confederates from the state. Most of the State Guard now went over to the enemy, and with them went Buckner, John Morgan, afterward so famous as a guerrilla chieftain, and John Breckinridge, who had lately been Vice-President of the United States. The loyalty of these men to the Confederacy thus seems to have outweighed their loyalty to their own state, which had now decisively and finally arrayed itself on the side of the Union.

Kentucky declares for the Union.

General Polk's designs upon Cairo had already been anticipated and foiled by Federal troops assembled in Illinois. There had just entered upon the scene a thoughtful and silent man, of whom our story has already caught a glimpse upon a street-car in St. Louis, rebuking a flippant secessionist. Ulysses Simpson Grant was then thirty-nine years of age. He was the eldest son of a leather-dealer, of Scottish descent, and was born at Point Pleasant in Ohio on the 27th of April, 1822. He was educated at West Point, and was present in every battle of the Mexican War except Buena Vista. In his humble rank of lieutenant he had been distinguished for personal gallantry so far as to attract the attention for a moment of General Scott, the commander-in-chief, and of his staff-officer, Robert Edward Lee. In 1854, having reached the grade of captain, he gave up his commission and engaged thereafter in business as wool-dealer, auctioneer, real-estate agent, achieving little success, until the outbreak of hostilities in 1861 found him at Galena in Illinois, earning a scanty subsistence in the leather trade. At that time he was regarded as a broken and disappointed man, for whom no one would have dreamed of predicting a brilliant future.

When the President's call for troops came in April, Grant assembled and drilled a company of volunteers at Galena, and presently led it to

Springfield, the capital of Illinois. He then wrote a very modest letter to the War Department at Washington, saying that since he had been educated at the expense of the Federal government, he now felt it his duty to offer his services, and he accordingly asked for a commission. No notice was taken of this letter. Disappointed here, Grant went to Cincinnati, where McClellan was in command of the Ohio volunteers, hoping that he might obtain a place on that general's staff. But after calling twice at headquarters and not finding the general, he returned baffled but not disheartened to Illinois. There his zeal and skill in organization soon became so conspicuous that the governor placed him in command of a regiment, with which he marched to northern Missouri and put himself under the orders of General Pope. The Federal army was now increasing its dimensions so rapidly and suddenly that there was a great demand for general officers, and men who had been trained at West Point and seen active service were sometimes promoted straightway from the grade of captain to that of brigadier-general, as had been the case with Lyon. Members of Congress from Illinois, who had observed Grant's zeal and efficiency, now recommended him to President Lincoln for promotion, and he was accordingly made brigadier-general while Fremont was holding the chief command in the West.

When the cardinal position at Cairo was threatened by Polk, Grant seized it and made it his headquarters on the same day that Polk occupied Columbus. Grant thus gained an initiative which he was not slow in using. Polk's position at Columbus blockaded the Mississippi river up to that point; by next seizing Paducah, he would blockade the lower Ohio likewise, and command the mouths of the Tennessee and the Cumberland, two broad rivers which served as indispensable military highways leading for hundreds of miles through the central portion of the Confederacy. The bishop sent scouts to inspect Paducah, but Grant was again beforehand, and occupied the town just at the moment when *Grant seizes Paducah.* the good state of Kentucky was throwing off the incubus of secession. His behaviour in this affair was characteristic. Comprehending the military situation at a glance, he telegraphed to Fremont that he should strike at Paducah unless withheld by positive orders. Then he went on and seized the position, and on returning to Cairo found Fremont's despatch authorizing him to make the attempt if he felt strong enough. We see here the same qualities which we had observed in Lyon, — the ardour and quickness to strike, combined with the sagacity which knows where to aim the blow. With Paducah in Union hands, it was no longer possible for the Confederates to gain a defensive line along the Ohio river without a desperate battle. Shortly afterwards the movement was completed by sending General C. F. Smith to hold the mouth of the Cumberland. Grant now asked permission to attack Columbus, but the request was unheeded. Several weeks were passed in organizing and drilling the troops, while Polk strengthened the bluff at Columbus with earthworks mounting 142 heavy guns. Strong fortifications were also begun by the Confederates lower down the river at New Madrid and Island Number Ten, and still lower at Fort Pillow.

On the 1st of November, while Fremont was advancing against Price as above mentioned, Grant was directed to make demonstrations on both banks of the Mississippi, in order to prevent Polk from sending troops into Missouri. At the same time he was ordered to detach a small force to aid in the pursuit of the guerrilla chieftain Thompson. For this duty Grant detailed 3000 men under Colonel Oglesby, while with about the same number under his own command he sailed down the river under convoy of two gunboats, and landed soon after daybreak of November 7 on the Missouri shore some three miles above Columbus, at a point where he was screened by thick woods from the view of the enemy. Just opposite Columbus, and completely commanded by its guns, were three wooden shanties built on a low flat, scarcely above the level of the water. The place was named Belmont, on the same principle that will sometimes lead well-meaning parents to christen a little brunette daughter "Blanche." To this point Polk had just sent General Pillow with 2500 men, intending to cut off the detachment under Oglesby. Perceiving the aim of this movement, Grant decided to frustrate it by an immediate attack. Few of the men on either side had ever been under fire, but they fought very well for nearly four hours, until Pillow retreated in disorder and the Union troops took possession of his camp.

Battle of Belmont.

It was now time for them, having struck their blow, to get away from Belmont at once, for under the hostile guns of Columbus the place was untenable. But the undisciplined Union soldiers, elated with victory, dispersed to pillage the camp, shouting and cheering, while their officers, scarcely less raw than themselves, made speeches presaging the speedy overthrow of the rebellion and the summary hanging of Jeff Davis "on a sour apple tree." Finding the language of command insufficient to restore order, Grant set fire to the camp, while the batteries at Columbus, seeing it now occupied only by foes, opened a heavy plunging fire. These energetic warnings sufficed to bring the men to their senses, and falling into place again they started in good order for the boats.

But meanwhile Pillow had rallied his defeated troops, and being joined by three fresh regiments from across the river, had succeeded in taking a position between the Union men and their boats, so as to cut off their retreat. For a moment there were symptoms of confusion in the Federal ranks, which Grant allayed by remarking that victorious soldiers who had cut their way in could cut their way out again. A spirited charge soon repulsed the enemy, who disappeared from sight as he had done before, — but this time only to await the arrival of the high-decked steamers which were crossing the river crowded with reinforcements and bringing General Polk himself upon the scene.

These fresh troops arrived in time to assault the Federals in flank just as they were reaching the shore, but it was too late to cut them off. Their embarkation was effected, not without much confusion and the loss of some parties who had been sent to bring in the wounded, but they carried away two of the cannon which they had captured, as well as a few prisoners. Grant was the last to leave the field, and narrowly escaped capture or death. As he sat on his horse, covered with a cloak which disguised his rank, Polk saw him and exclaimed, "There's a Yankee, my boys, if you want to try your aim!" The last Federal steamer was just unmooring, but Grant's horse slid down the bank on his haunches, a plank was thrown out, and the general trotted aboard amid a hail of musket-balls, which for the most part flew harmlessly over the deck. As the men were all embarked, the gunboats now poured grape and canister into the Confederates on shore until they sought shelter in the woods. Late in the evening Grant reached Cairo, having accomplished his main purpose in occupying Polk's attention and diverting reinforcements from the Confederate army in Missouri. The wary bishop now kept his men together at Columbus in anticipation of further attacks.

Whether in the life of Grant or in the history of our Civil War, the fight at Belmont was but a slight incident; yet at one time it provoked much discussion. Both sides claimed a victory. The Federals claimed it as having won the morning's fight, as having effected their object, and as having come away after inflicting a heavier loss upon the enemy than they had sustained themselves. The Confederates claimed it as having at last compelled the Federals to withdraw in hurry and confusion. Public opinion at the North adopted the Confederate view of the

Comments on Belmont.

case, and seeing nothing but the fact of an advance in the morning followed by retreat in the afternoon, hastened to the conclusion that this was another fiasco like Big Bethel and Ball's Bluff. Whenever an engagement occurred at that early period of the war, the northern people looked for overwhelming victory followed by a long stride southward; they cared little for demonstrations and diversions, and having met with a long series of slight reverses, the importance of which was much exaggerated, they were naturally in a captious and fault-finding mood. The affair at Belmont was accordingly made the theme of angry sarcasm, and although this mood was soon dispelled by the great victory at Fort Donelson, the sarcasm was revived in later years with far less excuse, when Grant became a candidate for the presidency. Democratic newspapers in 1868 made much of Belmont, while indulging in criticisms that were as ill-considered as ill-natured. Grant's military object in the movement was sound, and, as we have seen, was accomplished. His conduct of the movement was excellent; but for his coolness and steadiness it would not have escaped the disaster so nearly incurred through the insubordination of the troops. Had they obeyed orders instead of stopping to riot in the enemy's camp, they would have been withdrawn as promptly as they had advanced, instead of waiting for the enemy to rally and gather reinforcements; and the affair would have worn the aspect of a brilliant dash instead of a repulse. Such untoward incidents are characteristic of fights between perfectly raw troops. But the affair showed at the same time of what excellent fighting stuff these novices were made. It was hotly contested on both sides. The Federal loss was 485 in killed, wounded, and missing; the Confederate loss was 641. Compared with the forces engaged, these figures show boldness and persistence; in the Revolutionary War such an affair would have ranked as a very considerable battle.

In defence of the battle of Belmont no more pithy and incisive comment has ever been made than the simple remark with which Grant himself, in his "Memoirs," dismisses the subject: "If it had not been fought, Colonel Oglesby would probably have been captured or destroyed with his 3000 men. Then I should have been culpable indeed."

CHAPTER II

FORT DONELSON AND SHILOH

EVENTS were now crowding upon the scene which made Belmont and all that had gone before seem insignificant. Baffled in their hopes of gaining the Ohio river, the Confederates had established their defensive line in southern Kentucky, stretching from Columbus on the Mississippi to Cumberland Gap in the Alleghanies. The weak spot in this line was the part where it was crossed by the Tennessee and Cumberland rivers, which afforded access to the Federal navy. It was thought that the ascent of these streams might be blocked by fortresses, as Polk had blocked the descent of the Mississippi; and to this end Fort Henry was erected on the Tennessee, and Fort Donelson, about twelve miles distant, on the Cumberland. Both strongholds were within the state of Tennessee, a little beyond the Kentucky border, just where the ascending courses of the two parallel rivers begin to diverge. Ninety miles northeast of Fort Donelson, the post of Bowling Green, forming a salient in

The first Confederate line of defence.

the long line, was held by General Buckner. At an equal distance to the east of Bowling Green, General Zollicoffer, in an entrenched camp at Mill Spring, formed the right wing of the whole line, and guarded the approaches to the Cumberland Mountains. The chief command west of the Alleghanies had been given to Albert Sidney Johnston, who was then regarded in all parts of the country as one of the ablest of American soldiers. General Johnston was a native of Kentucky, of New England descent. A graduate of West Point, he had served with distinction in the Texan army in 1836, and afterward in the Mexican War, and in 1857 had conducted the memorable expedition to Utah. At the beginning of the Civil War he had been opposed to secession, and it was intended to offer him one of the highest commands in the Federal army. But when the state of Texas, of which he had long been a citizen, seceded, he did as so many others did and "went with his state." He was then in his fifty-ninth year, handsome in person and winning in manner, of lofty character, heroic courage, and undoubted ability. On assuming command he had completed the defensive line just described by throwing Buckner forward into Bowling Green, and was now busily employed in collecting an army sufficient to hold so vast a territory. Opposed to his left was

Albert Sidney Johnston.

Grant, at Cairo, now acting under orders from Halleck, at St. Louis. Opposed to his centre and right was the army which had been assembled in northern Kentucky under Don Carlos Buell. Five divisions of this army, under Generals McCook, Crittenden, Nelson, Wood, and Mitchel, lay to the northward of Bowling Green. A sixth, watching the extreme rebel right, was commanded by George Henry Thomas, of Virginia, one of the greatest soldiers produced by the Civil War, as well as one of the most attractive characters in American history since George Washington. General Thomas had been educated at West Point, and had served with distinction in the Mexican War. As a Virginian of Virginians he was confronted with the painful question of allegiance which beset Lee and <small>George Henry</small> both the Johnstons and so many other <small>Thomas.</small> high-minded men; but in his case love for the Union prevailed over his intense attachment to his native state; and he became such a power in the Federal army that Virginia, which fought so hard to dismember the Union, may now congratulate herself that in giving us Thomas she also did much to help save it. A man of rare and exquisite refinement, whole-souled devotion to duty, perfect sincerity and perfect modesty, he was every inch a soldier. His military judgment was unerring, and when he struck it was with the blow of a trip-hammer. We shall see him growing in fame and in achievement until at Nashville, in the concluding period of the war, he annihilates a great Confederate army on the field of battle. His first victory was similar in completeness, though small in scale. On the 19th of January, 1862, in a short, sharp fight near Mill Spring, in which Zollicoffer was killed, Thomas destroyed the Confederate force and cleared all that part of Kentucky at a single blow. By this victory the Federals gained Cumberland Gap and were brought within support of the loyal population of eastern Tennessee; the eastern extremity of Johnston's line was demolished, and his salient at Bowling Green was threatened on its flank. But still graver ill fortune was preparing for him in the other direction, where Grant was about to take the initiative.

Battle of Mill Spring.

As Colonel Preston Johnston tersely observes, in his biography of his father, "there has been much discussion as to who originated the movement up the Tennessee river. Grant *made* it, and it made Grant. It was obvious enough to all the leaders on both sides." Sherman, Buell, and Grant agreed in urging it upon Halleck, but McClellan, general-in-chief, thought it should be postponed for a while, until after eastern Tennessee should have been occupied. Halleck seems

56 *The Mississippi Valley in the Civil War*

to have understood the value of the movement, but when Grant asked permission to make it, Halleck silenced him so sharply as to make it appear that he deemed it a gross blunder. Halleck thought the enterprise should not be undertaken with less than 60,000 men; but Grant persisted, and Commodore Foote, commanding the gunboat flotilla, added his solicitations, until at last the requisite permission was obtained; and on February 2 Grant and Foote started up the Tennessee with 17,000 men and seven gunboats. The success of the movement was due to its promptness, as is usual in warfare, in which more strikingly than in any other pursuit of life we see the truth of the adage that time is money. Fort Henry was doomed by the mere quickness of the movement. General Tilghman, the commandant, had but 3400 men, and saw at once that it was too late for reinforcements to reach him. Accordingly he sent most of his force over to Fort Donelson, remaining himself with a small detachment to cover the retreat. This was sound policy and apparently the only course open to the commander of Fort Henry; the struggle must be made at Fort Donelson. General Tilghman worked his few men and guns admirably, and after a brief bombardment by the fleet he surrendered Fort Henry with only 96 men. A convenient base was

Capture of Fort Henry.

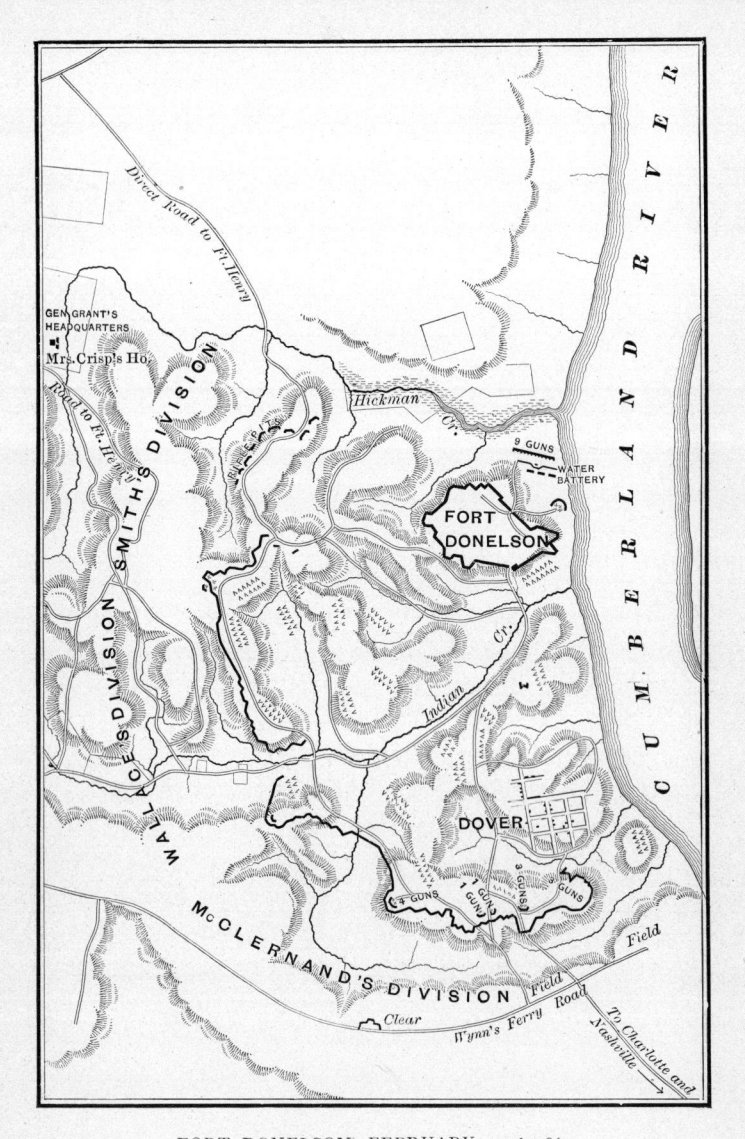

FORT DONELSON, FEBRUARY 13-16, 1862

Fort Donelson and Shiloh

thus established against Fort Donelson, to which the Union forces now hastened.

Fort Donelson was situated on a plateau near the great bend of the Cumberland river, elevated about one hundred feet above the shore-line. It "consisted of two water-batteries on the hillside, protected by a bastioned earthwork of irregular outline on the summit, enclosing about one hundred acres."[1] To the north of it Hickman creek, flowing into the Cumberland and filled at this season with backwater, formed an impassable barrier. About half a mile to the south Indian creek emptied into the river, and just south of Indian creek stood the little town of Dover, whence ran the road to Nashville by way of Charlotte, affording the only available line of retreat in case of an overwhelming land attack. To the west or rear of fortress and town the country is cut up by several small brooks flowing into Hickman and Indian creeks, and leaving a series of ridges from fifty to eighty feet in height and for the most part parallel to the river. Starting from Hickman creek on the north, at a point rather more than a mile from the river, a continuous line of ridges was fortified with rifle-pits and abattis difficult to penetrate. Broken only at one spot by the valley of Indian creek, this line of defences was carried

Position of Fort Donelson.

[1] Davis, *Rise and Fall of the Confederate Government*, ii. 28.

southward and eastward as far as the river, enclosing the town of Dover and commanding the road to Charlotte. Nine batteries were placed at intervals along the line.

This strong position was occupied by an army of 18,000 men, commanded by General Pillow, an officer whose vanity far exceeded his merit. Second in command was General Buckner, an excellent soldier, whose relations with Pillow were not altogether cordial. On the 13th of February, the day after Grant arrived with his army, a third general, senior in rank to Pillow, came in and took command. This was John Floyd, lately secretary of war under President Buchanan. He was a person unfit for any such responsible position; and Johnston clearly made a capital mistake in sending him there at a critical moment.

Its commanders.

Fort Henry had fallen on the 6th, and Grant, realizing the need of striking quickly, had hoped to attack Fort Donelson on the 8th; but the roads were flooded, supplies were slow in coming, and the fleet had a long distance to travel in descending one river and ascending the other. The sun was setting on the 12th when the divisions of McClernand and C. F. Smith, numbering about 15,000 men, arrived before the works. A third division of 2500 men, under Lew Wallace,[1] had been left at

[1] An able officer, since better known as the gifted author of *Ben-Hur* and *The Fair God*.

Fort Henry, but this was brought up next day, as the forces were insufficient to surround the works. During the 13th the investment was completed. McClernand held the Charlotte road with his right and stretched his left nearly as far as Indian creek. On his left came the centre division under Lew Wallace, and beyond, stretching northward to Hickman's creek, was stationed C. F. Smith with the left wing. The line was still a slender one, and Grant's conduct in coming up so quickly had been marked by audacity. It is seldom in history that a force behind entrenchments has allowed itself to be quietly invested by a force no greater than itself. If the enemy had harassed him on the march from Fort Henry, or vigorously attacked him on the morning of the 13th, it might have interfered seriously with his plans; but during those two days the Confederates behaved as if paralyzed. Grant's conduct indicates that he gauged the calibre of Pillow and Floyd, and took it into the account. When his lines were completed on the 13th, he ordered an attack by way of feeling the enemy's strength. None of the works were carried, but McClernand's hold upon the Charlotte road became firmer.

Investment of Fort Donelson.

The night was a dismal one for the soldiers. Their supplies were delayed, and food was getting scarce. The weather had been warm, and many of these inexperienced men had forgotten or thrown away their blankets. Now the temperature dropped to twenty degrees below the freezing-point, while the camps were swept by a furious storm of snow and sleet. Many were frost-bitten, some were frozen to death, in others were sown the seeds of fatal disease. The morning, however, brought the gallant fleet, convoying the transports with the provisions so sorely needed, and 5000 fresh troops, which were added to Wallace's division and essentially increased the strength of the besieging line. Commodore Foote, pushing up within 500 yards of the water-batteries, opened a furious fire, which succeeded in silencing several guns; but at length their plunging fire disabled his two best gunboats and compelled him to withdraw out of range, leaving the river above the fort still open to the enemy. The works on the river-front were knocked out of shape, but the fort seemed as far as ever from surrender, and at nightfall of the 14th Grant began to think it might be necessary to have recourse to siege.

<small>An artillery duel.</small>

But Floyd had held a council of war that morning in which it was decided that the situation was alarming, and that the best thing for the Confederates to do was to cut their way out, retire upon Charlotte, and reopen land-communication with

Nashville. The sortie was to have been made that day, but at Pillow's instance, it was postponed till next morning. Early on the 15th Grant had gone on board one of the gunboats to consult with Foote, who was suffering from a wound received the day before, and could not come ashore. Soon after daybreak Pillow hurled 8000 men upon McClernand's right, and after an obstinate struggle not only pushed him off the Charlotte road, but threw his whole line into confusion and drove him in upon Wallace. The avenue of escape was thus opened, and if the Confederates had taken immediate advantage of it, though they would have lost the fort, they could probably have saved their army.

Sortie of the Confederate garrison.

But Pillow, flushed with his success, now attempted altogether too much. He sent a despatch to Johnston, announcing a Confederate victory, and attacked Lew Wallace in the hope of rolling him up on Smith and turning the whole Federal position. In this he was aided by Buckner, but the Confederates were exhausted with their morning's work and made little headway. Presently there came a lull in the battle, and just at this moment Grant rode upon the field. There was no thought of siege in his mind then. He saw the state of affairs and the error the Confederates had committed; and he knew that at such critical moments success waits upon a bold initiative. He ordered Wallace to retake the positions lost in the morning, while Smith was to charge upon the entrenchments on the left. The veteran Charles Ferguson Smith, one of the truest men and finest officers in the Federal service, led the assault in person, inspiring his raw troops with his own dauntless courage. "I was nearly scared to death," said one of his soldiers afterwards, "but I saw the old man's white mustache over his shoulder, and went on." Under a withering fire of rifles they swept up the ridge and encountered the tangled boughs of the abattis. "No flinching now," shouted the old hero, waving his cap aloft on the point of his sword, "here's the way, come on!" and in a few minutes they had scrambled through and driven the defenders from their rifle-pits. The ridge was carried, and the right of the Confederate line was in our possession.

Ferguson Smith storms the Confederate entrenchment,

This achievement at once relieved the pressure upon the Federal right. Buckner brought over a whole division to drive Smith from the ridge he had taken, but all to no purpose; he could not stir him an inch. Meanwhile Wallace, assaulting the enfeebled forces on his right, pushed them back into

while Wallace cuts off their retreat.

their works, seized the Charlotte road, and occupied every yard of ground to the river's edge. The situation of the Confederates was far worse than in the morning. They had lost more than 2000 men in the battle, their escape was cut off, and Smith's position commanded their works.

In the night an extraordinary scene ensued. A council of war decided that nothing was left but to surrender. But Floyd, who was at that moment under indictment at Washington for embezzlement of public funds, declared he would rather die than surrender. "Yes," said Pillow, "there are no two men the Yankees want more than you and me, and they shall not have us." Floyd asked Buckner if they would be allowed to depart in case they should turn over the command to him. Buckner replied yes, if they should leave before terms of surrender were agreed on. So these unworthy chiefs forsook their men and escaped up the river on a small steamboat, while Colonel Forrest pushed his cavalry across a half-frozen marsh formed by backwater and got away, leaving part of his force in the hands of the wakeful foe. At daybreak Buckner sent a messenger to learn what terms would be accepted. "No terms," answered Grant, "but unconditional surrender. I propose to move immediately upon your works." The Confederate com- "Unconditional surrender."

mander complained of such treatment as "unchivalrous," but was fain to submit.

The surrender delivered up to Grant nearly 15,000 prisoners, with 65 cannon and 17,000 muskets. His loss in killed, wounded, and missing, had exceeded 3000, and that of the enemy had been not far from the same. For physical dimensions it was the greatest military achievement that the American continent had yet witnessed; but its strategic value was not to be measured by its physical dimensions. The two great rivers were laid open for hundreds of miles, Importance of the victory. so that Union gunboats sailed far into Alabama. The victory of Thomas at Mill Spring had already led Johnston to evacuate Bowling Green and retire upon Nashville. Now it was necessary to abandon Nashville also, for the great suspension bridge over the Cumberland was Johnston's only available line of retreat, and there was now nothing to hinder Foote from coming up to destroy it. If the army stayed in its jeopardized situation, he would be sure to come. There was a panic in Nashville. The state government fled, with the archives and all the money in the treasury, Johnston fell back to Murfreesboro, and just a week after Buckner's surrender a division of Buell's army occupied the capital of Tennessee. On the Mississippi river the results were equally decisive. By staying in Columbus, Polk would only invite the fate which had overtaken Buckner, and he accordingly retreated as far as Corinth, in Mississippi.

Thus the first Confederate line of defence was shattered throughout its whole length, and the silent man who had dealt such a blow stepped at once from obscurity into a national fame. The American people had happily had but little experience in military matters, and knew little of the dynamics of warfare; and when they saw position after position thus surrendered, and a wide stretch of country abandoned, as the immediate result of Grant's victory, the feeling was one of amazement, and a hopeful mood was enkindled that was as yet premature, because none could yet comprehend the enormous difficulty of the task which had to be performed. Grant had now won a foothold in the confidence of the people which did him and the country good service in the trying time to come, when at Vicksburg he was confronted with a problem immeasurably more complicated and difficult than that which he had now solved at Fort Donelson. In the gloomy record of the anxious and impatient year which had just passed, this great victory was the one bright spot. The victor became a popular hero, and the phrase "Unconditional Surrender," humorously associated with the initials of his name, became the watchword of the northern people, and the index of the policy which was to be pursued until the spectre of secession should be exorcised and the work of the men who founded this nation guaranteed in safety forever.

The correct and studious Halleck, who had been so slow to sanction Grant's forward movement, Halleck and Grant. now telegraphed to Washington, begging to have his own command so enlarged as to cover all the armies west of the Alleghanies, and added, with droll inconsistency, that "hesitation and delay are losing us the golden opportunity." President Lincoln immediately appointed Grant major-general of volunteers, and presently Buell, Pope, Smith, McClernand, and Wallace were raised to the same rank. On the 11th of March Halleck's command was enlarged according to his request, and divided into three departments, Pope in Missouri commanding the right, Grant on the Tennessee the centre, and Buell at Nashville the left.

A fortnight before these arrangements were made, Grant found it necessary to go for one day to Nashville, to consult with Buell, and during his absence some of his undisciplined men indulged themselves in marauding. On his return they were promptly arrested, but the news of the incident, magnified and highly coloured in an anonymous letter, led Halleck to send the following despatch to McClellan at Washington: "I have had no communication with General Grant for more than a week. He left his command without my authority, and went to Nashville. His army seems to be as much demoralized by the victory of Fort Donelson as was that of the Potomac by the defeat of Bull Run. It is hard to censure a successful general immediately after a victory, but I think he richly deserves it. I can get no returns, no reports, no information of any kind from him. Satisfied with his victory, he sits down and enjoys it, without any regard to the future. I am worn out and tired by this neglect and inefficiency. C. F. Smith is almost the only officer equal to the emergency."

Halleck sent this extraordinary despatch before complaining to Grant or giving him a chance to justify himself. No wonder that on receiving it McClellan should have felt bound to reply: "The future success of our cause demands that proceedings such as General Grant's should at once be checked. Generals must observe discipline as well as private soldiers. Do not hesitate to arrest him at once if the good of the service requires it, and place C. F. Smith in command. You are at liberty to regard this as a positive order, if it will smooth your way."

By Halleck's command the army had just been moved back from Fort Donelson to Fort Henry, preparatory to ascending the Tennessee river for the capture of Corinth. Halleck now availed himself of McClellan's message so far as to place Smith in command of the expedition, while he charged Grant with disobedience and directed him to remain at Fort Henry. Sorely astonished and hurt, Grant asked to be relieved of his command. An interchange of telegrams followed for several days, in the course of which Grant completely justified himself, and was replaced in charge of the expedition, greatly to the relief of Smith, who had been one of Grant's teachers at West Point, and thoroughly believed in him. Smith was shocked and amazed at this readiness of Halleck to condemn his subordinate unheard, and at the moment after a great victory; but the explanation is not far to seek. In common with many of the older officers, Halleck was strongly prejudiced against Grant, who had been somewhat under a cloud when he left the regular army. It is unquestionable that Grant shared with Daniel Webster, and many other men of strong and massive natures, a somewhat overweening fondness for John Barleycorn. The fact was made much of by ill-disposed people, and was of course duly brought to the attention of President Lincoln, who estimated it with his customary humorous shrewdness. "I should like," said Lincoln, "to find out the kind of whiskey he drinks: I would send a barrel of it to every one of my generals!" There is nothing to show that Grant's usefulness as a commander was ever impaired by this personal trait, but it seems to have been what Halleck had in mind when he acted so precipitately upon the anonymous letter.

Whiskey and war.

The little town of Corinth, in northern Mississippi, which was now threatened by the approach of the Union army, was the meeting-point of two great railroads that connected the Mississippi river and the Gulf of Mexico with Virginia and the Carolinas. By seizing this strategic point and driving the enemy from his positions on the river at New Madrid, Island Number Ten, Fort Pillow, and Memphis, the whole country would be laid open as far as Vicksburg. The task of opening the great river from above was entrusted to General Pope, with whom the greater part of Commodore Foote's fleet was now to coöperate; and an expedition was already fitting out for the capture of New Orleans and the conquest of the river from below. The task of taking Corinth was assigned to the united forces of Grant and Buell, which Halleck was to command

Strategic importance of Corinth.

in person. The Confederates were straining every nerve to secure this important position, and make it the base for an offensive campaign which should retrieve the disaster of Fort Donelson. General Beauregard, who had won such laurels at Bull Run, was sent to Mississippi, and had already occupied Corinth in force. Loud and bitter complaints were poured upon Johnston for losing Fort Donelson and Nashville, and the Confederate government was urged to remove him from his command; but Mr. Davis, after listening patiently to an angry delegation from Tennessee who begged him to give them a general, replied with great earnestness, " If Sidney Johnston is not a general, the Confederacy has none to give you." A special committee was appointed to inquire into the causes of the late disasters, and Floyd and Pillow were removed from command; but Johnston was retained in his high position, with Beauregard as his chief lieutenant, and by the end of March they had assembled at Corinth an army of nearly 50,000 men. Polk was brought thither on his retreat from Columbus, and Braxton Bragg came up with 10,000 men from Pensacola. This able general was a native of North Carolina. At the battle of Buena Vista, in
Braxton the Mexican War, he had by a timely
Bragg. movement saved from destruction the regiment of Jefferson Davis, and this service was

never forgotten by the President of the Confederacy, who always befriended Bragg through good and evil fortune. Bragg was a man of refinement in feature and expression, somewhat stern and reserved in demeanour, an excellent disciplinarian and organizer, but wanting in strategic power. To complete this gathering of the forces, General Van Dorn, scarcely recovered from his recent crushing defeat at Pea Ridge, was ordered to bring over his army from Arkansas; but although he moved with alacrity, he only succeeded in getting up one regiment in time for the coming battle.

Just before the misunderstanding between Grant and Halleck, General Beauregard sent a couple of regiments with a field-battery to take possession of the bluff at Pittsburg Landing, about twenty miles northeast from Corinth, but this force was driven away by two of Foote's gunboats. A few days later General C. F. Smith, coming Pittsburg up the river with his forces, selected Landing. this spot as the rendezvous for the two Union armies. Halleck had designated Savannah, on the eastern bank, nine miles below or northward from Pittsburg Landing, but Smith was authorized to make a different arrangement if he saw fit. When Grant arrived, he recognized the importance of the position and adopted it. Many persons found fault with him after the battle for taking position on the west side of the river, but the ablest critics seem to agree with the Count of Paris that the position was "extremely well chosen." It was Grant's theory of the campaign that he was to attack and crush the enemy, and the east side of the river was not the place in which to do this. It would not do to give up the bluff at Pittsburg Landing to Johnston and Beauregard. The position was an exceedingly strong one, and while the gunboats commanded the river Grant might expect to have sufficient means of transport at hand in case of disaster. It was his plan to wait in this position until the arrival of Buell's army, after which the united forces were to advance upon the enemy at Corinth. Meanwhile, as Buell was expected to arrive at Savannah, Grant kept his headquarters there for the present, but spent a large part of each day with the army at Pittsburg Landing.

The position was a quadrilateral nearly enclosed by natural obstacles, but open on the southwest, the side facing toward Corinth. The north was covered by Snake creek, emptying into the river a little below the landing. Owl creek, a tributary of Snake creek, enclosed the northwest side. To the southeast Lick creek flows into the river above the landing, and at that time its volume was greatly swelled by backwater. All three streams, indeed, were more or less flooded. The space included between them measured about three miles in either direction. The ground was uneven and thickly wooded. A number of small roads intersected it, and on one of these, running out toward Corinth near the right of the position, was a rude meeting-house built of logs and known as Shiloh church. The greater part of the army was arranged across the open front of the quadrilateral between Owl and Lick creeks which protected its two flanks. The right wing, near the crossing of Owl creek by the road from Pittsburg Landing to Purdy, was commanded by a general who for profound knowledge of strategy, and versatility of resource, must be ranked among the masters of the military art. William Tecumseh Sherman had succeeded Grant in command at Cairo, and now in the gathering of the forces had come to take charge of a division in the advance upon Corinth. On Sherman's left, and somewhat overlapping him to the rear, was McClernand, and next to him Prentiss, while Stuart's brigade of Sherman's division held the extreme left, resting upon Lick creek.[1] About a

Arrangement of Federal forces at Shiloh.

---

[1] These positions as marked on the map indicate approximately the relative positions of the Federal *camps* on Sunday morning, rather than the fluctuating lines of battle which were formed under fire.

mile and a half to the rear, stretching from a point slightly above Pittsburg Landing across to Snake creek, the divisions of Hurlbut and C. F. Smith were stationed in reserve; but the gallant Smith was never again to take the field. He had hurt his leg in jumping into a yawl, and this slight injury, joined with the effects of exposure at Fort Donelson, brought him in a few weeks to the grave. He was then lying ill at Savannah, and his division was commanded by William Wallace. Lew Wallace's division was five miles down the river at Crump's Landing, whence a road runs westward to the town of Purdy. Movements of the enemy were possible in this direction, and Wallace remained to watch the Purdy road. Another road parallel with the river connected Wallace directly with the right of the Union reserve by a bridge lately built over Snake creek.

The only quarter in which the Union army was exposed to assault was the open front between Owl and Lick creeks. At a later period of the war this line would doubtless have been entrenched, and the whole position made invulnerable. But the need of entrenching was not then so keenly felt as it came to be afterward. It took just such terrible affairs as Shiloh to reveal the need of it. For it was even in this strong position that Johnston resolved to attack and crush Grant's army

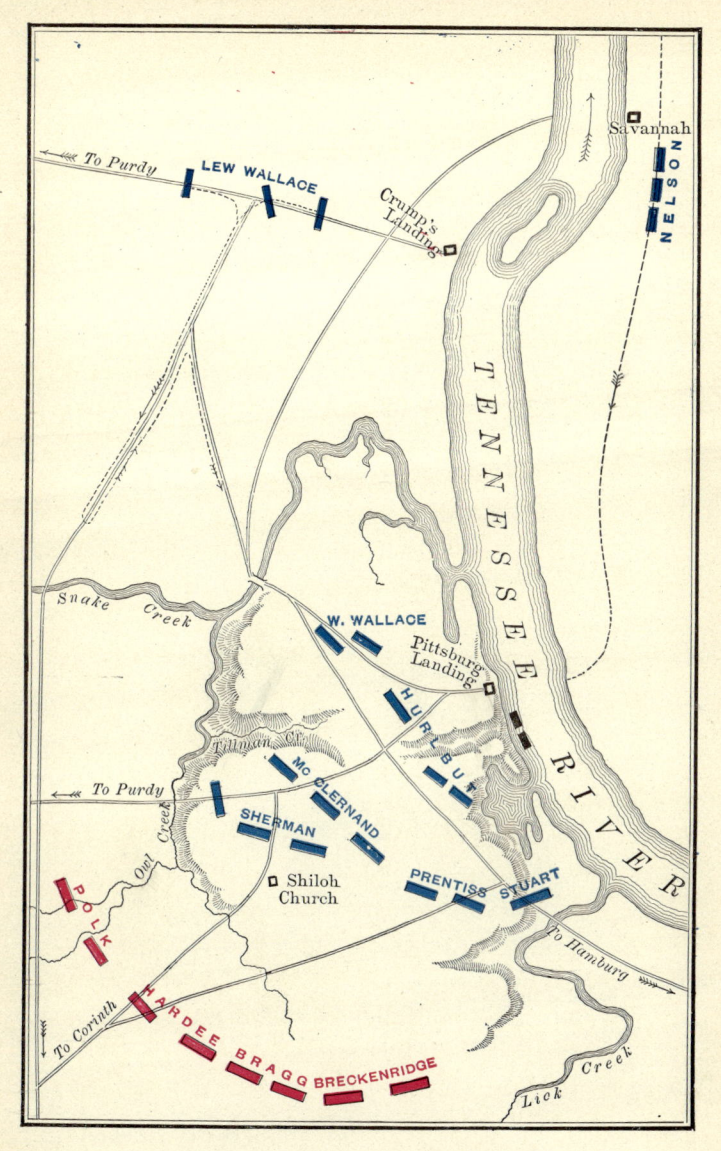

SHILOH, APRIL 6, 1862, MORNING

before Buell's should have joined it. Could this be done, it might repair the disaster of Fort Donelson and regain to the Confederacy the lost territory. *The eve of battle.* At the very least, it would save Corinth and restore the prestige of the southern arms. Johnston waited as long as he dared for the arrival of Van Dorn from Arkansas, with 20,000 men, but swollen streams and miry roads made him wait in vain. On the other hand, Buell's march from Nashville was delayed by unlooked-for obstacles. There was a freshet in Duck river, and a bridge had to be rebuilt, which took several days. In the early spring American roads are at their worst, and marching was slow. Still Buell made progress, and on Saturday evening, the 5th of April, the head of his foremost division, under Nelson, arrived at Savannah. At that moment the Confederate lines were already deployed and ready for battle in front of the Federal army, but hidden from view in the forest. The attack had been planned for Saturday morning, but some misunderstanding of orders had bred delay until it was too late to attack before the morrow. Beauregard now argued that the plan of surprising Grant's army had evidently failed, and he held the element of surprise to be so important that in its absence the attack had better not be made. It would be wiser, said Beauregard, to retire upon

Corinth; but Johnston persisted, and ordered the attack for next morning at daybreak.

Perhaps no other battle of the nineteenth century save Waterloo has been the occasion of so much difference of opinion as the battle of Shiloh. One of the points most hotly discussed has been the question how far the Federal army was taken by surprise on the morning of that bloody Sunday.

How far were the Federals surprised at Shiloh? Rumour had it for a while that the presence of an enemy was so far unsuspected that in Prentiss's camp, where Johnston's first blow fell, men were captured by wholesale in their beds. It has also been contended that the end of the day found the Federal army so completely shattered that nothing but Buell's timely arrival could have saved it from utter destruction or capture. A sober study of the documentary evidence seems hardly to justify such extreme statements; yet doubtless they come much nearer to the truth than Grant and Sherman, in their published Memoirs, are willing to admit.

So long as Grant felt it necessary or desirable to keep his headquarters at Savannah, it was doubly incumbent on him to secure the position of his army by every practicable means. If he thought it better to employ his raw troops in drilling than in throwing up earthworks, it was an error in judg-

Fort Donelson and Shiloh 77

ment excusable in view of his want of experience, but none the less an error. His inattention to the exposed front between Owl and Lick creeks is pretty clear proof that he was not expecting an attack in that quarter for the morning of Sunday, April 6. Had he been on the lookout for such an event, would he not have spent Saturday night at Pittsburg Landing instead of Savannah? and would he not have lodged some appropriate instructions with Lew Wallace, instead of waiting till Sunday morning?

<small>Grant was not expecting the attack on Sunday morning,</small>

These considerations have all the more weight since in Grant's absence from the field it was not at all clear who represented him there. Lew Wallace and McClernand were the only major-generals, so that the latter was ranking officer at the front. As Sherman's camp, however, was situated furthest forward, it would seem to have been especially incumbent on him to watch for indications of the enemy's presence in the neighbourhood. Here a cavalry force would have been useful, but for want of such aid the army was virtually blindfold. Under such circumstances it would seem that Sherman should have taken more than ordinary pains to learn all that could be elicited from the forest by pickets and scouts. His failure to do so, his evident fail-

<small>nor was Sherman.</small>

ure to realize the need for it, was simply a mark of inexperience. It is truly remarkable that an army of 40,000 Confederates should have approached on Saturday afternoon within a distance of two or three miles, and not have sharply aroused the attention of the Federal camps. The point is one on which General Sherman in later years was unduly sensitive. I have often heard him repudiate with scorn the charge of having been taken by surprise at Shiloh, and there can of course be no doubt as to his perfect sincerity of conviction.

The Federals were surprised. Nevertheless, the undeniable fact that when the Confederates attacked in full force on Sunday morning, the Federals were in camp and not in line of battle, would seem to furnish absolute demonstration that the attack was not expected.

The first Union officer to take the alarm was the West Virginian brigadier, Benjamin Prentiss, who on Saturday descried indications of the presence of cavalry in the neighbourhood and strengthened his pickets. Soon after five o'clock on Sunday morning the battle was begun by the *The opening attack upon Prentiss's division.* skirmishing of the rebel pickets with those of Prentiss; and scarcely had that general formed his division and thrown it a quarter of a mile forward, when it was struck by the mighty rush of the Confederates. On they came in three parallel lines, one following another at intervals of about half a mile. First came Hardee, with about 10,000 men, then Bragg, with 10,000 more; while the rear line comprised Polk's 10,000 to leftward and Breckinridge's 6000 to the right. When the full line of battle was developed, this arrangement brought forward Polk on the extreme left, by Owl creek, with Hardee as left centre, Bragg as right centre, and Breckinridge on the extreme right, by Lick creek. Besides these 36,000 infantry there were 4000 cavalry, scarcely effective in that tangle of forest. On the other hand, the Union army numbered about 40,000 men, but 7000 of these were with Lew Wallace at Crump's Landing, leaving 33,000 to confront the enemy's attack.

Grant was taking an early breakfast at Savannah when suddenly he heard the heavy firing, and forthwith started up the river, leaving a note for Buell. At Crump's Landing he found Lew Wallace awaiting him in a boat. Telling Wallace to hold himself in readiness for an immediate start, Grant hastened to the battlefield. Arriving at eight o'clock, and finding that the enemy had evidently massed his whole strength in our front, he sent a verbal order to Wallace to march at once. The distance was only five muddy miles, but after five hours of

<small>Grant's instructions and Lew Wallace's march.</small>

obstinate fighting, in the course of which the
Federal front was driven back more than a mile,
nothing had yet been heard from Wallace, and
two of Grant's staff — James McPherson [1] and
John Rawlins — were sent to look for him. The
cause of delay was a misunderstanding such as
one is continually meeting with in every-day life.
It had not occurred to Grant that Wallace would
move by any other route than the direct road from
the vicinity of Crump's Landing to the bridge
over Snake creek. But it happened that some of
Wallace's brigades had been thrown out for some
distance along the Purdy road, and it seemed to
him sufficiently direct to come by a route parallel
to that which Grant had in mind, crossing Snake
creek a couple of miles higher up. When Mc-
Pherson and Rawlins found him, he had nearly
reached the creek; but now he learned from them
that to pursue this route would be dangerous. It
would lead him to the point where the road from
Purdy to Pittsburg Landing crosses Owl creek, and
now that the Federal line had been driven back,
this would bring him on the field in an isolated
position, where he would be liable to be separately
attacked. It thus became necessary for Wallace
to retrace his steps for some three miles, and then

[1] Afterward commander of the Army of the Tennessee, and
one of the ablest generals in the war.

to take a cross road to the Snake creek bridge below. All this marching and countermarching used up the day, so that Wallace did not arrive upon the scene of action till seven in the evening. His was, comparatively speaking, a division of veterans, and its absence was severely felt. This serious peril might have been prevented had Grant in the first place sent to Wallace a businesslike written order, specifying his line of march. It is in such minute attention to details that great generalship largely consists. Napoleon in his best days left but little room open for contingencies and misunderstandings.

Johnston's plan of battle was very simple. It was to push back the Federal army in such wise as to turn its left flank, and to interpose Bragg and Breckinridge between that flank and the river. Thus by cutting off the Federals from Pittsburg Landing and driving them, in more or less disorganized condition, into the pocket formed by Snake creek, he might even hope to force them to surrender. The desperate valour and dogged persistency with which his first charges were received, however, were such as to make it doubtful whether one long day would suffice for his programme. We have seen how the first fury of the assault fell upon Benjamin Prentiss about half past five in the morning. That

Johnston's plan of attack.

general held his ground nobly, gaining time for the other divisions to form in line of battle; but presently the enemy pushed in between Prentiss and Sherman, whose left regiment soon gave way in disorder. This obliged Prentiss to fall back to save his right flank; and so he alternately stood firm and yielded a little, until he had been pushed back half a mile to a point where Hurlbut reinforced him.[1] When this was accomplished, it was nine o'clock, or three hours and a half since this division had first been struck.

Prentiss pushed back.

Meanwhile the disaster to Sherman's left wing, with the retirement of Prentiss, exposed McClernand's left flank, and he endeavoured to make a partial change of front to meet the danger; but under the fierce onset of the enemy, his line was driven back with the loss of six guns, and it was not able to recover itself and make a fresh stand until it had yielded nearly a quarter of a mile. By this time Sherman's third brigade, commanded by Colonel Hildebrand, had completely lost its organization and melted away, leaving on the ground more than

McClernand and Sherman pushed back.

---

[1] For many of these details I am indebted to General Buell's paper, "Shiloh Reviewed," in *Battles and Leaders of the Civil War*, i. 487–536; one of the most masterly pieces of military criticism that I have ever read in any language.

300 killed and wounded. The rest of Sherman's division fought with great obstinacy, and inflicted frightful loss upon their assailants; but the Confederates were so much stronger at the point of contact that mere heroism was of no avail against them, and by noon Sherman's division had ceased to exist as an organized body. Fragments of its regiments and companies took shelter among their friends of McClernand's division, which through these irregular accretions became quite an amorphous body, taking its orders indifferently from McClernand or from Sherman. After two hours more of desperate fighting, these generals retired their division across Tillman creek and took up a strong position along the road from Snake creek to Hamburg.

In this position their left flank was, in a measure, protected by the line of reserve which Hurlbut and William Wallace had maintained since an early hour of the day. Upon an advanced portion of this line Prentiss had retired, and toward the same point Stuart's brigade, on the extreme Union left, was driven, but not until thrice its own numbers had been massed against it. About the left centre of the Federal line was a wooded area with dense undergrowth, admirably adapted for defence; and there the indomitable Prentiss, reinforced by Stuart and by brigades from Wallace and Hurlbut, maintained his ground from nine in the morning till five in the afternoon. Again and again the Confederate assaults were repulsed with heavy slaughter. So savagely were they received that they bestowed upon the place the name of "Hornet's Nest." The long struggle at this point proved fatal to Johnston's scheme for turning the Federal left, and if among the Federal generals there is any one who deserves especial commemoration as having " saved the day," it is Benjamin Prentiss for the glorious stand which he made in the Hornet's Nest.

<small>The Hornet's Nest.</small>

It was in an open field on the eastern margin of this fiercely contested area, shortly after a spirited charge at about 2.30 P. M., that General Johnston was struck by a rifle-ball which cut an artery in the leg. The wound need not have been fatal. Although no surgeon happened to be near at hand, the general or any of his comrades might easily have extemporized a tourniquet that would have put him out of danger. But Johnston was so absorbed in his work that he took no heed of the wound until suddenly he sank and died from loss of blood. The command of the army then devolved upon General Beauregard, who was at that moment in the rear, at Shiloh church.

<small>Death of Johnston.</small>

The death of Johnston was a bitter loss to the

Confederacy. Jefferson Davis afterward declared his belief that "the fortunes of a country hung by the single thread of the life that was yielded on the field of Shiloh."[1] Johnston's death deprived us of the data requisite for testing the soundness of this opinion; but of the theory that if he had lived he would certainly have crushed the Federal army that evening, something may be said. The often repeated statement that Beauregard threw away what Johnston had won seems unfair to the former and inconsistent with the history of the remainder of the day. In point of fact, the Confederates had not yet won the battle.[2] The advanced division of Buell's army, under Nelson, was approaching on the further bank of the Tennessee river; and in order to gain a victory, it was absolutely necessary for the Confederates to capture Pittsburg Landing and cut off Grant's army from reinforcements. The long stoppage at the Hornet's

[1] *Rise and Fall of the Confederate Government*, ii. 69.

[2] Indeed, Johnston had not even gone to work in the way best fitted to carry out his plan of turning the Federal left flank. For that purpose his right wing ought to have been much more heavily massed, and his heaviest blow should have fallen upon Stuart rather than Prentiss. By following this line of action and pressing northward upon the Hamburg road, perhaps the Hornet's Nest might have been turned and Pittsburg Landing captured, which would have made the Confederate victory certain. It was a grave mistake to hammer for hours at the Hornet's Nest instead of pursuing the course thus outlined.

Nest had used up so much of the day as to leave scarcely time enough for this crowning achievement. After Johnston's death, more than two hours elapsed before the tremendous pressure upon Hurlbut's left flank compelled him to retire toward Pittsburg Landing, while a similar attack upon William Wallace's right wing pushed it back, disordered and partially crumbled. These events left the remaining Federal force in that part of the field, consisting of the remnants of Wallace's and Prentiss's divisions, with both wings in the air. Thus a little before six o'clock about six regiments, numbering over 2200 men, were encompassed and captured by the enemy. Prentiss was taken prisoner, and Wallace received a mortal wound.

<small>Capture of Prentiss.</small>

This great success for the Confederates was far from being an unmixed success, for the sending of so many captives to the rear entailed further delay when every minute was precious. The position at Pittsburg Landing was covered by a ravine partly overflowed with backwater. On bluffs overlooking this ravine a battery of twenty pieces was planted just as three Confederate brigades were advancing to the attack. As the enemy, flushed with victory, came on, these batteries opened upon them, while at the same time the gunboats Tyler and Lexington took part in the contest and enfiladed the

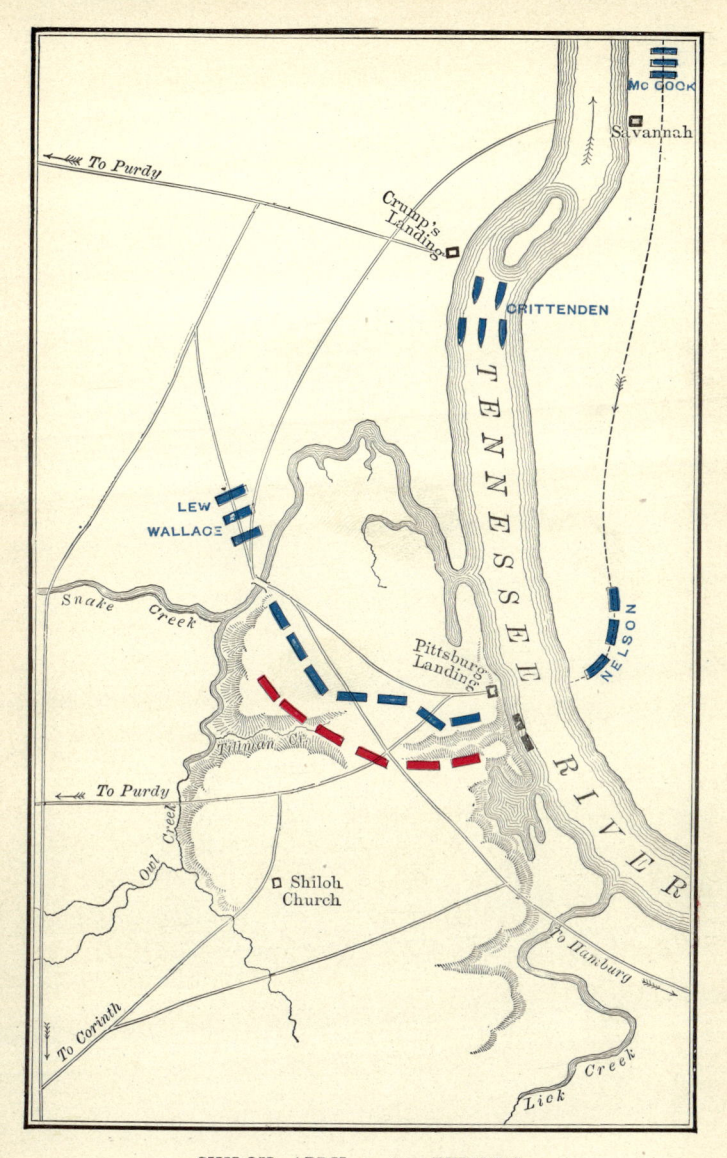

SHILOH, APRIL 6, 1862, EVENING

rebel lines with their giant balls. Moreover, Nelson's division was crossing the river, and Ammen's brigade, its first brigade, arrived upon the scene to support the Federal artillery. The Confederates were driven back, and presently orders from Beauregard were passed along their advanced lines directing them to desist from further attacks and to retire out of range of the gunboats. By some southern writers Beauregard has been severely censured for these orders; it is maintained that if he had ordered one last grand charge, it would surely have routed or destroyed the Union army. This opinion is open to grave doubt. If Beauregard could at that moment have put 6000 or 8000 fresh reserves into the fight against his weary antagonist, he might in all probability have routed him. But here at nightfall, after more than twelve hours of desperate fighting, his own men were as weary as the enemy; and it was now Grant, not Beauregard, who could bring fresh troops into action, for the big steamboats were delivering Nelson's men by the thousand at Pittsburg Landing.

Thus, in spite of their magnificent valour and dash, aided by the initial advantage of the surprise, the Confederates at the end of the day fell just short of victory. Their utmost efforts left the line of communication between Grant's army and the reinforcing army unbroken. Had Buell's arrival been further delayed, they might perhaps have completed their victory on Monday, but now the conditions were entirely changed. It was in an agony of rage and disappointment that Bragg at nightfall received Beauregard's orders to suspend the fight till morning. It is a principle often illustrated in war that when two armies have fought until their strength is well-nigh spent, the one that can soonest summon its jaded energies to a final assault is almost sure to win. Upon this principle Bragg would have risked everything upon a grand attack on Sunday evening. When Beauregard's staff-officer brought him the order to desist, Bragg inquired if he had already promulgated the order to other generals. The officer replied that he had. Then quoth the disconsolate Bragg, "If you had not, I would not obey it. *The battle is lost.*"[1] It is upon this view of the case that some writers have built the inference that Beauregard threw away the advantage which Johnston had virtually won. Of course nobody can tell what would have ensued had Bragg made his attack, but the general history of the

[1] See Colonel William Preston Johnston's interesting paper in *Battles and Leaders,* i. 568. A more correct view (as it seems to me) of the situation is given by General Beauregard in the following paper, i. 590, 591.

day supports Beauregard's view that it would have ended in a repulse. What was the fundamental fact in the case which prevented the Confederates from approaching Pittsburg Landing, the goal of their endeavours, until their commanding general judged the opportunity for seizing it to be gone? Doubtless that fundamental fact was the wonderful staying power of the Federal troops. Man for man, they were just as good fighters as the Confederates. The latter began with such an immense initial advantage, in the surprise, that it lasted them all day. From the outset the several Union divisions were placed at the dire disadvantage of forming under furious pressure, so that in many cases a line was swept from its ground while in process of formation. The rallying of such lines often brought fragments of one division into adherence to another, thus seriously disturbing the organization. During the entire day no opportunity was offered for making a firmly knit Federal line of battle. Gaps were made which allowed one division after another to be taken in flank and compelled to fall back. Had these things occurred upon open ground, a judicious use of the Confederate cavalry might have completed the disorganization of the Union army and routed it. Such a disaster was prevented by the broken and wooded country.

The fundamental facts in the case.

With this one circumstance in their favour the Federals, in spite of the tremendous disadvantage with which they started, disputed every inch of ground so obstinately that the day was not long enough for the Confederates to reach their goal, but just as it seemed almost within their grasp, the conditions were radically changed by the arrival of Buell's army. Such were the fundamental facts in Sunday's battle.

At seven in the evening the Federals preserved a sufficiently continuous line of battle from the vicinity of the Snake creek bridge to that of Pittsburg Landing. Its connections were preserved with Nelson on the left, and with Lew Wallace, who had just arrived at Snake creek, on the right. These reinforcements added to each wing about 7000 men, and Grant tells us that with his strength thus restored he should have assumed the aggressive on Monday morning, even without further aid. Probably he would have done so. It was characteristic of him not to know when he was beaten, and we have his own word that he never for a moment doubted of ultimate victory; but it was fortunate that his disorganized divisions were not called upon to assume the aggressive next morning without fresh support.

Arrival of Nelson and Lew Wallace.

We may now turn our attention for a moment

to the eastern bank of the Tennessee river, and observe how the relieving army arrived upon the scene. When General Buell reached Savannah, early Saturday evening, he found that Nelson's division had arrived there and gone into camp. Grant had not yet come down from Pittsburg Landing for the night, and Buell soon went to Nelson's camp, so that the two generals did not meet that night. Grant had already visited Nelson's camp and told that officer that he would send steamboats down for him on "Monday or Tuesday, or some time early in the week." Grant added, "There will be no fight at Pittsburg Landing; we will [i. e., shall] have to go to Corinth, where the rebels are fortified. If they come to attack us we can whip them, as I have more than twice as many troops as I had at Fort Donelson."[1] These remarks are in harmony with the other indications which show that Grant was taken by surprise on Sunday morning.

Grant's expectations on Saturday.

At sunrise on that memorable day Buell and Nelson were at breakfast when the sound of heavy firing burst upon their ears. Nelson's men were at once put in marching order, and Buell, finding that Grant had already started up the river, procured a small steamboat and followed him. Pre-

[1] Buell, "Shiloh Reviewed," in *Battles and Leaders*, i. 492.

sently a descending steamer handed to Buell a letter from Grant, in substance as follows: "The attack on my forces has been very spirited since early this morning. The appearance of fresh troops on the field now would have a powerful effect, both by inspiring our men and disheartening the enemy. If you will get upon the field, leaving all your baggage on the east bank of the river, it will be a move to our advantage, and possibly save the day to us. The rebel forces are estimated at over 100,000 men." Soon Buell found Grant upon a steamboat at Pittsburg Landing, and after a brief conference the two went ashore. Guides were sent to Nelson for his difficult march, and steamboats were collected at Savannah to bring up the divisions of Crittenden and McCook, the former of which was just arriving at that point. For the rest of the day both Grant and Buell were busy on the battlefield. The latter found much work to be done in rallying and reorganizing stragglers, and in preparing for the rapid disembarkation of his troops. As for Grant, we catch glimpses of him during the day in various parts of the field, now with Sherman on the right wing, now in the Hornet's Nest with Prentiss, now on the right again. We do not hear of any notable movement or tactical manœuvre performed by him, for the

His view of the situation at Sunday noon.

Fort Donelson and Shiloh 93

circumstances admitted nothing of the sort. The work for a commander consisted chiefly in myriads of readjustments here and there, sustaining the efforts of single brigades or regiments, or the fragments of such; and in this we cannot doubt that on all parts of the field the stubborn bravery of the men gained fresh inspiration from the indomitable spirit of their commander.[1]

In order to avoid the fire from the Union gunboats, which was kept up all night, the Confederates fell back about a mile and occupied the camps in which the Federals had slept the night before. The tents thus served to shelter them from the cold pelting rain which came down in torrents. The Federals lay in the mud, scantily protected by the leafless trees. General Grant, whose ankle had been badly bruised by a fall of his horse, sought refuge from the storm in a log-house; but the surgeons had taken possession of the place, and its sights and sounds were so doleful that the general soon retreated into the chilling rain.

A bivouac in the rain.

During the night the remainder of Nelson's division crossed the river, and Crittenden's came

---

[1] The last paragraph of General Buell's admirable paper (*Battles and Leaders*, i. 536), though apparently somewhat severe, is thoroughly borne out by the judicious criticism of Mr. Ropes, *Story of the Civil War*, ii. 84.

up from Savannah on steamboats, followed after an interval by McCook's, which arrived early in the morning. The steamboats also brought Nelson's artillery. These reinforcements numbered 20,000 men, and in organization and discipline they were confessedly superior to Grant's army; for they had been trained for several months under the eyes of Buell himself, who was unsurpassed as an organizer. As they arrived in succession, these divisions were arranged for the morrow's line of battle; Nelson on the left, next to the river, then Crittenden on his right, then McCook. Next came the remnants of Hurlbut's and McClernand's divisions, mended with fragments from those of William Wallace and Sherman; while the extreme right, near Owl creek, was occupied by the fresh division of Lew Wallace. Besides Buell's 20,000 men and Wallace's 7000, we may estimate at 10,000 the number of Grant's troops who had fought during the previous day and were now again brought into line. To oppose this force Beauregard had from 20,000 to 25,000 men, none of them fresh. Some reorganizing was necessary, and in the course of it there was some shifting of commands; so that Hardee occupied the extreme right, with Breckinridge on his left, then Polk, and finally on the extreme left, Bragg.

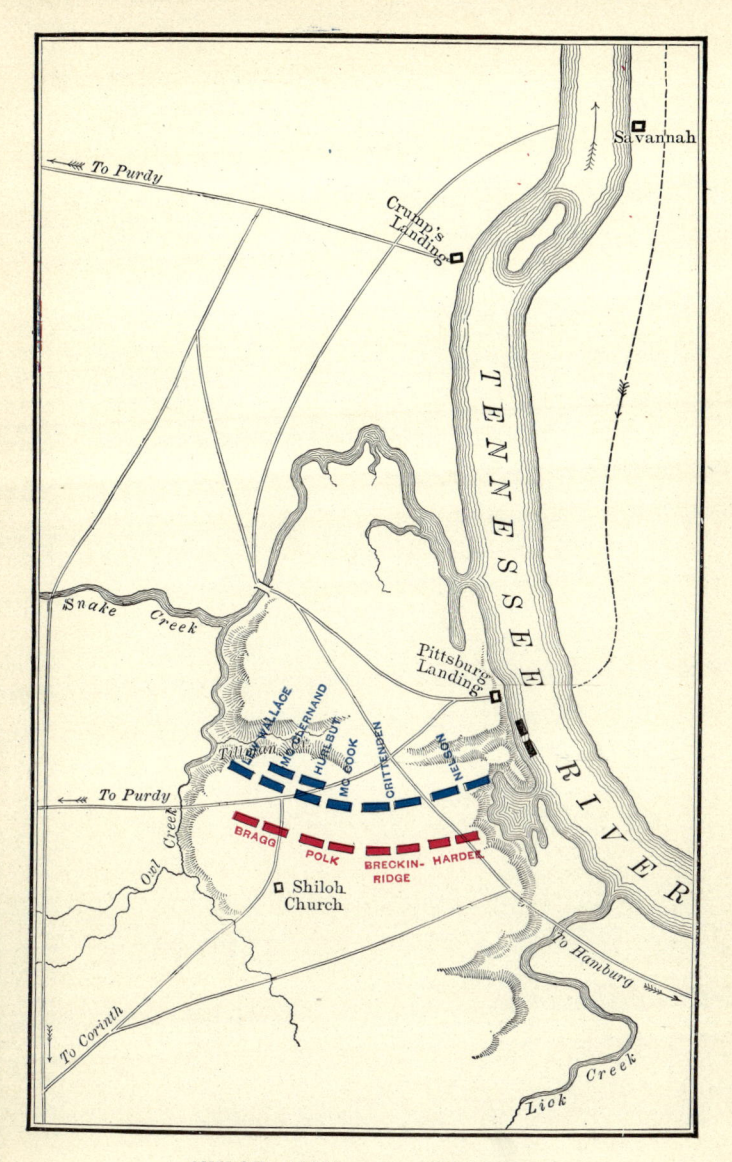

SHILOH, APRIL 7, 1862, MORNING

Fort Donelson and Shiloh 95

Victory for the Confederates was no longer to be expected, save through some extraordinary blunder of their antagonists. The entire experience of our Civil War shows that in fighting quality American soldiers from all parts of the country are so evenly matched that, under similar conditions, even a slight superiority in numbers ensures victory. A parity of conditions does not exist when the assailing party rushes against entrenchments and is shot down faster than it can advance; nor can it be said to exist when the commanders are so unequally matched as, for example, at Chancellorsville, where Lee's 60,000 men defeated Hooker's 120,000, because at every point of contact between the two armies during the battle, Lee's superior intelligence opposed superior numbers to those of Hooker. On the second day of Shiloh, where the conditions were nearly equal, there was nothing to interfere with the rule that victory takes sides with the heaviest battalions. The Union soldiers were also less fatigued. Beauregard was hardly entitled on Monday morning to expect victory, but a battle was preferable to an immediate retreat upon Corinth, harassed by an aggressive foe.

The contest opened soon after daybreak with Nelson's advance against Hardee along the Hamburg road. By seven o'clock Lew Wallace's division had forced its way across Tillman creek and occupied the heights to the south of it. By ten o'clock a fierce struggle was inaugurated about the road to Corinth, between the Purdy road and Shiloh church, and for six hours here the fighting was as severe as any that Sunday had witnessed. To break down Bragg's division, and to gain a firm hold of the Corinth road southwest of Shiloh church, would cut the Confederate connections with Corinth. To prevent such a catastrophe Bragg put forth his utmost efforts, returning the offensive with magnificent pluck and resource. In this great fight the decisive part was played by McCook's division on the spot. But scarcely less decisive was the pressure of Nelson and Crittenden against the rebel right, which obliged Beauregard to reinforce it at the expense of his left. To prolong the fight under such conditions would have been to invite destruction, and presently Beauregard skilfully withdrew his army, keeping up a show of resistance as long as possible in order to cover his retreat. By four o'clock he was making all haste toward Corinth.

Monday's battle.

The Union army made no attempt to pursue the enemy and complete his discomfiture. Why this should not have been done has never been satisfactorily explained. It would seem that the conditions were favourable for annihilating Beauregard's army. Bragg reported next morning that his troops were "utterly disorganized and demoralized," while Breckinridge declared, "My troops are worn out, and I don't think can be relied on after the first volley." Forage was short, and the horses were so exhausted that artillery had to be abandoned on the road. Buell's men must surely have been fresh enough to pursue, and so must Wallace's; and, moreover, Buell's fourth division, under Wood, had begun arriving upon the battle-field in the middle of the afternoon, and his fifth division, under Thomas, was coming up behind. Wood and Thomas brought 12,000 fresh men. It is difficult, therefore, to understand why Beauregard was not persistently followed up and harassed by from 20,000 to 30,000 pursuers. The responsibility, of course, rests with Grant, who never offered any sound explanation. He only tells us that he had not the heart to demand more work from his own jaded men, and he felt some delicacy about giving orders to Buell, whose senior he had been but a short time.[1] Such delicacy at such a moment shows, as Mr. Ropes says, an entire failure to rise to the height of the occasion. Fancy such an excuse from Frederick or Napoleon!

Why was there no pursuit after Shiloh?

[1] Grant's *Memoirs*, i. 354.

The failure, be it observed, is not a parallel case with the refusal of Meade to return the offensive after the repulse of Pickett's charge at Gettysburg; for in the latter case there were sound reasons for not putting in jeopardy the victory that was ours as things stood. A vigorous pursuit after Shiloh could not have imperilled the Union army in any way.

I suspect that the true explanation, after all, may be that our peace-loving people had not yet come to realize what a terrible affair war is, when truly effective, and especially when waged against our own kin. Under the compulsion of stern necessity we could fight against our brethren, but we could not feel toward them the indifference which Napoleon at Austerlitz felt toward the Russian fugitives upon the Satschan lake. We were satisfied with thwarting the hostile army, and did not appreciate the need for terminating its existence. Some such state of mind, on the part of our troops at Shiloh, seems to be implied in General Buell's remarks when he says, "I make no attempt to excuse myself or blame others when I say that General Grant's troops, the lowest individual among them not more than the commander himself, appear to have thought that the object of the battle was sufficiently accomplished when they were reinstated in their camps; and that in some way that idea obstructed the reorganization of my line until a further advance that day became impracticable." [1] This is not inconsistent with General Sherman's humorous reply when I once asked him why the retreating rebels were not pursued : " I assure you, my dear fellow, we had had quite enough of their society for two whole days, and were only too glad to be rid of them on any terms ! "

The American people, unused to warfare upon a great scale, were astounded at the news of this terrible battle. For the first time in the history of the western continent we were called to witness such slaughter as had marked the campaigns of Marlborough or Napoleon. On each side more than 10,000 men were killed or wounded, while on the first day the Union army lost some 3000 prisoners. In proportion to the total numbers engaged in the battle, these losses were enormous. Reckoning the Confederates (without their cavalry) at 30,000, Grant's army at 40,000, and Buell's three divisions at 20,000, we have a total of 90,000, with a loss of more than 20,000 ; more than two ninths, or approaching one fourth. "I saw an open field," says Grant, "in our possession the second day, over which the

Terrible slaughter.

[1] *Battles and Leaders,* i. 534.

Confederates had made repeated charges the day before, so covered with dead that it would have been possible to walk across the clearing, in any direction, stepping on dead bodies, without a foot touching the ground. . . . On one part bushes had grown up to the height of eight or ten feet. There was not one of these left standing unpierced by bullets. The smaller ones were all cut down."

Considering the rawness of most of the troops engaged, the battle of Shiloh was peculiarly significant. It tested American mettle. It showed what formidable fighters an industrial people, hating warfare, could suddenly become under the spur of necessity. On either side, moreover, it awakened such a feeling of respect for the other as had until that day remained dormant. It also dispelled some illusions. It showed the northern people that a few victories like Fort Donelson would not suffice to overthrow the Confederacy, but that the whole southern country would have to be conquered inch by inch. It took this tremendous battle to determine whether the results of the capture of Fort Donelson were to be permanently secured. As to this point Shiloh was decisive. The Federals were not thrown back upon Kentucky, but advanced into Mississippi, and laid siege to Corinth, the centre of the second Confederate line of defence.

Significance of the battle.

CHAPTER III

THE CAPTURE OF NEW ORLEANS

THE defeat of the Confederates at Shiloh put it out of their power to regain what they had lost at Fort Donelson. Giving up for the moment all hope of recovering Kentucky or holding any part of Tennessee west of the mountains, their task was limited to the maintenance of their second great defensive line, extending from Memphis through Corinth and Huntsville to Chattanooga.

All but one of the positions taken in flank by Grant's advance up the Tennessee river had been abandoned. At one point, however, the Confederates still maintained their foothold. This was at the great double loop of the Mississippi commanded by New Madrid and Island Number Ten, just at the corner of the four states of Missouri, Kentucky, Tennessee, and Arkansas. When Polk evacuated Columbus, he took with him 130 pieces of artillery and planted them in this position. Thus armed, Island Number Ten with its outposts hermetically sealed the river to ships descending from Cairo. Vast swamps on the east

Island Number Ten.

side of the river made it difficult to approach the island with an army. There was only one road by which an enemy could come, a very good road leading from Tiptonville six miles below in a direct line and on the narrow peninsula between the river and Reelfoot lake. On the other hand, if the Confederates should lose control of the river below New Madrid, this Tiptonville road was their only possible line of escape. But in order to close this road, it was necessary for the Federals not only to capture New Madrid, but also to run their gunboats and transports past the island itself, and this was thought to be impossible.

The island was garrisoned by 7000 men. A position so far in advance of the Confederate line was necessarily liable to be overwhelmed, and doubtless it would have been evacuated but for the belief that Federal gunboats could not pass it. On the 3d of March General John Pope arrived with 20,000 men on the western bank of the river, and erecting batteries at Point Pleasant, twelve miles below New Madrid, he cut off the supplies of the town and in ten days compelled it to surrender.

The enèmy's only line of escape was now the Tiptonville road, and Pope's problem was how to seize it, for his transports, under convoy of Foote's fleet, were all above the formidable island. The densely wooded peninsula opposite the island, made

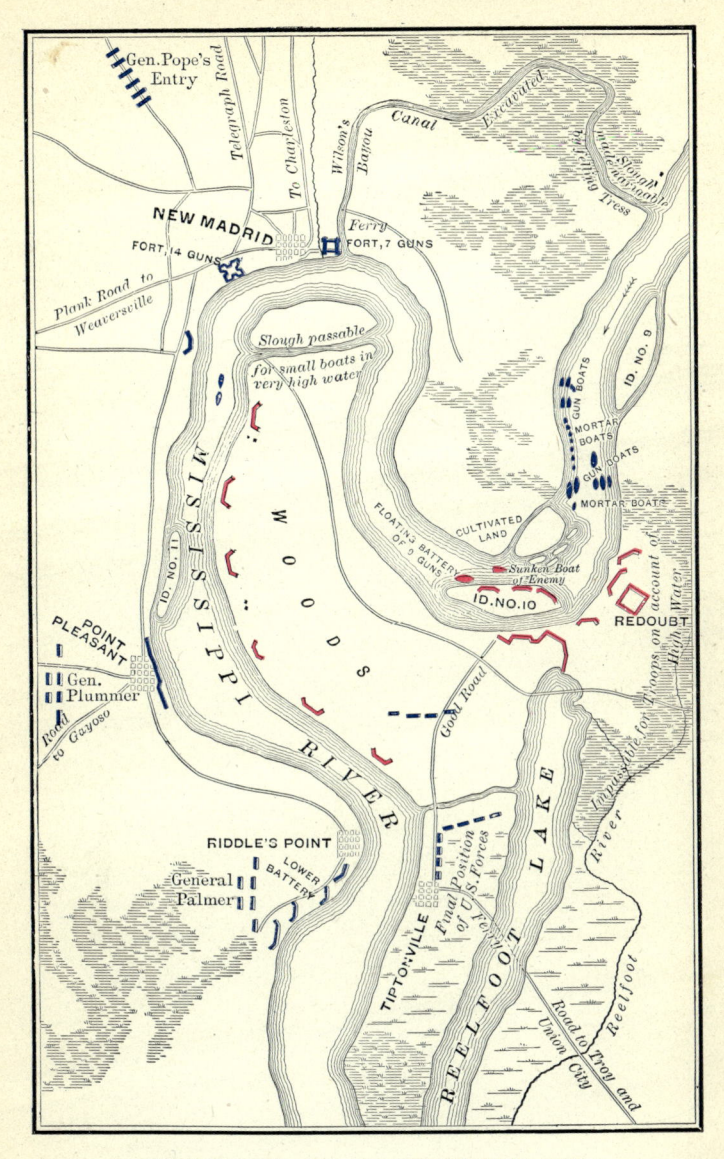

NEW MADRID AND ISLAND NUMBER TEN
MARCH 3–APRIL 7, 1862

by the great bend of the river, was at that time overflowed, and at some distance to the north was partially intersected by bayous. The whole peninsula was under water, and it was resolved to cut a navigable channel through the forest by sawing off the trees near the ground. <small>Sawing out a channel.</small>
The army contained an engineer regiment, composed entirely of skilled workmen, and this regiment with much labour accomplished the task. First the men, working in relays of three hundred, stood upon small rafts and cut off the trees about eight feet above the water. As fast as the trees fell, another set of men in small boats tackled them with ropes and they were hauled away by steamboats. When room enough was cleared in this way, a large raft was fastened to a stump, and from this raft a huge saw, attached to a pivot, was set working below the water so as to cut away the stumps close to the ground. Now and then in shallow places stumps were dragged up roots and all, and in some cases excavation was necessary. It was cold, wet work, but no one flagged or fell sick, and in nineteen days a channel six miles in length, fifty feet wide, and four and a half feet deep had been sawed through the submerged forest. By this extraordinary passageway the transports for Pope's army were taken safely across the peninsula and out again into the river at New

Madrid, without coming within a dozen miles of the heavy guns of Island Number Ten.

To crown this triumph of ingenuity a daring exploit now became necessary. The place where Pope intended to cross the river, below Point Pleasant, was guarded by Confederate batteries, which must first be silenced. One or two gunboats were needed for this, but none of the gunboats drew less than six feet of water, and consequently none of them could pass through the forest canal. The gallant Foote considered the risk of running by the island so great that he did not like to ask officers or men to undertake it, but Commander Henry Walke, of the Carondelet, was found eager to try the experiment. The boilers and other vulnerable parts of the ship were protected in every possible way by planks and chains and coils of heavy rope. A barge laden with hay was lashed in front of the magazine. The great guns were run in under cover and the portholes shut, the sailors, with pistol and cutlass, stood on guard in case of an attempt to board, and the boatswain was ordered to be ready to sink the ship sooner than let her fall into the enemy's hands. The escape-steam was led aft through the wheelhouse instead of puffing and sputtering through the smokestacks. And thus at ten o'clock on the night of April 4, enshrouded in the thick dark-

Exploit of the Carondelet.

ness of a gathering storm, the gallant Carondelet cast off her moorings and glided down the broad river, unseen and unheard. It was not until she was close to the island that her presence was betrayed. The soot in her smokestacks, no longer moistened by the escape-steam, took fire, and a tell-tale blaze sprang forth from their grimy tops. The enemy promptly took the alarm and began firing his heavy guns, the roar of which was soon drowned by louder peals of thunder, while glimpses of the passing ship were revealed from moment to moment in vivid flashes of lightning. But her bold and shrewd commander ran her so close to the island batteries that their ponderous balls flew harmlessly overhead, and before the gunners could lower their pieces and take accurate aim she had glided by, and the hour of midnight found her safe at New Madrid.

On Sunday the 6th and Monday the 7th, while the battle was raging at distant Shiloh, the Carondelet pounded to pieces the batteries on the eastern shore as far as Tiptonville, and was presently joined by the Pittsburg, which followed her example and ran the gauntlet of Island Number Ten at two o'clock on Monday morning. The Confederate garrison now made haste to evacuate their stronghold, but it was too late. During the evening Pope's army crossed the river and occupied the

Tiptonville road, whereupon the garrison surren-
dered at discretion. Three generals with 7000 men, 123 heavy guns, 35 field-pieces, 7000 stand of muskets, tents for 12,000 men, several hundred horses, and an immense quantity of ammunition, were captured in this brilliant operation, without the loss of a single man on the Federal side. The credit for the achievement was, as usual, given to the commanding officer,[1] and Pope for the moment acquired a reputation which seemed to rival Grant's, but which he was destined within six months to lose when confronted with a problem which abler men than he found insoluble, — the problem of outgeneralling Robert Lee and Stonewall Jackson.

<small>Surrender of the garrison.</small>

By the capture of Island Number Ten the Mississippi river was thrown open down to Fort Pillow, against which the army and fleets immediately proceeded. But Halleck now summoned Pope and his army to Pittsburg Landing, where all the Union forces were concentrating for the advance upon Corinth. There was no use in operating separately upon Fort Pillow, for Corinth once taken, it would fall of itself.

<small>Results.</small>

[1] The idea of sawing a channel through the submerged forest, the operation upon which everything else depended, originated with General Schuyler Hamilton, of New York, a grandson of Alexander Hamilton and great-grandson of Philip Schuyler. See *Battles and Leaders*, i. 462.

It will be observed that in the affair of Island Number Ten the decisive blow was struck by the Carondelet. Without the gunboats the operation could not have succeeded. The same was true, in the main, of Grant's movement against Forts Henry and Donelson, the whole significance of which, moreover, lay in the fact that it opened a vast stretch of country to an invasion in which the river fleet was an indispensable instrument. The sparse population of the states which were the theatre of war, their extensive area, and the poorness of their roads made it pecul- iarly necessary for the armies to con- trol the rivers and railways. To get sufficient food from the country trav- ersed was usually impossible, and all the opera- tions of the war, especially in the West, derived their peculiar character from the necessity of maintaining long lines of communication, the cut- ting of which would entail speedy famine. The great rivers which flow in all directions through the heart of the continent, sustaining on their broad waters the movements of fleets, thus early impressed upon this American war a novel and interesting feature, to which there is no parallel in European history. The rivers afforded lines of operation in many respects more secure than the railways, since they could not be cut, and here the

Importance of rivers and the river fleets.

immense superiority of the northern states in ships and machinery came early in the struggle to turn the scale slowly but surely against the Confederacy. These formidable gunboats, with their powerful guns, were like floating fortresses which could be moved in two or three hours to longer distances than an army could march in a day; and while it was but seldom that they could capture fortified places without the aid of a land force, at the same time this combination of strength with speed made them an auxiliary without which the greater operations of the war could hardly have been undertaken.

In a still wider sense it is true that but for the navy and its gallant commanders it would have been impossible to put down the rebellion. The work done by the navy was truly Titanic. There was something romantic in the boldness with which President Lincoln and Mr. Seward, at the outbreak of hostilities, quickly announced their intention of blockading three thousand miles of coast, all the way from the Potomac to the Rio Grande.

The United States navy in the Civil War. Europe laughed at the idea; such a thing had never been done by the greatest maritime powers, and the United States had very few warships, most of them antiquated and all about to become so.

Yet within a few months this stupendous blockade was made effective. It isolated the Confederacy from all the rest of the world, and made its overthrow possible. In those days we had a great and growing merchant marine, before our abominable tariff and navigation laws killed it. The American flag was seen in nearly all the ports of the world, our hardy sailors were to be found on every sea, and we had a small band of brave and intelligent naval officers trained in a school of peculiar excellence.[1] With such resources, aided by our Yankee versatility and our mechanical appliances, a navy especially adapted to the needs of the occasion, and unlike anything ever seen before, was created as if by magic. The famous old ships-of-the-line and frigates, a few of which are still lying in our navy yards, were of no more use than the catapults and cross-bows of the Middle Ages; and even such steam-frigates as the Roanoke and Minnesota, which only five years earlier had ranked among the finest warships afloat, were now at once rendered powerless by the invention of armoured rams and gunboats. Of its old materials the government made such use as it could, while it called upon inventors for new designs, and meanwhile bought up every craft floating in American waters

[1] The events of our war of 1898 with Spain show that there has been no falling off from the lofty standard of achievement fixed by Hull and Perry and Farragut.

that could in any wise be promptly adapted to fighting and pressed into the service. Large steamers of 2000 tons burthen, swift little river and harbour tugs, Fulton ferry-boats casemated in iron and armed with formidable guns, tall Mississippi steamboats, squat mortar-boats, turtle-shaped rams with powerful engines and deadly beaks, went to make up an immense fleet of such nondescript appearance as would have aroused the skeptical wonder of a Nelson, but well-fitted, in the hands of sagacious and daring men, for the varied and difficult work which it had to perform. With such vessels as these, usually aided by detachments from the army, the government went on seizing the enemy's seaports and strengthening its grip upon his coast-line, until by the end of the war every considerable maritime town in the Confederacy had passed into northern hands.

In this important warfare the South laboured from the outset under insurmountable disadvantages. Of the naval officers who followed their states into rebellion, there were some, such as Semmes and Buchanan, of eminent ability. But the South had only two shipyards, the most important of which, at Norfolk, was soon lost. She had no merchant-shipping or sea-faring population, very few machine-shops or skilled mechanics, and her supply

Naval inferiority of the South.

of iron was soon cut off by the blockade. Under these circumstances, though the Confederates worked with the zeal and determination which characterized all their proceedings, they necessarily effected but little. With the aid of their agents in England, favoured by the culpable negligence of Lord Palmerston's government, they succeeded in launching a few formidable privateers and inflicting upon our foreign trade an injury which, though serious enough, has been greatly exaggerated, and was indeed a mere trifle compared to that which we have since inflicted upon ourselves by idiotic legislation concocted in the lobbies of Congress. Such privateering could have no military significance save in so far as it might cripple our resources for attack; and this it did not do to any appreciable extent. In the defence of their rivers and harbours the Confederates showed their unfailing gallantry; but their ships were few, their engines of inferior make and liable to accident, and their commanders on the whole unequal in training to the officers of the Federal navy.

Early in the war the United States government became impressed with the necessity of capturing New Orleans. The place was of the first importance, both in itself and in its strategic relations. With a population of 170,000 souls, it was by far the largest city of the Confederacy, and it contained, moreover, more machine-shops and trained workmen than any other. It was important to deprive the enemy of these resources. The city was comparatively near to Mexico, which was threatened with occupation by the forces of France, a power whose attitude toward the American Union was distinctly hostile. Above all, New Orleans barred the ascent of the Mississippi river to Union fleets, and if the rebellion were ever to be suppressed, every inch of the Mississippi must be conquered and held. Beyond it lay the three revolted states of Texas, Arkansas, and Louisiana, which could not only put 100,000 men into the field, but could at the same time raise food enough to feed the whole Confederacy for countless ages. These states must be lopped off, and the rest of the southern country blockaded on its west side as well as on its coasts. Besides this, the Confederate hold upon the Mississippi seriously crippled the commercial resources and thus indirectly the military strength of all the northwestern states. The Confederate leaders counted much upon this, and some of them, in their first sanguine dreams, hoped that the imperative need of using this pathway for trade would presently compel the northwestern people to join them. Thus reinforced they might control the

Military importance of New Orleans.

continent, leaving the northeast, and especially thrice-hated New England, out in the cold.

However exaggerated such hopes may have been, there could be no doubt as to the necessity that the United States government should seize New Orleans as soon as possible. Every month of delay made the enterprise more difficult. *Need for prompt action.* Early in the summer of 1861 the city was virtually defenceless, and it has been said, on high authority, that any three warships could then have entered the river and ascended it to Cairo without serious opposition. That the government then made no attempt to seize and fortify the great defensible points on the river is one proof among many of the slowness with which the people came to realize that they were entering upon a desperate struggle for national existence. The action of the Confederates was also dilatory, for they found it hard to believe that the United States government was about to put forth all its energies to subdue them, and the first effect of their victory at Bull Run was to create a false sense of security. Nevertheless they worked faster than the Federals, and after Fort Donelson their efforts were redoubled. The works on the lower Mississippi grew daily in strength, and in a few months they might fairly hope to render their great city impregnable.

Among the persons who first discussed with the Federal government a definite plan for the capture of New Orleans was Commander David Dixon Porter, a man to whom eminent naval ability came by inheritance, for he was son of that famous Captain Porter who had first carried the American war-flag on the Pacific ocean, and after a glorious cruise had at length succumbed in an unequal struggle with two British frigates in the harbour of Valparaiso, in one of the fiercest sea-fights of the War of 1812. In the spring of 1861, while watching the mouths of the Mississippi, Commander Porter studied the situation, and on arriving in Washington six months afterward he spoke of the importance of capturing New Orleans to President Lincoln, who did not need to be reminded of the subject by Porter or anybody. His first remark was that, of course, such a piece of work could not be done too soon. "The Mississippi," said Lincoln, " is the backbone of the Rebellion; it is the key to the whole situation. But we must have troops enough not only to hold New Orleans, but to proceed at once toward Vicksburg, which is the key to all that country watered by the Mississippi and its tributaries. If the Confederates once fortify the neighbouring hills, they will be able to hold that point for an indefinite time, and it will require a large force to dislodge them." With these prophetic words Mr. Lincoln urged on the preparations with all possible despatch. A fleet of warships mounting more than 150 guns was fitted out, and accompanied by a strong squadron of mortar-boats. A land force of 13,000 men was collected and placed under command of General Benjamin Franklin Butler, of Massachusetts, concerning whose military qualifications one need only say that it was fortunate, so far as the capture of New Orleans was concerned, that the conditions of the case were such as to give all the serious work to the fleet.

For the chief command of that fleet a hero was chosen who in the naval annals of the English race will take rank second to none unless it be Nelson. In that terrible fight at Valparaiso, when the Essex was forced to strike her colours to the Phœbe and the Cherub, there was to be seen on the deck of the hard-pressed American vessel a boy of fourteen years, already distinguished for coolness and daring, whose name was David Glasgow Farragut. A native of Tennessee, descended from an Aragonese family once prominent in the island of Minorca, he had in early childhood been adopted into Captain Porter's family, and had entered the navy in 1810. During his half-century of service he had won the highest reputation among his bro-

<small>David Glasgow Farragut.</small>

ther officers. In 1833, when South Carolina undertook to put her theory of nullification into practice, it was Farragut whom Andrew Jackson sent to Charleston harbour to enforce his famous decree that "the Union must be preserved." When the Civil War broke out, Farragut's southern friends tried their best to induce him to join them, but he quickly silenced them with the uncompromising reply: "Mind what I tell you! You fellows are going to catch hell before you get through with this business!" In spite of this determined attitude, the government is said to have hesitated about entrusting him with such an expedition as that against New Orleans. It was feared that, however loyal, he might perhaps show less zeal in such an enterprise than a man of northern birth and associations. But Gideon Welles, secretary of the navy, with his able assistant, Gustavus Fox, reinforced by Montgomery Blair and Porter, who knew him so well, overcame these doubts, and on the 20th of January, 1862, Farragut was put in command of the great expedition.

The capture of New Orleans is remarkable as the last victory won entirely by wooden vessels. It was the crowning exploit of the old-time navy. While the expedition was fitting out, there occurred that memorable battle in Hampton Roads in which the genius of Ericsson suddenly revolutionized the naval warfare of the world. None of Farragut's ships were armoured; none could have stood against such a foe as the Merrimac. His flagship the Hartford, of 25 guns, belonged to a type already passing away, like the still more picturesque and imposing seventy-fours and frigates which had preceded it. To the same Farragut's class belonged the Brooklyn, Rich- fleet. mond, and Pensacola, and these were followed by one side-wheel sloop, three screw corvettes, and nine screw gunboats, each carrying two guns on pivots. Attached as auxiliaries to this squadron were nineteen bomb-vessels, each armed with one 13-inch mortar, and these were accompanied by six gunboats, three of which were double-ended ferry-boats from New York. This auxiliary flotilla was placed in charge of Commander Porter, and a distinct and special part of the work was assigned to it.

The city of New Orleans is situated on the east bank of the Mississippi, 110 miles from its mouth. To bar the approach of a hostile fleet, the Confederates had strengthened and equipped the two old government fortresses at the Plaquemine Bend, ninety miles below the city. The course of the winding river at that point is nearly east and west. On the left or north bank stood Fort St. Philip, and on the right bank, some 800 yards farther downstream, was Fort Jackson. The latter was a casemated work, built in the form of a star, and armed with 75 guns. Fort St. Philip was an open work, with strong brick walls covered with sod, and mounted 53 guns. Both forts were well supplied with food and ammunition, and each held a garrison of 700 men. The guns were not so heavy as one might suppose, for while there were a few that threw missiles of 80 pounds weight, nearly half the number were only 24-pounders. Even these, however, were dangerous to wooden ships, and such was the confidence of the rebels in the strength of these fortresses that they did not believe a hostile fleet could get past them. They were much more afraid of possible attacks from above, and as the Confederacy was ill-supplied with heavy cannon, they preferred to send as many as possible to points farther up the river. Between the two forts and the city of New Orleans other defensive works had been begun, but were inadequately armed, and could do little to check the progress of an enemy who had once run the gauntlet between Jackson and St. Philip.

Forts Jackson and St. Philip.

For further obstruction the Confederates stretched across the broad river between the forts a row of heavy schooners well anchored with sixty fathoms of cable and held together by stout iron chains. Their masts were unshipped and cast overboard without being entirely cut loose, so that drifting hither and thither with their tangled mass of rigging, they might foul the screws of any steamers that should come too near. Above the forts were a dozen Confederate warships, mostly wooden and of light armament. The cigar-shaped ironclad ram Manassas, carrying one 32-pound carronade which fired straight ahead, might have been formidable but for the weakness of her engines, which prevented her acquiring much impetus. The most dangerous rebel vessel, had she been ready for action, was the Louisiana, an ironclad with sloping sides carrying 16 very heavy guns; but Farragut's movements were so prompt that the night of the battle found her still manned with diligent workmen and unfinished. This small fleet was nominally controlled by Commander John Mitchell, of the Confederate navy; but six of the ships belonged to a force known as the river defence fleet, and were commanded by a merchant captain, whose behaviour was afterward deemed insubordinate. The land defences were in charge of General Duncan, and under him Lieutenant-Colonel Higgins commanded Fort Jackson. The department-commander was General Mansfield Lovell, whose headquarters were at New Orleans. All three were able officers, but ill-supported. Lovell's

The Confederate rams.

whole force in the city consisted of 3000 raw troops without arms enough to go around, so thoroughly had every corner been ransacked for forces with which to strike the heavy but unavailing blow at Pittsburg Landing.

In spite of these disadvantages the Confederates felt sure of victory, and indeed the task set for Farragut was so difficult that only the highest skill and daring could have performed it. His wooden vessels, carrying 177 guns, had to contend with 128 guns in strong fortresses and 39 guns carried by vessels partly armoured. According to Admiral Porter, who thus concisely states the case, " it is generally conceded by military men that one gun in a fort is about equal to five on board of a wooden ship, especially when . . . the forces afloat are obliged to contend against a three-and-a-half-knot current in a channel obstructed by chains and fire-rafts." [1] After making all due allowances, therefore, the Confederates might easily feel that the odds were in their favour. They worked night and day in strengthening their defences, and another fortnight might have made them impregnable. But Farragut pushed on his preparations with desperate energy. There was great difficulty at first in getting his larger vessels over the bar, but by the 16th of April these obsta-

[1] *Battles and Leaders*, ii. 33.

cles were surmounted and all was in readiness for the bombardment. Commander Porter anchored his bomb-vessels around the bend of the river, close to the right bank, from three to four thousand yards below Fort Jackson and behind a thick wood. The mastheads were dressed with bushes, and thus became indistinguishable from the treetops. In such wise the bombardment began on the morning of the 18th, and was kept up with great fury for five days and nights, during which the mortar fleet fired 16,800 shells, or more than one to every minute. The aim was excellent. Nearly every shell was lodged inside of the fort, which at the end of this time was riddled like a worm-eaten log. Huge masses of sand-bags still protected the magazine, however, and, although several guns were silenced, Fort Jackson as yet gave no sign of surrender. As for Fort St. Philip, it had suffered comparatively little damage. *Bombardment of Fort Jackson.*

This preliminary bombardment was a pet scheme of Porter's, to which Farragut seems to have attached small importance, though he was willing to give it a trial. Porter was so keenly alive to the danger which the fleet would incur in running past the forts that he deemed it necessary to begin by forcing them to surrender, and this he hoped to do *Difference between Farragut's view and Porter's.*

with his bomb-shells. Moreover he disapproved of the policy of ascending the river while leaving hostile forts in the rear unreduced. On the other hand, Farragut was ready to take the risk of passing the forts, and believed that as soon as the city of New Orleans should be in our possession, the forts, thus isolated, would have no alternative but to surrender. The progress of Porter's bombardment soon convinced Farragut that it was not worth while to wait for the forts to be disabled. But before he could ascend the river, the line of dismantled schooners which barred the passage must be broken. On the night of the 20th, while the bombardment was briskly going on, this important task was undertaken by Lieutenant Caldwell, with the small gunboats Itasca and Pinola. A

<small>The Itasca's exploit.</small> torpedo connected with an electric battery was lodged under the bows of one of the swaying hulks, but the wires broke prematurely and no explosion took place. The Itasca then tried to grapple the hulk and set it on fire, but manœuvring in the strong swift current she became entangled for a moment, and losing control of herself turned inshore and ran aground in a very dangerous position. With much difficulty her consort dragged her off, and now the adventurous little craft, seizing victory from this untoward accident, steamed cautiously upstream by the eastern

bank with just enough water to float in, till she passed outside and above the line of hulks. Then deftly turning, and crowding steam, aided by the full momentum of the current, she steered boldly down upon the chains that stretched between the third and fourth hulks and held them together. As she struck with prodigious force, her bows were lifted quite clear of the water, and when they came down again the stout chains snapped asunder, the current pushed the great hulks far apart to right and left, the gallant Itasca passed through unscathed, and a gateway was opened for the whole fleet to pass up.

At two o'clock in the morning of April 24 Farragut hoisted his red-light signal, and the whole squadron steamed slowly up the river. The vital parts of the ships — their engines and magazines — were protected by chain cables and sand-bags, their light spars were sent down, and every needless encumbrance removed. Captain Theodorus Bailey led the way in the gunboat Cayuga, closely followed by the sloops Pensacola and Mississippi, the corvettes Oneida and Varuna, and the gunboats Katahdin, Kineo, and Wissahickon. As the Pensacola passed through the breach in the line of hulks, the batteries in both forts opened upon the fleet with a tremendous roar. Then Commander William Bain-

The advance up the Mississippi river.

bridge Renshaw, with the Westfield and four other gunboats, came up within two hundred yards of Fort Jackson, and with a hailstorm of grape and canister drove the Confederates from their guns; while the heavy broadside of the Pensacola replied effectively to the fire of Fort St. Philip. The Manassas attempted to ram the Pensacola, but missing her, kept on and inflicted a slight wound upon the Mississippi. In such wise Bailey's foremost vessels got past the forts with little injury and engaged the enemy's ships above, while the two swift corvettes followed and joined in the fight. One of them, the Varuna, delivered a shot which burst the boiler of a Confederate transport crowded with troops, and presently with her shells set three other ships on fire. She was then attacked by two rams, both of which she defeated and disabled, but not until the enemy's iron beak had crashed through her wooden side. Running into shallow water, her crew and gallant commander, Charles Stuart Boggs, were rescued by her consort the Oneida, while her two crippled opponents were set on fire and abandoned. Three ships were wrecked or sunk by the Cayuga, one or two ran aground in attempting to flee, and one escaped to New Orleans.

Meanwhile Farragut in the Hartford, followed by the Brooklyn, poured his broadsides into Fort St. Philip, driving the gunners under cover while the great ships slowly passed by. More than two hundred guns were now firing at once, with noise like an earthquake, and the dark sky was veiled in darker clouds of smoke, fitfully illumined here and there by spasmodic flashes. Presently the whole scene was shown up in the lurid glare of a blazing raft which a brave little tugboat was pushing straight down upon the Hartford. After passing the fort with thirty-two shots in her hull and rigging, the flagship was now exposed to her greatest danger. In turning her helm to avoid it, she grounded on a shoal, and there received the shock of the huge mass of burning pine-knots. The crackling flames instantly caught her and danced half way to her mastheads, while shells from St. Philip's water-batteries still kept dropping and bursting on her deck. At this perilous moment the great captain to whom the battle had been entrusted showed all the qualities of which he had given promise fifty years before, when as midshipman he trod the blood-stained deck of the Essex. Walking calmly up and down, his hands behind him, the old man gave his orders with a cheery voice that made every one ashamed of fear. "Steady, boys, steady," he cried, with his pleasant smile, "there's a hotter fire than this, you know, for those who flinch from duty!" His coolness and the admirable discipline of the crew quelled all the dangers. The fires were put out, and the staunch ship, freed from the shoal, sailed on up the deep channel, with other good work still before her.

The flagship's consort, the Brooklyn, following closely in her wake, was presently struck by the ram Manassas, and an ugly gash was made in her side six feet below the water-line. But nimble carpenters bolted heavy planks over the wound, and she kept on her way. The crisis of the battle was now safely passed. All but three of the gunboats of the rear division, under Captain Henry Bell, made a good passage into the waters above St. Philip, whose gunners were by this time weary and disheartened. One of the three unfortunates was the Itasca, which had so nobly played the part of pioneer. Her boiler was pierced by a shot, and she drifted downstream, running ashore just below the mortar fleet, and landing most of her crew in safety. In less than an hour and a half from the commencement of the action, Farragut's squadron had run the gauntlet, the forts were turned, and the doom of the Confederacy's proudest city was sealed. As the ships glided up the river, the noise of battle hushed, the undaunted Manassas Fate of the Manassas. was descried through the dull twilight of the April morning, pushing after them like a grim, forlorn hope. The Mississippi, which she had rammed, was ready to clear off the score, and turned quickly upon her to run her down. But the agile ram sheered away from the blow and gained the shore, where her crew abandoned her. The Mississippi then pounded her with shot till she drifted away with the current, wrapped in flames, which presently caught her magazine and blew her into atoms.

All but three of the rebel ships now lay at the bottom of the river or floated in charred fragments on the tide. The Louisiana stayed moored to the shore above St. Philip, where she had been of little use. Two others crouched under what was left of Fort Jackson. The victorious fleet kept on up the river, silenced the batteries at Chalmette, hard by the spot where Andrew Jackson had vanquished a British army in 1815, and swept around the bend which brought them before the wharves of New Orleans, where all was clamour and confusion. General Lovell had retreated northward with his handful of troops, leaving the city in the hands of its mayor. Amid the clangour of church-bells the citizens had been busy since daybreak burning great bales of cotton, and destroying the munitions of war which they had heaped together and the half-built gunboats on which they had been working night and day. Innumerable fragments thickly strewed the surface of the river with a seething scum. Mr. Cable, the novelist, then a young lad, stood by and witnessed the scene as the ships drew near. "The crowds on the levee," he says, "howled and screamed with rage. The swarming decks answered never a word; but one old tar on the Hartford, standing with lanyard in hand beside a great pivot-gun, so plain to view that you could see him smile, silently patted its big black breech and blandly grinned."

A plank was thrown from the Cayuga, and Captain Theodorus Bailey, with Lieutenant George Hamilton Perkins, regardless of the knives and pistols of the raging mob, walked through the streets to the City Hall and demanded surrender. The mayor sought to gain time by evasive answers. Until Butler's troops should arrive, Farragut could not occupy the city, though his guns could destroy it, and the mayor, taking advantage of his forbearance, kept the state flag of Louisiana flying for five days more. Meanwhile Porter, who had stayed with his bomb-vessels below the forts, summoned them to surrender, and on General Duncan's refusal he renewed the bombardment. This was not relished by the garrisons, and on the night of the 27th they all, except one company of devoted planters, rose in mutiny and began spiking their own guns. Next

Surrender of the forts.

morning General Duncan surrendered. While the terms were arranged in the cabin of the Harriet Lane, with flags of truce flying at her masthead and on both the forts, the Louisiana, by accident unmoored, came blundering down with the current, all aflame, her shotted guns discharging to right and left, until she suddenly blew up, rolling the Harriet Lane over on her beam-ends, and shaking all the officers out of their seats. A moment later the explosion would have killed friend and foe alike. It was simple carelessness on the part of the men who were destroying the useless hulk.

The surrender of the forts allowed the transports with Butler's troops to ascend the river. On the 29th, while they were expected but before their arrival, a small detachment of marines from Farragut's fleet landed in the city and hoisted the stars and stripes over one of the public buildings. Scarcely had they left the spot when a man named Mumford hauled down the flag for the populace to trample under foot and drag through the mud. The marines returned and hoisted another, and guarded it till May 1, when Butler arrived and took possession of the city, which he ruled till the middle of the next December. The selection of such a man for such a command was a needless though unintentional insult to the conquered city. Where a military rule, at once stern and just, is required by circumstances, it is far better to have a true soldier than an unscrupulous politician, bent upon money-making and intrigue. In fairness to Butler it must be said that his administration was in some respects intelligent and able. Order was preserved, and the streets were so much cleaner than ever before that the demon of yellow fever was banished for some time. But there was an amount of confiscation unparalleled elsewhere during the war; and a swarm of adventurers, with Butler's connivance, made their fortunes in speculating with the property thus seized. The hanging of Mumford, for his insult to the Federal flag before the city had been regularly occupied by our troops, was an act of extreme severity, although the victim appears to have been a creature on whom our sympathy would be wasted. As the Count of Paris says, "The death of Mumford is the only stain on the brightest page, perhaps, in the history of the United States, — the page on which it is written that neither after final victory nor during the course of this terrible war, while the citizens were giving their lives by thousands in defence of the Union, has any political offence (save in this one instance) been expiated in blood."

This military execution, the speculating in sequestrated property, and the notorious "woman order" were the incidents in Butler's rule which attracted most attention. Relying on the forbearance which Americans habitually exercise toward even the meanest of the female sex, some foolish women in New Orleans, well-dressed and rating themselves as ladies, sought to vent their spite by making faces at Federal officers on the street, calling them names, and spitting at them. To stop such behaviour Butler issued an order " that hereafter, when any female shall, by word, gesture, or movement, insult or show contempt for any officer or soldier of the United States, she shall be regarded and held liable to be treated as a woman of the town plying her avocation." Never, perhaps, was a military order more successful in effecting its immediate purpose; but the furious rage with which it was greeted throughout the South may easily be imagined. Had its wretched author, however, understood in the smallest degree the feelings of gentlemen, had there entered into his constitution so much as a single fibre of true manhood, he would have seen that this vile edict insulted no one else so grossly as the officers and soldiers under his command. Such an outrage ought to have led to his immediate recall. It was doubtless silly in Jefferson Davis, after Butler's departure from New Orleans, to

The "woman order."

issue a proclamation denouncing his former political ally as a felon who might be hanged without ceremony; but after making due allowance for the extravagant bitterness of war-time, it seems a not unnatural commentary on the behaviour which earned for the military governor of New Orleans the familiar sobriquet of "Beast."

The value of prompt action in warfare has never been better illustrated than in Farragut's capture of New Orleans. The blow was dealt before the enemy had completed his preparations for defence, and while his energies were distracted by the concentrated advance of the Federal army upon Corinth. Its political value was great; it nipped in the bud one of the many schemes of Napoleon III. for recognizing the independence of the Confederacy. Its military value, in opening the lower Mississippi, was equally great, and would have been still greater if the army had coöperated with like skill and promptness. The capture of New Orleans, taken in connection with the capture of Corinth, ought to have entailed the immediate fall of Vicksburg and the complete conquest of the Mississippi river; and but for the flagrant imbecility which then directed the movements of our western armies, it would almost certainly have done so. But we have now to enter upon a melancholy tale.

CHAPTER IV

FROM CORINTH TO STONE RIVER

ON the 11th of April, 1862, four days after the hard-won victory of Shiloh, General Halleck arrived at Pittsburg Landing and took command in person of the forces there assembled. On the 21st General Pope arrived with his army, fresh from its capture of Island Number Ten. With the three armies of Pope, Grant, and Buell thus united, Halleck had an effective force of more than 100,000 men. This force was organized by Halleck into right wing, centre, left wing, and reserve. All of Grant's army, except the divisions of McClernand and Lew Wallace, which were taken out and replaced by Thomas's division from Buell's army, formed the right wing, and was commanded by General Thomas. The remainder of Buell's army, forming the centre, was still commanded by General Buell. General Pope with his army formed the left wing. The reserve was made up of the two divisions of McClernand and Wallace, with McClernand in command. In this arrangement, it

Halleck's advance upon Corinth.

will be observed, there was no place for Grant. His talents were got rid of for the moment by appointing him second in command over the whole, a position more honourable than useful, since no specific duties were assigned him. With this grand army Halleck started at the end of April, creeping slowly forward, entrenching at every step, and restraining the ardour of his generals, until after nearly a month he had safely accomplished the twenty miles from Pittsburg Landing to Corinth! His adversary Beauregard, soon gauging the calibre of the Federal commander, retired inch by inch, keeping his skirmishers well forward and presenting as bold a front as possible. His total effective force, including the troops of Van Dorn, who had joined him just after Shiloh, amounted to scarcely more than 50,000 men. He was outnumbered two to one, and ought to have been surrounded and captured. He understood that Corinth could not be held; all hope of that had really been lost when he withdrew his beaten army from the field of Shiloh. The most he could do was to save that army from capture, while delaying the enemy as long as possible; and this he did very well indeed. He had thrown up extensive works as if with the intention of withstanding a siege at Corinth; but before Halleck had fairly closed in upon him, he

Beauregard evacuates Corinth.

From Corinth to Stone River 135

had evacuated that town and retreated upon Tupelo, a station sixty miles south on the railroad leading to Mobile.

Pope's forces were sent in pursuit, while their commander was confined to his tent by illness, about five miles from Halleck's headquarters. Despatches came in to the effect that the woods were full of Confederate stragglers, and it was hoped that at least 10,000 would be captured within a day or two. This intelligence Pope forwarded to Halleck, and it quite turned his head. Translating hope into reality, Halleck telegraphed to Washington that "General Pope, with 40,000 men, is thirty miles south of Corinth, pushing the enemy hard. He already reports 10,000 prisoners and deserters from the enemy, and 15,000 stand of arms captured." Great were the rejoicings throughout the North, *Much cry and little wool.* but they gave place to indignation a few days later, when it appeared that this brave story was but a new version of the three black crows. No prisoners were taken worth mentioning, Beauregard's army was still intact, and Pope was generally blamed and ridiculed for a wild statement which he had in no way authorized. With praiseworthy desire not to embarrass his chief, Pope bore this popular censure in silence, and it was not until after the end of the war that he even asked Halleck for an explanation, which that general, with some frivolous excuses, declined to give. Pope's conduct in this affair shows true generosity, but what shall be said of the superior officer who thus allowed a subordinate to become his scapegoat and uttered never a word to clear him?

Chagrined and disgusted as the northern people were at Beauregard's easy escape, nevertheless the occupation of Corinth was an event of great importance. It broke through the second Confederate line of defence, and gave the Federals possession of the only railroad which directly connected the Mississippi river with the seaboard of Virginia and South Carolina. It also turned the positions of Fort Pillow and Memphis on the great river, just as the capture of Fort Donelson had turned the position of Columbus. On the 5th of June, just a week after the fall of Corinth, the Federal fleet found Fort Pillow abandoned. This river fleet, which had coöperated with Grant and Pope, was now commanded by Commodore Charles Davis, as the wound received by Foote at Fort Donelson had grown worse and obliged him to retire. Foote was a commander worthy of a navy that boasted a Farragut and a Porter, and in Davis he had a worthy successor. The fleet had been strengthened by the addition of four powerful rams constructed by Colonel Ellet of the army, a man of venturesome courage, under whose separate command they had been somewhat oddly placed. From Fort Pillow this strong armada hastened downstream to Memphis, which the fall of Corinth had already made untenable, but which the Confederate Commodore Montgomery had too chivalrously determined not to abandon without fighting to the death. Against Davis's five gunboats and Ellet's four rams he could bring eight gunboats, some of them armed with beaks; and on the 6th of June, at six o'clock in the morning, under the high bluff crowded with anxious citizens gathered in the blazing sunshine to watch the scene, he advanced to the trial of arms, which was short, sharp, and final. At half past seven the spectators dispersed to their homes, the men muttering curses, the women in tears. Of their eight gunboats three were captured, three were sunk, and one was blown up; only one had escaped. One of the Federal ships was seriously injured, and two or three men were wounded, but not a man on that side was killed. Memphis surrendered that day, and thus the Mississippi was opened as far down as Vicksburg. *(Naval battle of Memphis.)*

After his capture of New Orleans, Farragut had proceeded up the river, receiving the surrender of Baton Rouge, the capital of Louisiana, and other towns; but on the 18th of May his progress had been stopped at Vicksburg, 400 miles above New Orleans by water and 400 below Memphis. The position of that town was such that it could not be taken without the coöperation of a larger land force than Butler was able to spare, and so it became necessary to wait for the fall of Corinth. But after that event, as before it, Halleck dawdled instead of striking. On the 28th of June Farragut's fleet ran past the guns of Vicksburg without serious damage and effected a junction with that of Commodore Davis just above the town. Nothing could be done without an army, and Farragut asked Halleck for troops, but could not get any. Precious time was thus slipping away, while the enemy was putting every minute to good use. General Van Dorn, detached from the army which Beauregard had withdrawn to Tupelo, made all haste to Vicksburg, taking Breckinridge and his division along with him, and worked day and night building fortifications and collecting cannon.

Van Dorn fortifies Vicksburg.

Moreover, so far from losing heart on account of their crushing naval defeats at New Orleans and Memphis, the undaunted Confederates were making ready to attack the victors upon their own element. Fifty miles up the Yazoo river, which empties into the Mississippi just above Vicksburg, they were building a formidable ironclad ram, which they hoped would do as much mischief as the Merrimac had done and threatened at Hampton Roads, and Farragut had no Monitor at his disposal. This famous ram, the Arkansas, was built like the Merrimac, though smaller in size, and if her engines had been sufficiently powerful, she might have wrought fearful havoc to the Federal fleet. At her first appearance, on the 15th of July, she attacked and put to flight the Tyler and Carondelet, and, running under the friendly guns of Vicksburg, where Commander William Porter, with the Essex, tried in vain to destroy her, she became a perpetual menace to our ships.

The Confederate ram Arkansas.

By the end of July, as no troops could be obtained, and the crews were suffering from fever, it was decided to abandon offensive operations, and Davis withdrew his ships 300 miles up the river to Helena, while Farragut returned to New Orleans. The energetic Van Dorn at once sent Breckinridge with 6000 men and the Arkansas to recover Baton Rouge and bring back the state government, besides securing the mouth of Red river. The capital was defended by a detachment of 4000 of Butler's troops, with the ram Essex and a couple of gunboats. In the fight which occurred on the 5th of August at one o'clock in the morning, the Confederate troops were repulsed with a loss of 500 men, the machinery of the Arkansas broke down, and when she was attacked by the Essex, her commander ran her ashore, landed his crew, set her on fire, and turned her adrift. Like so many other rebel vessels in these waters, her career came to an end in a deafening explosion. Nothing daunted, however, by this reverse, Van Dorn seized and fortified the village of Port Hudson, a few miles above Baton Rouge but below the mouth of Red river. By thus holding Vicksburg and Port Hudson, the Confederates controlled the 250 miles of river between them, and through the Red river obtained their supplies from the trans-Mississippi region as promptly and securely as ever. Until they could be ousted from these two strongholds, in spite of the splendid naval victories above and below, the work of clearing the Mississippi river was but half accomplished; the "backbone of the rebellion" was not yet broken. Many more lives were yet to be sacrificed, many more homes made desolate, before that great object could be attained.

Destruction of the Arkansas; Van Dorn fortifies Port Hudson.

The lesson of the summer of 1862 is a mournful one. It shows us how far the self-devotion of a noble people and the valour of able commanders could be neutralized by incompetence at the head of affairs. Corinth had fallen on the 29th of May and Memphis on the 6th of June. Halleck had

100,000 men elated with success, while his adversary, Beauregard, had 50,000 dispirited by a long series of reverses. At any time between the first of June and the middle of July a force of 20,000 men, coöperating with the fleets of Farragut and Davis, which were ready and waiting for them, might easily have taken Vicksburg and saved a whole year of anxious and arduous work in this quarter. *Lost opportunities.* There was nothing to prevent Halleck from sending such a force by rail to Memphis and thence down the river, and their landing at Vicksburg would have met with no such resistance as Sherman encountered six months later. But Halleck's mind was not large enough to take in the whole theatre of war between the Mississippi and the Alleghanies. Thus far the advance of the Union armies from Fort Donelson up the Tennessee river to Corinth had operated directly to open the Mississippi river by taking its fortified places in flank; and with New Orleans now in our possession, nothing but the occupation of Vicksburg was necessary to complete the conquest.

But in this vast theatre of war, there was another region that needed to be looked after; there was another strategic point scarcely less important than Vicksburg. This was the mountain fastness of Chattanooga, commanding eastern Tennessee and all the northward avenues by which an army starting from the centre of the Confederacy might hope to recover some of the lost ground in Tennessee and Kentucky. Halleck at Corinth was 300 miles distant from Vicksburg on the one hand, and 200 miles from Chattanooga on the other.

<small>Importance of Chattanooga.</small> It was as important for him to occupy the latter as the former, lest the enemy, despairing of direct success against overwhelming odds in Mississippi, should seek to retrieve the situation by boldly returning the offensive and throwing his whole force northward into eastern Tennessee and Kentucky. For two other reasons it was desirable to possess Chattanooga as the key to eastern Tennessee. First, it would interpose a Union army between the rebel forces in Virginia and in the West, and thus prevent their easily reinforcing one another. Secondly, the people of eastern Tennessee were devoted to the Union, they were subjected to grievous persecution on that account, and ever since the first outbreak of hostilities, President Lincoln had been impatient to relieve them. Halleck, therefore, was imperatively called upon to reach out his left hand to Chattanooga while seizing Vicksburg with the right. It was indeed a long reach, but he possessed both the stronger force and the interior lines. With all the difficulties of

the task, a Napoleon would have made light work of it. A moderately good general would have made sure of one prize, even at the risk of losing the other. But what shall be said of the generalship which could throw away such advantages of strength and situation, and tamely allow the enemy, dividing his weaker force and moving upon exterior lines, to gain *both* the coveted positions! Let us observe the manner in which this awful disaster was brought upon us.

Besides the army of 50,000 under Beauregard, the enemy had 12,000 men under Kirby Smith at Knoxville in east Tennessee, watched by 9000 Federals under George Morgan at Cumberland Gap. He had also a garrison of 2000 men at Chattanooga, and this was watched from Huntsville in Alabama by 7000 Federals under an able commander, the astronomer Ormsby Mitchel. This general had just accomplished one of the most brilliant raids that were made on either side during the war. At the beginning of June he held a hundred miles of the railroad between Corinth and Chattanooga, some portions of which were torn up, and on the 7th of that month one of his brigades even went so far as to erect batteries on the north bank of the Tennessee, opposite Chattanooga, and begin bombarding the town. But with only 7000 men, Mitchel

Mitchel's raid.

could not hope to retain such advantages. If Halleck had now promptly reinforced him with 30,000 or 40,000 men under Buell, Chattanooga might have been seized at once and held against all comers. Halleck would still have retained 70,000, or at least 60,000, with which to crush all opposition in Mississippi and proceed overland to Vicksburg, drawing his supplies either by boat or by rail from Memphis.

Now Halleck did despatch Buell toward Chattanooga, but in such a fashion as to render the movement useless. The question arose by what line of railway should Buell obtain his supplies when once he should have occupied the mountain citadel. Should they come from Memphis through Corinth and Huntsville, or from Louisville by way of Nashville and Murfreesboro? The former line was parallel to the enemy's front, the latter was perpendicular to it, and all sound military considerations required that the latter should be chosen. So thought Buell, whose judgment in such matters was most excellent, but Halleck overruled him, and insisted upon his taking the line from Memphis to Chattanooga and putting the railroad in thorough repair yard by yard as he went. Under these imperative orders Buell started from Corinth on the 10th of June with 40,000 men, and after six weeks of rail-

Why Buell was "slow."

road-building reached by the end of July a position from which he could threaten Chattanooga.

Meanwhile Halleck lay idle at Corinth, as if on the defensive, with his army of 60,000 men still outnumbering the enemy, who retreated from before him. He gave most stringent orders to Pope not to press the Confederate army in such wise as to run risk of a battle, and summed up his theory of the situation in these memorable words: "I think the enemy will continue his retreat, which is all I desire." The <small>Halleck's imbecility.</small> enemy was indeed rapidly moving the bulk of his army southward to Mobile, but he could not be expected to show such an accommodating disposition as to throw himself into the Gulf of Mexico! It is usually safe to suppose in warfare that your enemy will not do as you desire. General Beauregard, who was not a favourite of Jefferson Davis, was now removed from command, and his place was taken by Braxton Bragg. As soon as Bragg saw the manner in which Buell had been started eastward, he boldly divided his own forces. Leaving 15,000 men under Van Dorn, as the nucleus of a force with which to cover Vicksburg, he retreated upon Mobile with 35,000, and thence sped by rail straight to Chattanooga, which he reached and occupied in advance of Buell on the 29th of July.

By this masterly move Bragg suddenly gained the initiative and threw the Union armies upon the defensive, along the whole line. Holding Chattanooga, he seriously threatened Buell, who with Mitchel's division now had 47,000 men, but was obliged to spare 20,000 in small detachments to guard the long railroad, leaving only 27,000 ready for the field. Against this force, by summoning Kirby Smith from Knoxville, Bragg could at any moment throw 47,000 men. To relieve Buell from this embarrassment, 20,000 more men were sent from Corinth to take the place of those who were guarding the railroad, leaving only 40,000 for the work in Mississippi. Against these, by bringing together Lovell and Price, with other troops from Arkansas, Van Dorn was presently able to oppose 32,000. It was not long before Bragg's activity awakened such alarm that the army at Corinth was still further depleted to send reinforcements to Buell, so that it became quite out of the question for it to undertake any offensive operations. Thus it was that Halleck frittered away his golden opportunity; thus was his great army scattered to little purpose; thus did he allow the enemy to seize both the strategic centres west of the Alleghanies, and to prolong the Civil War at least a twelvemonth. And to crown all, the ridiculous line of communication for

How his army was scattered.

the sake of which everything had been thus indiscriminately sacrificed was almost immediately rendered useless by the events which forced Buell northward into Kentucky

On the 16th of July, before the nature or extent of the mischief had become apparent, Halleck started for Washington. President Lincoln felt the need of a general-in-chief for all the armies of the United States, in the hope of securing unity of operation. *Halleck appointed general-in-chief.* Comparatively little had been accomplished thus far in the East, whereas much had been accomplished in the West; and it seemed logical to choose the western commander-in-chief for the supreme control of the armies. The departure of Halleck left Grant in command at Corinth. Pope was now called eastward to take charge of the forces hitherto scattered about in northern Virginia, and his place was filled by one of his division-commanders, William Stark Rosecrans, who after distinguishing himself in the early campaigns in West Virginia had taken part in the recent advance upon Corinth. On arriving at Washington, Halleck's supreme capacity for doing the wrong thing was illustrated by a step which threatened the Union cause with speedy and irretrievable wreck. The Seven Days' battles near Richmond had seriously damaged McClellan's army, but still left it in a position which must compel Lee to remain about Richmond. Lee would gladly have fought for another week and given 20,000 men to get McClellan's army away from the James river; and what he so earnestly desired Halleck now did for him by removing it by sea to northern Virginia, in the hope of making Washington more secure.[1] While this clumsy movement was going on, Lee was at once let loose, with all his force, to overwhelm Pope, threaten the Federal capital, and invade the loyal states.

The northern people did not generally at the time appreciate the relations of cause and effect in this tide of calamity which so suddenly rolled over the country and seemed for a moment to be undoing all that had been done. But the Confederate generals appreciated it thoroughly, and the imbecility so manifest at the head of our armies made them very bold indeed. Now that Bragg had

[1] McClellan's plans were apt to be sound, although he was, to an astonishing degree, inefficient in action. His intention, which Halleck overruled, was to seize Petersburg as a point from which to operate against Richmond, just as Grant tried to do, two years later. Had McClellan done so, it is safe to say that no invasion of Maryland by Lee would ever have been heard of. See Ropes's *Civil War*, ii. 235–243, where this point is very clearly set forth. The Count of Paris truly says that Halleck's order, withdrawing McClellan's army from the James river, was more disastrous to the Federal cause than any of the defeats inflicted by the enemy. See his *Civil War in America*, ii. 249.

saved Chattanooga and gained the initiative, he meditated the reconquest of Tennessee and Kentucky, and, emulous of Lee, he lost no time in starting. During July and August the cavalry raids of Morgan and Forrest spread terror and confusion through those two states. Morgan and Forrest. They cut railroads, seized telegraph offices and sent misleading despatches over the wires, carried off horses and mules by the thousand, and once in a dash upon Murfreesboro captured 1700 troops and a battery of artillery. Buell sent Nelson to look after them, but that enterprising commander was free to confess that chasing cavalry with infantry was not very inspiriting work. Buell had long since earnestly called the government's attention to his perilous deficiency in cavalry, but could get no assistance.

At length in the last week of August, while Lee was crushing Pope in Virginia, the forward movement began. Kirby Smith took his 12,000 men over the mountains by a pass which enabled him to turn Cum- Kirby Smith defeats Nelson. berland Gap and compel the Federal force to evacuate it and retreat upon the Ohio. He then struck across Kentucky to Richmond, where Nelson with 7000 men undertook to check his advance. In a sharp fight in which about 900 were killed and wounded on each side, Nelson was totally defeated and a third of his force was captured. Smith then advanced upon Cincinnati.

While this was going on, Bragg had come out of Chattanooga and crossed the Tennessee river. The sagacious Thomas saw that a movement into Kentucky was intended, and advised Buell to check it by occupying Sparta. But instead of doing so, Buell, who feared an attack on his right, concentrated his forces at Murfreesboro. Profiting by this error, Bragg slipped past Buell's left, crossed the Cumberland river at Gainesville, and marched straight toward Munfordville, a station on the Louisville and Nashville railroad through which Buell obtained his supplies. Munfordville was garrisoned by 4000 men. To reach it Buell had to travel 105 miles on the arc of a circle through Nashville and Bowling Green, while Bragg had only to travel 68 miles on a straight line forming the chord of this arc. Determined in no event to abandon Nashville, Buell left Thomas there with three divisions and hastened northward; but Bragg's shorter route enabled him to reach Munfordville and capture its garrison before Buell had passed Bowling Green. Bragg was now three marches nearer than Buell to Louisville, and everybody supposed he would instantly come up and capture that city, so important not only for its size and wealth, but

Bragg invades Kentucky.

also as the only base of supply from which Buell's 40,000 men could be fed.

In the states north of the Ohio the excitement was at fever heat, and everywhere the outlook seemed gloomy enough. Within a few weeks the President had called for 600,000 men, half of them to serve for three years and a half as nine months' militia; in case of necessity conscription was to be resorted to. People forgot Fort Donelson and New Orleans; it seemed as if all the gains had been cancelled. Those who held that the South could never be conquered now regarded their opinion as borne out by facts; and there were a few in whom party prejudice was so strong as to make them rejoice in this conclusion. While such short-sighted people wagged their heads, militia turned out in thousands to defend the threatened points, and the streets of Louisville and Cincinnati were the scene of busy military preparation.

<small>Panic at the North.</small>

But the wave of rebel invasion had already spent its force. On the 17th of September, the day on which Munfordville was captured, Lee was slightly defeated in the murderous battle of Antietam and compelled to turn his back upon Maryland. Perhaps the news of this reverse may have impressed upon Bragg the necessity of caution. His army had not been cordially received by the people of Kentucky. He found himself in a hostile country.

He was indeed on Buell's line of communications, in a position where defeat would be ruinous to Buell. But by the same token, defeat at the hands of an army lying south of him would be ruinous to himself, and his force did not outnumber Buell's. Louisville was not quite defenceless, and to attack it with the chance of being assailed in the rear would be to court destruction. Accordingly Bragg desisted and turned eastward to join Kirby Smith, who after threatening Cincinnati had retired upon Frankfort. Here was the weak point in the Confederate strategy. If, after his victory at Richmond, Smith had moved toward Louisville, so as to unite with Bragg upon Buell's line of communications, they might have hoped to crush him as thoroughly as Pope was crushed at Manassas.[1] As it was, they met at

Defect in the Confederate strategy.

[1] In this connection Mr. Ropes very properly comments on "the folly, which both the Union and the Confederate governments were so constantly committing, of having more than one commanding officer in one theatre of war." Bragg might have sent for Kirby Smith to come from Lexington (about 100 miles) and join him in giving battle to Buell at Munfordville. Smith, "although an independent department-commander, had offered to serve under Bragg in this campaign. Still, the fact that Bragg was not the sole commander in this region unquestionably hampered his movements. . . . Smith was not summoned, and Bragg did not feel himself strong enough to attack Buell alone." Ropes's *Civil War*, ii. 403. Thus the supreme opportunity for the Confederates in this invasion of Kentucky was lost by them.

Frankfort, the state capital, and amused themselves with the inauguration of a rebel governor, while Buell, who had marched on to his base at Louisville and largely reinforced his army, was now ready to turn and rend them. On the 30th of September, just as he was starting, there came an order from Halleck, relieving him from command and appointing Thomas in his place. But magnanimous Thomas, who understood the situation much better than either Halleck or the newspapers, protested so seriously against this injustice that the order was revoked.

Upon Buell's advance Bragg fell back. At Perryville, on the 8th of October, portions of the two armies came into collision. There was a severe fight, in which nearly 5000 men were killed and wounded on each side, but it decided nothing. Bragg retreated southeasterly and escaped into east Tennessee through Cumberland Gap, whence he made his way back to Chattanooga, and presently advanced upon Murfreesboro. Instead of fruitlessly chasing him through the Gap, the Federal commander, anticipating his movements, proceeded to Nashville, whence a new campaign might best be begun.

Battle of Perryville.

While on either side of the Alleghanies the Union armies had thus been baulked of the coveted prizes of Richmond and Chattanooga, and the loyal states were for a moment invaded by the enemy, there was one point where the Union line did not fall back, but every inch of ground once conquered was firmly held. That point was Corinth, where Grant remained in command. Grant had so many miles of railroad to guard, and his force was so much weakened by sending troops to aid Buell, that it was impossible for him to undertake any extensive operations. His first active movement was to send Rosecrans with 9000 men and Ord with 8000 to attack Sterling Price, who was isolated with 14,000 men at the village of Iuka, twenty miles southeast of Corinth. They were to attack him on opposite sides and crush him between them, but as often happens with such schemes, there was a lack of coördination in the movements. The battle was prematurely fought between Price and Rosecrans, and although Price retired from the field with heavy loss, he made good his escape and succeeded in joining his forces to those of Van Dorn. It could hardly be called a victory for the Federals.

Battle of Iuka.

With his army thus concentrated, Van Dorn now resolved to inflict such a blow upon Grant as would compel him to retire down the Tennessee river. His plan was bold but well-considered. Grant's forces were small for the extent of country he was directed to occupy. He had 7000 men at

Memphis under Sherman, 12,000 at Bolivar under Ord, 23,000 at Corinth under Rosecrans, and a reserve of 6000 at Jackson, where — as the most convenient point for communicating with these different forces — he had his headquarters. Van Dorn's total force was 22,000 men, and with it he boldly undertook to defeat Rosecrans and capture the works at Corinth. This would oblige Grant to retreat, and it was hoped it would throw him back as far as Fort Donelson. Accordingly, on the 3d of October Van Dorn attacked Rosecrans, and a very obstinate battle ensued, in which fortune seemed at first to favour the Confederates, but after two days of fighting they were defeated with a loss of 5000 in killed, wounded, and prisoners. The total Union loss was about 2500. After this serious defeat the Confederates could no longer hope to take the offensive against Grant. On the contrary, it left him free to assume the aggressive and begin upon his first movement against Vicksburg. For this ill-fortune Van Dorn was unreasonably blamed by Jefferson Davis, who at once superseded him by John Clifford Pemberton, a general in every way his inferior. On the other hand, Rosecrans won great increase of fame, and three weeks after his victory he was appointed to an independent command.

Battle of Corinth.

Van Dorn superseded by Pemberton.

It was inevitable that some of our generals should be made to serve as scapegoats for the disasters and panic of the summer. Popular indignation demanded victims, and at such times the blows are very apt to fall in the wrong places. If Halleck could only have been removed from the chief command and comfortably immured in some Old Woman's Home, what a relief it would have been to a long-suffering people! But the fates showed little discrimination in their awards. One of the most shameful pages in American history is that which records the unrighteous condemnation of the able and faithful Fitz John Porter, a wrong which has been tardily and partially rectified. As for Pope, who had shown himself totally unfit to command an army, his removal came none too soon. Of McClellan's incapacity, both in strategy and in tactics, the Maryland campaign had furnished the crowning proof, and the only reason for regretting him was the amazing selection of Burnside as his successor. The case of Buell was entirely different. It is true that the public had in great measure lost confidence in him; it was vaguely felt that somehow or other he ought to have prevented Bragg from invading Kentucky, or else that he ought not to have allowed him to get away from Kentucky without a crushing defeat. While a war is going

Buell made a scapegoat.

on, it is difficult to see below the surface of events. We now know, however, that it was Halleck who was responsible for Buell's failure to anticipate the rebels in seizing Chattanooga. With the enemy in possession of this place and holding eastern Tennessee, it is difficult to see how any general, without a decided superiority in numbers, without a suitable force of cavalry, and with a line of communications 300 miles long, could ensure himself against such mischief as that which for a moment overtook Buell. His retreat upon Louisville and his subsequent pursuit of the enemy were admirably managed, and the state of his army during the whole campaign bore testimony to his rare ability.

Unfortunately for Buell, however, he had made two powerful enemies, in Oliver Morton, governor of Indiana, and Andrew Johnson, whom President Lincoln had appointed military governor of Tennessee. Morton's services to the Union cause were so great that he stood high (and deservedly so) in the favour of President Lincoln. At the same time he was a man of relentless and domineering temper, and could never be made to understand that the Indiana troops in Buell's army owed obedience primarily to their general and not to the governor at Indianapolis. He would send his staff-officers

Buell's enemies, Morton and Johnson.

into the army to look after the interests of the Indiana men, exchange their arms without the knowledge of their commanders, and keep up a communication concerning various matters which were none of their business.[1] Buell was not the man to endure such infringements of discipline, and when he suppressed them he incurred the deadly hostility of the passionate Morton. As for Andrew Johnson, he wished to have all the other objects of the war postponed or sacrificed to the occupation of eastern Tennessee, and he hated Buell for entertaining broader views. Moreover, Buell was a strict disciplinarian, and insisted that war should be conducted upon civilized principles, and not upon those of Vandals and Bashi-bazouks. So when one of Mitchel's brigades, in the summer of 1862, wantonly sacked the town of Athens, in Alabama, Buell visited the offence with wholesome severity; by sentence of a court-martial the brigade was broken up and distributed, its commanding colonel was dismissed, and other officers were variously punished. For these praiseworthy measures Buell was loudly abused in public meetings and by many of the newspapers. He was accused of sympathizing with rebels, and foul imputations upon his loyalty were caught up and used against him by Morton and Johnson. In Octo-

[1] See Fry, *The Army under Buell*, p. 86.

ber the pressure in various ways brought to bear upon President Lincoln had come to be such that he yielded to it and consented to Buell's removal.

So industriously had Buell been maligned that it was said that everybody had lost confidence in him except Thomas! But Thomas's opinion on such a matter was probably worth more than that of any other man in the United States. He could feel keenly what a pity it was for the country to lose the services of such an accomplished and high-minded soldier.[1] The immediate occasion of Buell's dismissal furnishes a striking commentary upon the military obtuseness which then reigned at Washington. When Bragg retreated through Cumberland Gap, Halleck insisted that Buell should follow and

Buell superseded by Rosecrans.

---

[1] I am glad to be able, in support of my opinion of Buell, to cite the words of Mr. Ropes, one of the most acute and learned military critics of the nineteenth century: "It cannot be doubted that the cause of the Union was seriously injured by withdrawing Buell from the command of this army. Buell was as able a general as any in the service. Had he at the first — that is, on Nov. 1, 1861 — been placed in chief command in the West, it is not too much to say that the Confederate army of the West would have ceased to exist before June 1, 1862, and that thereafter a regiment of Union troops could have marched without opposition from Nashville to Chattanooga and Knoxville." *Civil War*, ii. 414. The reference to Nov. 1, 1861, is to the date of Halleck's appointment to the chief command in the West.

chase him around the circle, instead of moving to Nashville to head him off; and because Buell refused to lend himself to such a silly scheme, he was removed, and Rosecrans, fresh from the victory at Corinth, was put in his place.[1]

When Rosecrans took command at Nashville, October 30, this pretext for Buell's removal was ignored, and the new general was allowed to continue in the course begun by his predecessor. An immediate offensive was demanded by the circumstances. People were angry because Bragg had got off so easily. On the other hand the southern people were abusing Bragg for failing to conquer Kentucky. It is so easy in war-time for people at their cosy firesides to blame sorely tried soldiers for not doing the impossible! A battle was therefore necessary both for Bragg and for Rosecrans. The long campaign begun in July must be brought to a decisive issue. After all their marches and countermarches the two armies were face to face in middle Tennessee, and it was now to be seen which could annihilate the other.

[1] There is little direct evidence to show why Rosecrans received the appointment instead of Thomas, who had been appointed a month before. But Thomas had declined that appointment, and may have been supposed to be too much in sympathy with Buell. Moreover, since the important victory at Corinth, there was a visible disposition to look upon Rosecrans as "the coming man."

Rosecrans was at Nashville, where his first care was to repair the railway connecting him with his base of supplies at Louisville. Bragg had concentrated his forces at Murfreesboro, whence he sent the indefatigable Morgan on flying excursions to tear up rails and break down bridges in Rosecrans's rear; and for want of a sufficient cavalry, Rosecrans, like Buell, found it hard to check these performances. The longer he stayed quiet, the worse the nuisance was sure to become; and after due preparation he marched out of Nashville, on the day after Christmas, to attack and overwhelm the enemy.

The town of Murfreesboro is a station on the Nashville and Chattanooga railroad, thirty miles southeast from Nashville. A mile to westward of the town the road to Franklin crosses Stone river, a sluggish tributary of the Cumberland. The sinuous river, and the railroad and turnpike straight as arrows, all run northwesterly and near together, through dense cedar-brakes interspersed with occasional clearings. It was this triple line of turnpike, railroad, and stream that was now to be made the scene of some of the most obstinate fighting of modern times. Bragg's army was drawn up in line of battle at an acute angle with the river and mostly to the west of it. The left

The battlefield of Stone river, or Murfreesboro.

wing under Hardee and the centre under Polk were west of the river, and on the further side, to ward off any flank movement upon the town of Murfreesboro, was the right wing, composed of Breckinridge's division of Hardee's corps separated from its fellows. The general direction of the line west of the river was nearly north and south, with the left wing advanced southwestward. On the east side Breckinridge's division was considerably refused to the northeast. Such was the Confederate line of battle, — an arrangement apparently faultless and fully adequate to the work which Bragg had planned.

The Union army was drawn up to westward of the river in a line somewhat zigzag, but for the most part parallel to the enemy's front.

The arrangement of our troops at Stone river.

The right wing under McCook stretched from the Franklin road to the Wilkinson turnpike. It consisted of three divisions, — first Johnson's, resting on the Franklin road with its right refused in a crotchet, and then Davis's ; the third, which connected with the centre at the Wilkinson pike, was commanded by a young officer named Philip Sheridan, who had lately won his first laurels at Perryville. The centre, commanded by Thomas, consisted of two divisions, Negley's and Rousseau's, but in the plan of battle Palmer's division of the left wing practically formed

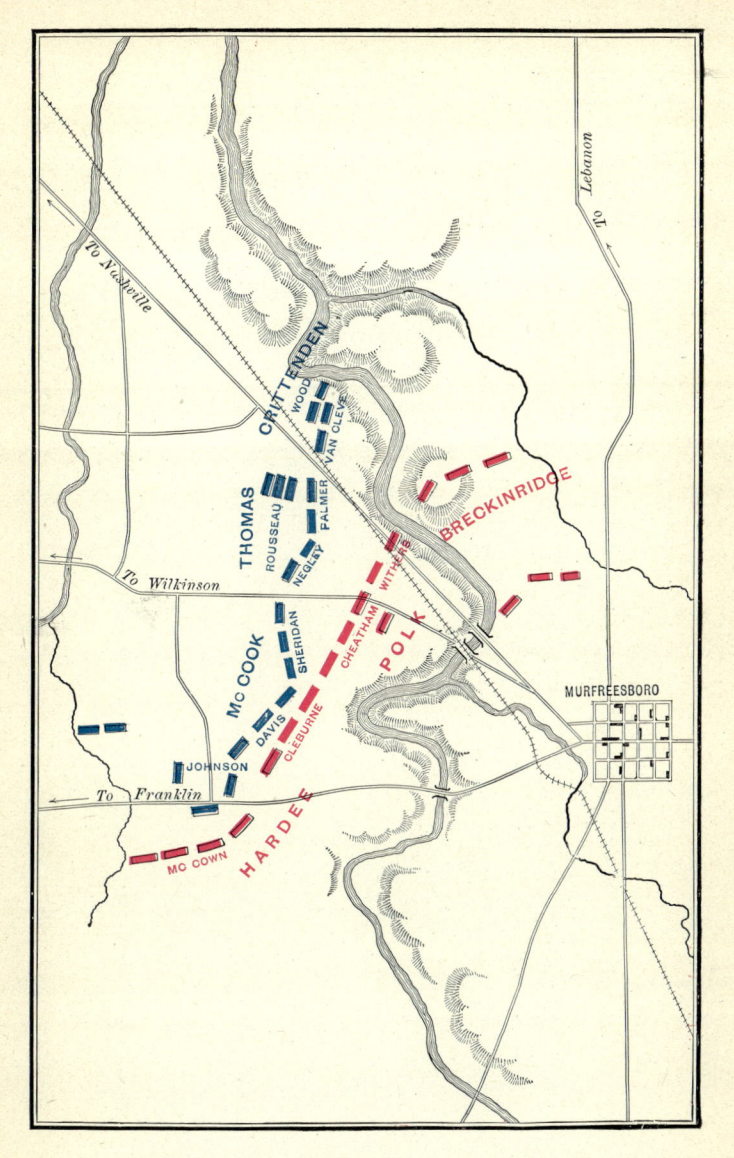

STONE RIVER, DECEMBER 31, 1862, MORNING

part of the centre. Negley and Palmer were drawn up in line between the Wilkinson and Nashville pikes, with Rousseau stationed in the rear as a reserve. The remainder of the left wing under Crittenden, consisting of Wood's and Van Cleve's divisions, reached from the Nashville pike across the railroad and rested its left on a bend in the river. Each line of battle, Union and Confederate, was about three miles in length, and each contained in infantry and artillery about 40,000 men.

It was well said by Frederick of Prussia that more than half the secret of winning battles lies in knowing how to take position. Rosecrans's arrangement was well adapted to his purpose save in one quarter of the field, but the defect in that quarter was a grave one. His plan of attack was brilliant and bold. It was to throw the two divisions of Wood and Van Cleve across the easily fordable river and crush the single division of Breckinridge. At that point is a commanding ridge upon which Union artillery, once posted, would enfilade the whole Confederate line. With the aid of this galling fire it seemed certain that Thomas, with his two divisions and Palmer's, would defeat the Confederate centre; while the Union left, continuing its turning movement, would pass through Murfreesboro and occupy the Franklin road, thus cutting

Rosecrans's plan of attack.

off the enemy's retreat. In other words, the Union army, pivoting upon its right, was to be swung around in a semicircle, enveloping and destroying the enemy. It was for this purpose that Rosecrans massed his troops so heavily upon his left. In space the Wilkinson turnpike divided his line in the middle, but nearly two thirds of his weight was to the left of this. This was well, provided the right wing were strong enough and so advantageously placed as to be able to hold its ground. If the pivot were to be shaken out of place, the whole turning movement would be spoiled and the army thrown upon the defensive.

It was all the more essential that the right wing should be made secure, since the arrangement of Bragg's troops was such as to indicate that an attack would be made in that quarter. In fact, Bragg's plan of battle was almost precisely the same as that of Rosecrans. With his left somewhat heavily massed and thrown forward, he intended to overlap and crush the Federal right. Swinging around his whole force west of the river with Polk's right as its pivot, he would come in upon the Federal rear, fold the army back against the river, and, seizing the Nashville turnpike, cut off their retreat. The two plans being thus substantially identical, each general having a heavy force opposed to the weaker wing of the other, it

Bragg's plan of attack.

followed that he who could soonest deliver his blow would be likely to achieve success. In this respect the position favoured the Confederate general. Rosecrans, in delivering his blow, must throw two divisions across the river, which, though not a serious obstacle, would still occasion some slight delay. In front of Bragg's left there was not only no obstacle, but the forest formed an impenetrable curtain, under cover of which his men could approach the Federal right without being observed.

Under these circumstances it was imperatively necessary for Rosecrans to use extraordinary diligence in placing his right wing. This he can hardly be said to have done, and the error which he failed to rectify spoiled his plan of battle and came within an ace of destroying the Union army. The error was that McCook's line was too long and thin and faced too much to the east, thus coming too near the enemy. If it had been refused half way back to the Wilkinson road, so as to face nearly south, it might at the same time have been more heavily massed. The enemy would have had to move farther to reach it, and could not have struck it in flank without stretching out his own line so far as to weaken himself. It could also have been more easily reinforced, in case of necessity, by Rousseau's division in reserve. Rosecrans under-

Faulty position of the Union right wing.

stood all this, and told McCook that he did not like his facing so much to the east. At the same time he did not press the matter, but left too much to the discretion of the corps-commander, who was over-confident, and assured him that in the event of an attack he could hold his ground just as he was for three hours. Herein was Rosecrans's one terrible mistake. Absorbed in preparing the offensive movement with his left, he did not give sufficient attention to his right. He ought to have visited the spot in person and insisted upon McCook's rectifying his position. One reason why Napoleon almost invariably won his battles was that he did not leave such important matters to subordinates, but overlooked all manner of details with his own eyes and made sure they were right. If he seemed sometimes to take fearful risks, it was generally after he had very thoroughly verified his premises. If Rosecrans had been a really great general, he never would have staked so much upon another man's judgment.

Other officers beside the commander-in-chief remarked upon the faulty arrangement of the right wing. On the eve of the battle General Sheridan, accompanied by one of his brigade-commanders, General Sill, visited McCook's headquarters and earnestly assured him that the arrangement was liable to invite disaster. But McCook did not profit by the warning. His line was not only not withdrawn, but it was not even properly guarded. When the storm of battle burst upon it at daybreak next morning, the 31st of December, it found Johnson, the first division-commander on the right, a mile and a half in the rear at his headquarters; and with him was Willich, the commander of the right brigade of his division, so that there was literally nobody in front to give orders to the troops. Baldwin's reserve brigade was too far in the rear to be of any use. The guns were ill-guarded, and some of their horses had been led to a distance to be watered.

McCook's want of vigilance.

Upon this scene of gross negligence fell the sudden shock of two Confederate divisions, one of which was led by Patrick Cleburne, the ablest division-commander in all the Confederate army west of the Alleghanies. The Confederate attack was superb and irresistible. Their men rushed forward like an overwhelming torrent, and in a few minutes Johnson's whole division was swept from the field with the loss of eleven guns, and fled in wild disorder toward the Wilkinson road.[1] This catastrophe uncovered the right of Davis's division, and upon this the victorious Confederates charged in heavy masses,

Rout of two divisions.

---

[1] The crotchet upon which McCook placed so much reliance was of course too thin and frail to withstand such an attack in mass.

striking it at once in front and flank. The resistance here was much more effectual. The redoubtable Cleburne was twice driven back by a murderous fire, but no bravery could compensate for the advantage of position which the rebels had gained, and after an obstinate struggle Davis's division was routed and driven across the Wilkinson turnpike, leaving Sheridan uncovered to receive the next furious onset of the enemy.

While the battle was begun thus inauspiciously on the right, Rosecrans had been carrying forward his plan of attack with the left. Part of Van Cleve's division had already crossed the river, and Wood with his men was preparing to follow, when the terrific roar of battle from the other end of the line made every one start with surprise, not unmingled with dismay. It indicated a much more sudden and violent attack than they had reckoned on. Presently word came that McCook was hard pressed, but it did not reveal the extent of the calamity; and Rosecrans, loath to admit the necessity for changing his plans, sent word to McCook to dispute every inch of ground. In a few minutes his own attack would set everything right. But the enemy had secured the initiative, and held the game in his hands. The surging volume of sound moved steadily northward, and drew nearer and nearer

Union army thrown upon the defensive.

with alarming rapidity. The first of McCook's three hours had hardly elapsed when a message came announcing the rout of two divisions and the loss of nearly all the field south of the Wilkinson road. The bold plan of attack must now be abandoned, or the enemy would gain the Nashville turnpike before the morning's disaster could be remedied, and thus our line of retreat would be cut off. The Union army was thrown upon the defensive, and the question for the moment was how to ward off impending ruin. The army must change front, and a new line of battle must be formed facing southwest. Crittenden was accordingly ordered to withdraw Van Cleve from beyond the river and send him westward to the railroad, while Wood was to follow and take place on his right so as to defend the Nashville road. Rousseau's reserve division was moved southward to support Sheridan.

It was a terrible moment. The cedar thickets in Sheridan's rear, between the Wilkinson and the Nashville roads, were swarming with fugitives, the shattered remnants of Johnson's and Davis's divisions. The Confederate centre, hitherto silent, opened a heavy fire upon Sheridan and Negley, while their victorious left was hurled upon Sheridan, whose defeat would now complete the destruction of the Union right. But in young Philip

Sheridan the advancing rebels encountered an officer of very different mettle from those they had disposed of that morning. When he found his flank uncovered by Davis's retreat, he withdrew his right and ordered his left to push back the enemy at point of bayonet; and while this charge, superbly conducted by Colonel Roberts, drove off the enemy in disorder, he used the precious moments in forming a new front at right angles to his old one and facing southward. In this new position he met the returning shock of the rebel infantry, and held them at bay for two hours. Then finding them again outflanking him, he faced his two right brigades to westward, so that his division and Negley's together formed something like a semicircle convex toward the south, and for another two hours the enemy's efforts to break this line were fruitless. The fighting was now terrific. Maddened by this obstinate resistance, Bragg massed the entire left and centre of his army against these two divisions, but was thrice driven back with frightful slaughter. At length, with his cartridge-boxes empty, his brigade-commanders all killed, and 1800 men laid low, the noble Sheridan saw that he must retreat. One more desperate charge with cold steel, and before the enemy had recovered he withdrew his men to the rolling plain west of the Nashville road where

Sheridan's magnificent fight.

the new line of battle was forming. "Here we are," he cried, as he met Rosecrans galloping up, — "here we are, all that are left of us." His magnificent resistance had saved the day.

The crisis, however, was not yet passed. To form a whole army in new line of battle under the fire of an advancing enemy flushed with success is an operation calculated to tax the highest powers of a general. The enemy's repeated and determined assaults left no respite. The whole right wing was now gone, and the brunt of the fight was taken by the centre under Thomas. With Sheridan's retirement, Negley was next outflanked and obliged to retreat. Rousseau's division, which had been sent to Sheridan's support, was also driven back. But Thomas was not to be conquered. On rising ground just west of the Nashville turnpike and commanding the field, Rosecrans was already forming his new line facing southwestward. The divisions of Johnson, Davis, and Sheridan were again set in order, with those of Van Cleve and Wood, 12,000 fresh men, to sustain them; and on the crest of the knoll Rosecrans gathered his artillery in heavy masses. To gain time for this formation, and to preserve its continuity with Palmer's division, which was now

Thomas stands invincible,

while Rosecrans forms a new battle-front.

the extreme left, between railroad and river, it was essential that Thomas should stand immovable as a rock. He rallied the divisions of Negley and Rousseau, and called Van Cleve to bring up one brigade to his support. Van Cleve came on the double quick, just in time to meet the rebel onset. The fighting at this critical point was perhaps the hottest of the day. One of Rousseau's brigades lost 26 officers and 611 men out of a total of 1566. Four times the Confederates with marvellous gallantry returned to the assault, and four times their ranks were so woefully torn with grape and canister that they fell back baffled and at last somewhat disheartened. Their hopes of victory were beginning to be dashed. The stubborn resistance of Thomas, added to that of Sheridan, had gained so much time that the new line of battle was approaching completion, and occupying so strong a defensive position that the work of Bragg's army must virtually be begun over again.

The division of Palmer, however, had become more and more enveloped in battle since the first withdrawal of Rousseau and Negley. By a concentrated assault upon Palmer, the enemy, whose original plan was now manifestly failing, might break through the Union left and take the new line in flank. But Palmer handled his men very finely, and the fighting was here as stubborn as

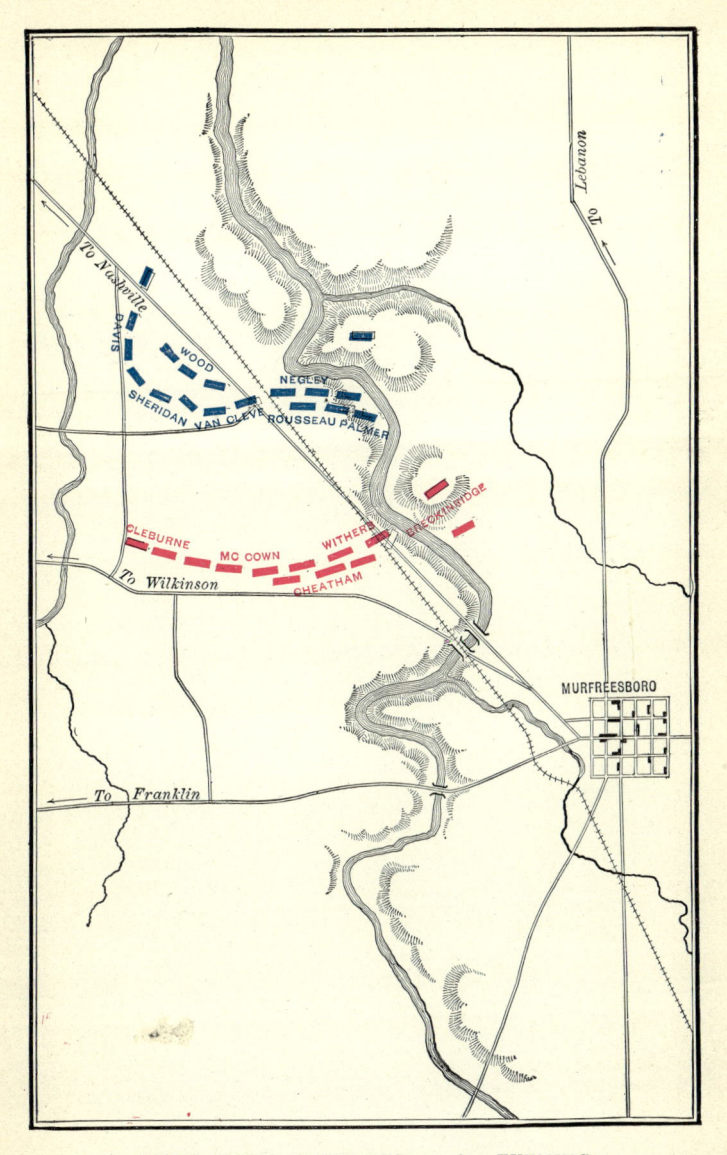

STONE RIVER, DECEMBER 31, 1862, EVENING.

anywhere in Thomas's part of the field. The most furious struggle was for the possession of a grove known as the Round Forest, which was regarded as the key to the Federal left. The Confederates, urged on by their bishop-general, Polk, performed prodigies of valour. *Terrific struggle; Palmer holds the Round Forest.* One of their regiments returned to the charge till it had lost 207 men out of 402; another, surpassing even this wonderful record of heroism, kept on till it had lost 306 out of 425. But all in vain. Palmer's grip on the Round Forest could not be shaken, and at length Polk sent across the river to Breckinridge for reinforcements. Up to this time Breckinridge's men had not been engaged. Crittenden had withdrawn his divisions cautiously, keeping up some show of menace, and Bragg had not yet deemed it prudent to weaken his right wing. Rosecrans's first movement, therefore, though nipped at the start, had played a useful secondary part in neutralizing a large force of the enemy.

At two o'clock in the afternoon Breckinridge sent over four brigades to Polk's assistance, and the attack on the Round Forest was renewed. It was unsuccessful, and the Confederates were so roughly handled that they did little more here till four o'clock. Then summoning all their energies, they rushed forward in one last determined effort.

Here, as Rosecrans hurried to the spot, a cannon-ball grazed him and carried away the head of Colonel Gareschè, his chief of staff, who was riding at his side. Making his way to the front, the commander ordered a bayonet charge, which broke the Confederate line and ended the battle in this quarter. During the progress of this series of deadly struggles at the Round Forest, the remainder of the Confederate army attempted to break down the new Federal line of battle by an attack in front. Unless this could be accomplished, all the successes of the morning went for nothing. But the new line was too strong to be carried. As the Confederates approached, their ranks were beaten down by a hurricane of grape and shrapnel and musket-balls, against which nothing human could stand. So great was the destruction that the assault which was just beginning was never made, but the baffled foe sought shelter in the woods, and the noise of battle ceased.

The Confederates baffled.

Thus ended the first day of the great fight at Stone river. It decided nothing except that both commanders had failed to carry out their plans. Rosecrans's plan had been foiled at the outset by the vigour and promptness with which Bragg struck the vulnerable point in his line. Bragg's plan had come very near succeeding, but was at length ruined by the stubbornness and resource of Sheridan, Thomas, and Palmer, and the skill with which Rosecrans reconstructed his order of battle. The two armies were still on a par in strength, being about equally exhausted. If either was to be crushed, the work must be begun anew, and Rosecrans now held such a position that little could be hoped from a direct attack upon him. The enemy's superior cavalry, indeed, had already begun to operate against our line of communications, to which our army was now parallel; and there was some fear lest he might follow up the movement in force and cut us off from our base. Rosecrans, however, rightly judged that the Confederate army was in no condition to attempt this. During the cold, clear night a council of war was held, and some of the generals earnestly advised him to retreat to Nashville. But Rosecrans would not hear of such a thing.

Results of the first day.

This determination proved very disconcerting to Bragg next morning. He had misinterpreted the bloody repulse of the afternoon, supposing it to be, like Sheridan's last bayonet charge, a device for facilitating retreat; and accordingly he imagined that he had won the battle. When he got up on New Year's Day and found the Union army still in position, it was a great disappointment. Little was done that day. Bragg spent it in reconnoitring to ascertain if his adversary was still present in full force. Rosecrans prepared to resume the offensive, and accordingly sent Van Cleve's division with one of Palmer's brigades to seize the heights upon the east side of the river and plant batteries there, according to his original plan. This movement, which threatened the town of Murfreesboro and Bragg's communications, was unopposed and apparently not discovered until the next day. The batteries enfiladed the whole of Polk's line, and it was necessary for Bragg either to storm the position or take his army away. On the afternoon of January 2, Breckinridge was sent back to the east side of the river and entrusted with the attack. At first Breckinridge was successful against Van Cleve; but Negley's division coming to the rescue, led by Colonel John Miller, its senior brigade-commander, the Confederates were presently overpowered. Their line was exposed to the raking fire of 58 guns from the Union batteries west of the river, and after half an hour Breckinridge retreated, leaving 1700 men of his division killed and wounded. During the night both armies began massing forces east of the river. Bragg sent over Cleburne's division, while Rosecrans sent the whole of Crittenden's corps, together with Davis's division,

Renewal of the battle.

Retreat of the Confederates.

and occupied the heights so firmly that it was idle to think of dislodging him. Nothing was done next day till toward midnight, when Bragg began his retreat to Shelbyville and Tullahoma. The retreat was unmolested.

The losses at the battle of Stone river were nearly the same as at Shiloh, — about 10,000 men on each side, or one fourth of the total infantry and artillery force engaged. Such a proportion of loss ranks it among the most stubborn battles of modern times. In point of bravery it is impossible to award the palm to one side more than to the other. It was simply Greek against Greek. As at Shiloh, the Confederates seemed at first to be bearing down all opposition; and as at Shiloh, they were at last compelled to retire from the field. Of the two battles Stone river seems in some respects the more interesting, as it was much the less simple in its conditions. There was more opportunity for the display *Comments.* of something like grand tactics, and here, except for the great initial mistake, Rosecrans showed signal ability. Pity that the mistake should have been so grave as to cause all this fertility of resource to be expended in the work of retrieving disaster! But for that well-nigh fatal error, Rosecrans might probably have gone forthwith to Chattanooga. As it is, the battle of Stone river seems less clearly a Federal victory than the battle of Shiloh. The latter decided the fall of Corinth; the former did not decide the fall of Chattanooga. Offensively it was a drawn battle, as looked at from either side. As a defensive battle, however, it was clearly a Union victory. It saved Nashville and tightened the Federal grasp upon Tennessee, and from this time forward, except for a brief period in the following autumn, the initiative in the great western theatre of war remained with the Union armies.

CHAPTER V

THE VICKSBURG PROBLEM

OF all the great rivers in the world, the Mississippi is perhaps the crookedest. A ship sailing over its waters will often travel a distance of thirty miles to reach a point eight or ten miles distant from its starting-place. This crookedness is not like that of the New England stream that flows in graceful curves through deep valleys worn down into the granite by long ages of rubbing and grinding under the pressure of glaciers. The Mississippi flows through a soft alluvial soil, in which it cuts fresh channels to right or left at the occurrence of the slightest obstacle to its direct progress. It is thus continually leaving its old bed for a new one, so that its long course is marked by countless swampy islands and peninsulas, while on either side may be seen stagnant crescent-shaped lakes, the remnants of its abandoned channels. The Mississippi water is so crowded with fine particles of reddish-brown alluvial mud that when dipped up in a tumbler it looks like diluted chocolate, and

Physical characteristics of the Mississippi river.

when poured out again leaves a thick slimy sediment in the tumbler. Of this alluvium great quantities are caught on its loop-like banks, until they gradually grow higher than the country beyond them, forming frail natural dikes, through which the contained water frequently bursts in devastating floods. Against such calamities the inhabitants of lowland towns on the banks of the Mississippi seek to protect themselves by erecting artificial dikes, known in the parlance of that once French region as "levees;" and when the imprisoned river sometimes asserts itself and washes away a part of the levee, the "crevasse" is as terrible to the dwellers on those flats as the avalanche or the landslide to people who live on the sides of steep mountains.

As a result of such freshets, the land on either side of the Mississippi is intersected by a network of bayous or sluggish streams as crooked as the river itself, and sometimes so long and deep as to be navigable for miles by vessels of considerable size. The strip of country thus creased and channelled in every direction, which forms the basin of the mighty stream, averages some forty miles in width. It is filled with cypress swamps, interspersed with dense forests of cottonwood, sweet gum, magnolia, sycamore, and tulip, beneath which the ground is thickly covered

The bayous.

with impenetrable masses of creeping vines. In such a country operations with an army are quite impracticable; at no season is it possible for a large body of men to secure a foothold. At the same time it is impossible to erect upon these low, flat shores fortifications fit to resist a naval force like that which captured New Orleans. Through the devious windings of the river the Federal gunboats could plough their way unmolested from point to point, controlling its navigation and possessing it as a military highway.

But to this peculiar state of things, which was general throughout the lower Mississippi basin, there were a few notable exceptions. On its eastern side, for hundreds of miles, the valley is bounded by the lofty plains of Tennessee and Mississippi, which terminate in precipitous bluffs; and here and there, though at long intervals, the river sweeps up close to the bluffs and washes their base for several miles. Such is the case at Columbus, Fort Pillow, Memphis, Vicksburg, *The bluffs.* Grand Gulf, and Port Hudson. All these places stand on the summit of bluffs rising from 80 to 200 feet sheer above the turbid water. They afford foothold for an army approaching from the rear, but on the other hand they are unassailable by fleets on the river. A ship's guns cannot be elevated sufficiently to inflict fatal damage on such places, which on their part can return such a plunging fire as is difficult for the strongest ship to endure. It was therefore only by fortifying these places that the Confederates could hope to retain their hold upon the Mississippi river. As soon as they lost one of them, they lost the river down to the next similar point, except in the single case of Island Number Ten, where the conditions were peculiar. When they lost Columbus and Island Number Ten, there was no other foothold for them above Fort Pillow; and when this and Memphis were taken away from them, there was no place where they could make a stand against the fleet until Vicksburg was reached.

But of all points on the great river this was the strongest to resist either fleet or army. To the fleet it was practically inaccessible, to the army it was nearly so. A little below the mouth of the Yazoo river the Mississippi makes one of its great bends, turning abruptly to the northeast, and after flowing five miles in that direction it turns with equal abruptness to the southwest, enclosing a peninsula less than two miles in width. Opposite the northern portion of this low peninsula stands the

Vicksburg and Port Hudson.

city of Vicksburg, crowning the bluff at a height of 200 feet above the water. For eleven miles below Vicksburg the river washes the foot of the cliffs. Then it sweeps away from them westward, and after three gigantic double bends again strikes the line of bluffs at Grand Gulf, which is only twenty-five miles below Vicksburg as the crow flies, but sixty miles by the river. Immediately below Grand Gulf the river once more leaves the bluffs, not to touch them again till it reaches the village of Port Hudson, two hundred and fifty miles farther down. Grand Gulf and Port Hudson, both of which were strongly fortified, might be regarded as outworks of Vicksburg, but of these Port Hudson was far the more important. For between it and Vicksburg the great Red river empties into the Mississippi, and the Red river was the highway by which the states of Texas, Louisiana, and Arkansas were connected with the central and eastern portions of the Confederacy. As a recruiting-ground for the rebel armies, these three states were able to supply 100,000 men; but still more than this, they were an inexhaustible granary from which the Confederacy was furnished with food, and while all its coasts were rigorously blockaded, its only communication with the outer world was through Texas and Mexico. To sever from the Confederacy its three trans-Mississippi states, and to blockade it on this side as closely as on its sea-coast, was an object of paramount importance. It would destroy nearly half its resisting power. To do this, it was not enough for Union fleets and armies to possess the mouth of the Mississippi and the whole of its course above Vicksburg. It was necessary to control every part of it, and especially this region about the mouth of the Red river. This stream was the great avenue between east and west, jealously guarded on either side by Vicksburg and Port Hudson, which were like two powerful bastions reciprocally flanking and protecting each other.

Between these two points the Mississippi river was entirely in rebel hands. Farragut's fleet at New Orleans could not pass above Port Hudson, nor could Davis's fleet at Helena pass below Vicksburg, without incurring great danger in running by the batteries. Nor was there any use in taking such risk unless to coöperate with an army acting between the two places. But no Union army could land on the eastern bank of the river at any point between Port Hudson and Vicksburg without severing itself from every source whence supplies could reach it. As long as Port Hudson was in rebel hands, a Union army could not operate upon Vicksburg from below without risk of speedy starvation; for the guns of Port Hudson closed the way to all supplies coming up the river, and the guns of Vicksburg itself frowned off all supplies attempting to come down.

<small>Unapproachableness of Vicksburg from the south</small>

The Vicksburg Problem

While thus quite inaccessible from the south, Vicksburg was, for other reasons, no less inaccessible on the north to an army approaching from the river. Above the city the hilly range on which it stands swerves northeasterly and quite away from the Mississippi, but near to its tributary, the Yazoo. Twelve miles above Vicksburg the waves of the Yazoo break upon the base of Haines Bluff, which commands all the river approaches at long cannon-range. As long as the Confederates held Haines Bluff, no army could land north of Vicksburg without being torn to pieces by a fire to which it could not effectively reply.

and from the north.

Thus the "Queen City of the Bluff," as southern people were fond of calling it, might indeed smile, in its royal sense of security, on all the difficult country around it. Unapproachable by its steep front on the Mississippi, by its left which Port Hudson covered, or by its right which was guarded by Haines Bluff, it could be assailed only in the rear; and here too the country, extremely rugged and broken by deep ravines, presented formidable obstacles to an enemy. While thus from its situation Vicksburg had come to be the mainstay of the Southern Confederacy, its strength was such that it was likened to Gibraltar. The task of taking it was as arduous as had ever been set before a general.

That the obstacles had been allowed to accumulate to such an extent was due, as we have seen, to the imbecility with which the Union armies were managed in the summer of 1862. When Farragut and Davis were patrolling the river on either side of Vicksburg in June, a force of 20,000 men, coming down from Memphis and landing north of the city, could not have failed to take it, for the approaches were not yet fortified and the Confederates had but a handful of men there. But although Farragut persistently begged, he could get no help from Halleck, who was trifling away the precious moments at Corinth, and scattering his 100,000 men in such wise as to accomplish nothing in any direction. On the other hand, if we had had a few more troops at New Orleans, it would have been easy to send a small force up the river and take Vicksburg from the south, for the Confederates did not seize Port Hudson till August. The energetic and quick-witted Van Dorn was not slow to catch the golden opportunities which we thus wantonly threw away. His men worked with exemplary vigour, and every day that saw Vicksburg and Port Hudson unmolested by Federal troops saw also their fortifications and outworks grow more and more impregnable.

A lost opportunity.

It was toward the end of October, 1862, that General Grant began to feel his hands free for a clutch at Vicksburg. His headquarters were then at Jackson in Tennessee; the centre of his army was a little south of Jackson at Bolivar, his right wing was at Memphis, his left wing at Corinth, and his base of supplies far up the Mississippi river at Columbus. His army consisted of 7000 men at Memphis under General Sherman, 19,200 at Bolivar under General Hurlbut, 17,500 at Corinth under General Schuyler Hamilton, who had there succeeded Rosecrans, and 4800 at Columbus under General Dodge, — in all 48,500 men. Heavy reinforcement was soon to be expected from the new levies which were collecting in response to the President's call in July for 300,000 men. Since Halleck's departure for Washington in July had left Grant in command of this army, he had so many points to occupy, in pursuance of Halleck's orders, that it was impossible to undertake any offensive operation. Under these circumstances Van Dorn had aimed a bold and skilful blow at Grant's left wing at Corinth, hoping to destroy it and force him to retreat down the Tennessee river; but the scheme, as we have seen, had ended in a bloody defeat at the hands of Rosecrans. But the losses of that battle had been more than made good by new levies and exchanged prisoners, so that Van Dorn now had 24,000 men. Besides these there

Grant's position and forces at Corinth.

were 6000 at Vicksburg, 5500 at Port Hudson, and about 2000 at Jackson in Mississippi, making for the total Confederate force about 37,500 men, under General Pemberton, by whom Jefferson Davis, after the defeat at Corinth, had unwisely superseded Van Dorn.

With his army properly concentrated, Grant felt ready to advance against this inferior force, and on the 26th of October he wrote to Halleck, proposing to abandon Corinth after destroying the railroads all around it, and then to concentrate his force at Grand Junction and move upon Vicksburg by way of the Mississippi Central railroad. This was the correct thing to do, but the suggestion did not find favour with Halleck, who was apt unduly to exaggerate the value of places as such, and to forget that after all it is the destruction of the enemy's army that is the primary object in warfare. Before the victory at Shiloh had decided that Corinth was to be ours, that little town was a point of intense strategic interest. But now that it had been definitely gained with all its fruits, including the fall of Memphis and the opening of the Mississippi down to Vicksburg, there was no good reason for continuing to occupy it in force. Strategic points can be held by covering them as well as by leaving men to defend them, and a movement of

Grant's first movement against Vicksburg.

Grant's whole army upon Pemberton, pressing him down through the state of Mississippi, would have effectually covered Corinth. Halleck seems never to have answered Grant's letter or taken any notice of his suggestion; so that being left without instructions, and unauthorized to abandon Corinth or any other point held by his army, Grant tried to see what could be done under these embarrassing circumstances. By weakening his forces at Corinth and Bolivar, he got together about 30,000 men near Grand Junction, and prepared to advance against Pemberton. But he was so puzzled and delayed by incomprehensible telegrams from Washington that he did not get started until the 24th of November. By this time reinforcements had arrived at Memphis, and Sherman was ready to move thence toward Grant and join him on the Tallahatchie river. As the Union army advanced, the Confederates fell back, continually skirmishing, until they reached the town of Grenada, behind the Yallabusha river. Grant with his forces united advanced as far as Oxford, forty miles north of Grenada.

This first movement of Grant was an attempt to approach Vicksburg in the rear, and either compel its evacuation, as had happened in the case of Columbus and Memphis, or attack it in the quarter where it was *The outflanking strategy.*

least invulnerable. Be it observed that this was a continuation of the same strategy which he had employed with such success from the moment he set out to attack Fort Donelson. Without approaching the Mississippi river, but simply by a victorious advance along a line parallel to it, he had effectually conquered it all the way from Cairo to Vicksburg. One after another the great bluffs which the Confederates had been at such pains to fortify had fallen of themselves in consequence of blows dealt not on the Mississippi river, but on the banks of the Tennessee and Cumberland. The victories at Forts Henry and Donelson necessitated the fall of Columbus. The victory at Shiloh, involving the fall of Corinth, necessitated also the fall of Island Number Ten, Fort Pillow, and Memphis. Island Number Ten, indeed, was taken with all its garrison by General Pope; but had Pope never attacked it, the fall of Corinth made it untenable, and it would have been evacuated; the fortress would have fallen, though the garrison would have escaped. This series of conquests of fortified places, simply through victories at distant points which outflanked them, was a beautiful though perfectly obvious piece of strategy. Grant's further advance toward the capital of Mississippi, along a line parallel to the river, was in illustration of the same principle. The presence of his army at Jackson would seriously threaten the Confederate hold upon Vicksburg. But the conditions of the case were now very different, and the progress of the army, which had heretofore been comparatively easy, was soon rendered extremely difficult by reason of the increasing length of its line of communications. In order fully to appreciate this point, let us consider for a moment how enormous was the task of supplying our armies in the Civil War, and how narrowly their movements were thereby restricted.

In the densely populated countries of Europe an army can often subsist upon the country through which it marches, but this was seldom the case with our armies in the southern states. Their food and ammunition had to be brought to them, and it was seldom possible for them to move more than a few miles from the line by which these supplies were brought. As Wellington once said, every army moves, like a serpent, upon its belly; and the clumsiness of such kind of movement, under the conditions which obtained in our Civil War, may best be illustrated by a little arithmetic. The weight of food, ammunition, and other supplies required by each soldier averaged 4 pounds daily. A single wagon, therefore, carrying a load of 2000 pounds and dragged over bad roads by six mules or draught

The task of supplying an army.

horses, would supply 500 men, provided it could make the trip both ways between the army and its base on the same day. If the army were one day's march from its base, so that the wagon must come one day and return empty the next, it could only supply 500 men every alternate day, or 250 daily. If the army were two days' march from its base, the wagon could only furnish supplies at the rate of 125 men daily, or 4 wagons to 500 men. To supply an army of 50,000 men, therefore, at two days' march from its base, required 400 wagons. Such an army ordinarily had at least 8000 horses for its cavalry and artillery, and each of these animals consumed 25 pounds of forage daily, which made a load for just another 400 wagons. These 800 wagons were drawn by 4800 mules or draught horses, which in turn required 180 wagons to carry their forage. These 180 wagons were drawn by 1080 animals, which were fed by 48 additional wagons, and so on. Adding the figures, we find that for such an army as Grant had in Mississippi in December, 1862, nearly 1100 wagons, drawn by 6600 animals, were needed to keep it supplied at two days' march from its base; while at three days' march, nearly 1900 wagons, drawn by 11,000 animals, were requisite. Such an army could not travel more than two or three days without shifting its base along the line of some railroad or river; and obviously this movable base must be securely connected by river or rail with some permanent base established in a region entirely under Federal control. We thus get a realizing sense of the prodigious importance of railroads in our Civil War. Had the rebellion occurred a few years earlier, before our long lines of railway had been built, its suppression by military means would have been physically impossible.

Indispensable as railways were, however, in supplying our armies in their long expeditions, they were far inferior to rivers in respect of security. Aided by the formidable gunboats, the Federal armies could advance to any distance along the banks of a navigable river, obtaining their supplies with promptness and regularity from flat-bottomed transports, which could almost anywhere be pushed up to the shore and quickly unloaded. *Rivers preferable to railroads.* Owing to the naval superiority of the Federals, these river lines of communication could not be cut by the enemy. On the other hand, the railroads afforded lines of communication, the insecurity of which rapidly increased with their length; as it was easy for the enemy's cavalry, in which he was usually superior to the Federals, to make bold incursions in the rear of our armies and tear up the track for miles. The effect of such a sudden stoppage of supplies was enough to paralyze all military operations. Imagine the food supply cut off for several days in time of peace from cities of the size of Hartford or Worcester, and you get an inadequate illustration of the peril of a great army severed from its base and isolated in the midst of lonely and hostile forests. To guard against such dangers was one of the most difficult tasks allotted to the Federal commanders, especially in the western theatre of war, where such immense distances had to be traversed. Accordingly we find that, while the Federal advance was always sure and decisive when supported by a river, it was apt to be precarious when the sole reliance was a long line of railway.

We can now fully understand why it was not easy for Grant in the state of Mississippi to continue the series of brilliant movements by which he had heretofore caused so many rebel river-fortresses to fall without taking the trouble to go and assault them. Hitherto his own forward progress had been secure, for it had rested upon the Tennessee river. Now it had become insecure, for it depended upon the integrity of every mile of a long line of railway. When Grant reached Oxford, on the 5th of December, he had his immediate base of supplies at Holly Springs, and his permanent base at Columbus, 180 miles distant. It was impossible to

Grant's insecure position at Oxford.

guard so long a line, and in order to advance upon Grenada and beyond, it was necessary to make some different arrangement. Memphis was admirably situated for a permanent base, and a railroad ran directly from that point to Grenada, where it joined the Mississippi Central. Unfortunately it had sustained serious damage, and Halleck had instructed Grant not to have it repaired. His movement was evidently regarded with disfavour at Washington, and the telegrams sent by Halleck were so bewildering that at this stage of the proceedings Grant felt it necessary to ask the question, "How far south would you like me to go?" After more or less discussion by telegraph, he at length received permission to plan his own campaign.

Thus armed with discretionary power, Grant held a conference with Sherman, in which two plans were thoroughly discussed. The one alternative was to keep on in full force to Jackson and threaten Vicksburg in the rear; the other was to divide the army, sending Sherman back to Memphis, and thence down the river to effect a landing just north of Vicksburg, while Grant should so manœuvre as to detain Pemberton upon the Yallabusha. There were sound objections to such a division of force, inasmuch as the enemy would possess the interior line whereby to mass his strength against either Grant or Sherman. In this instance, however, no serious risk was apprehended, since Grant felt able, even with his force diminished, to meet the enemy in battle; while Sherman, on the other hand, in case of ill-fortune, could retreat upon his ships. To move on in full force to Jackson would necessitate the adoption of Memphis as a base, and the thorough repair of the railroad between that city and Grenada; and this would consume precious time, during which the Confederates might be reinforced and Vicksburg was sure to grow stronger. For this reason mainly it was decided to adopt the other alternative and divide the army. Sherman accordingly returned to Memphis, organized his expedition, and on the 20th of December started down the river under convoy of the gunboat fleet, in the command of which Davis had lately been succeeded by Admiral Porter.

Sherman's movement against Vicksburg.

The fear that the Confederates in Mississippi might soon be reinforced was well founded. On the 24th of November the Confederate President had appointed Joseph Johnston to the chief command of all the forces between the Alleghanies and the Mississippi, with his headquarters at Chattanooga. A week later Mr. Davis himself visited Vicksburg and Jackson, and saw that reinforce-

ments were sorely needed; and here it is interesting to observe that the Confederate authorities could meddle and bungle as effectively as the government at Washington. *Mr. Davis's mistake.*
They had not yet given up all hope of retrieving the disaster at Pea Ridge and invading the state of Missouri; and to this end a considerable force had been assembled in northern Arkansas, which on the 7th of December was thoroughly defeated by the Union generals Blunt and Herron at Prairie Grove. Offensive movements in that quarter being thus decisively checked, Johnston thought that the reinforcements needed in Mississippi might best be taken from the Confederate army in Arkansas, thus sacrificing a comparatively small and remote interest in behalf of one that was great and immediate. But Davis was unwilling to do this for fear of political disaffection in Arkansas. He preferred to take the reinforcements from Bragg's army at Murfreesboro, and did so in spite of Johnston's solemn warnings. On the 20th of December Bragg accordingly sent 10,000 men to reinforce Pemberton in Mississippi. The great battle at Stone river was fought eleven days later; and when we consider how closely that battle was contested and how narrowly the Federal army was saved from destruction, it seems probable that if those 10,000 men had been at hand, Bragg would

have won a decisive victory, and the whole course of the war in the West would have been changed most disastrously for the Union cause. So much good was already achieved for the Federals in consequence of Grant's assuming the offensive, slow and hampered as his movements had been.

But Bragg did more for Pemberton than merely to send him reinforcements. On the 11th of December he sent the brilliant trooper, General Nathan Forrest, with 2500 cavalry, across the state of Tennessee to cut Grant's communications with Columbus. Grant was warned of this movement by a telegram from Rosecrans, but Forrest's blows were difficult to parry, and Grant had then no cavalry commanders equal to such a task. In one of the most effective raids of the war, Forrest destroyed sixty miles of railroad, besides cutting the telegraph lines so effectually that from the 19th to the 30th of December Grant was quite isolated from the rest of the world.

<small>Forrest's raid.</small>

At the same time Pemberton ordered a raid on his own account. Van Dorn, with all the cavalry in the army, some 3500 in number, rode around into Grant's rear and made a dash at Holly Springs, where a great mass of supplies, valued at $1,500,000, had been accumulated for the use of the Union army. The place was commanded by a

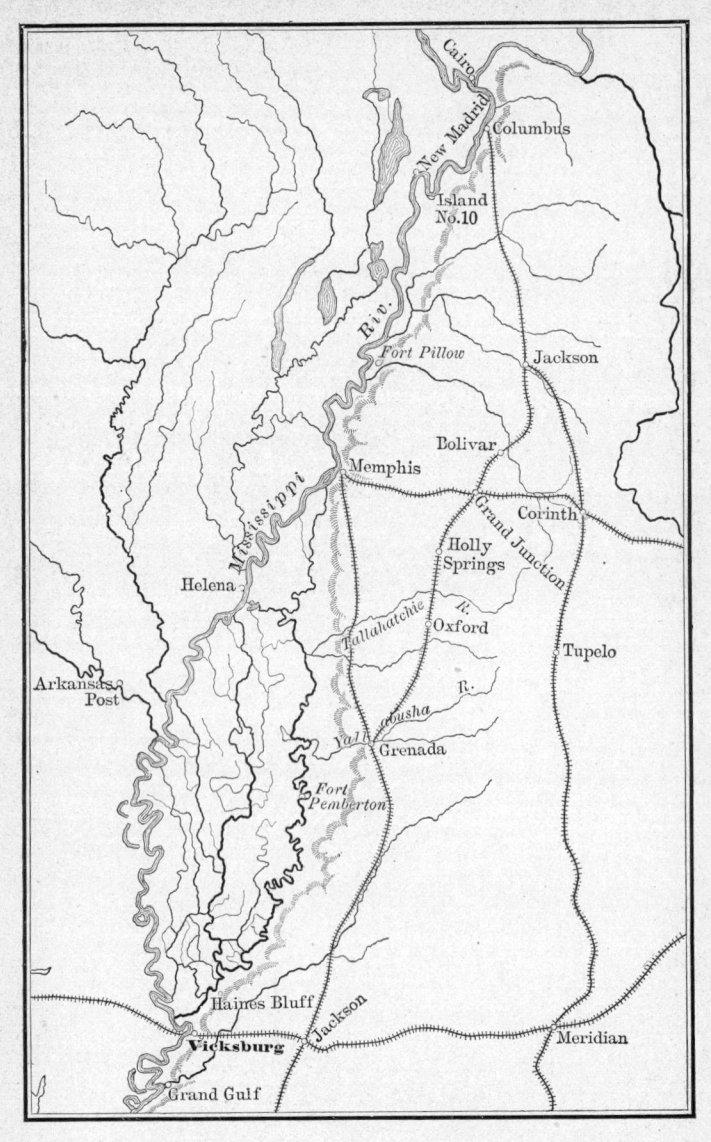

GRANT'S FIRST MOVEMENT AGAINST VICKSBURG
NOVEMBER 24, 1862–JANUARY 10, 1863

Colonel Murphy, whom Grant had duly warned of the danger and instructed to defend his post to the last extremity. But at daybreak of the 20th, the very day after receiving this order, Murphy allowed himself to be taken by surprise, and surrendered the town, with his whole force of 1500 men, with scarcely a show of resistance. For this shameful conduct he was dismissed the service, but the damage was done. Van Dorn burned all the stores, and making a long detour returned safely to his army.

Van Dorn captures Holly Springs.

Grant was now in a very uncomfortable situation. That which he most dreaded had come to pass. Van Dorn had destroyed his accumulated stores, and Forrest had destroyed the only road by which other stores could come to replace them. There was nothing to be done but retreat, and the cutting of the telegraph made it impossible to notify Sherman of this movement. To support the army on its retreat, it was necessary to try the experiment of living upon the country. When some women of the neighbourhood came to Grant's headquarters and tauntingly asked him where he expected to get food for his soldiers, he quietly reminded them that their barns and granaries seemed to be well stocked. "What!" they ex-

Grant retreats to Grand Junction.

claimed, frightened and crestfallen, "you surely would not lay hands on private property!" The general regretted the necessity, but assured them that they must not expect him to starve his army on their account. Fortunately, the mishap occurred while the army was in a region of abundance. It ate up everything animal or vegetable that could serve as food on its retreat of eighty miles to Grand Junction, stripping the country for fifteen miles to right and left. Before the 8th of January communication had been opened with Memphis, and on that day Grant received a despatch from Halleck, informing him that Sherman had been defeated before Vicksburg, and directing him to go at once to the rescue with all the available force at his command. Accordingly on the 10th Grant went to Memphis, and began his preparations for moving his army down the river to Vicksburg.

Meanwhile Sherman steadily pursued his course, in total ignorance of what was happening to his chief. He started from Memphis on the 20th of December, with 32,000 men and 60 guns, steamed down the Mississippi to the mouth of the Yazoo and thirteen miles up the Yazoo, and landed his troops near Chickasaw bayou, on the low flats in front of the range of bluffs just north of Vicksburg. This lowland, regularly submerged at cer-

Sherman's defeat at Chickasaw bayou.

tain seasons, was intersected by a labyrinth of bayous and stagnant lakes in such wise that there were only five paths along which an army could advance toward the bluffs, and these paths were so completely commanded by the Confederate guns as to be impassable. The outlook was not promising, but it was the only point north of Vicksburg where a landing could be made at all, and accordingly it must be tried. Sherman's theory of the campaign was based on the expectation of surprising the enemy and securing a foothold upon the bluffs, where he might maintain himself until Grant could join him. There were no topographical maps upon which he could rely, and he did not know how completely the Confederates had crowned the bluffs with batteries. The enemy, moreover, having watchful scouts all up and down the banks of the river, had observed him every moment since his departure from Memphis; and the bluffs were guarded by 12,000 men, who in that position were more than a match for 100,000 assailants on the swampy ground below. The ground, indeed, was so bad that Sherman's 32,000 men were twice as many as he could use to good effect. Under these circumstances he ordered an assault, and was right in doing so, inasmuch as the facts here stated were not fully known to him, and could not be ascertained save by trial. On the 29th of December the assault was made. It was as ably and gallantly conducted as any operation of the war, but was doomed to failure from the outset. Two brigades, one of which was commanded by Francis Blair (our old friend of the Camp Jackson days), made their way up to the enemy's works, but recoiled for want of support; and presently the attack was abandoned. It cost Sherman nearly 2000 men killed and wounded, while the Confederates lost 187. It was not safe to stay upon the lowland, for a very slight rise in the river might at any time flood it and drown the whole army. On the 2d of January, therefore, convinced that the enterprise was hopeless, Sherman moved his troops down to the mouth of the Yazoo, where he met General McClernand, who had been sent to take command of the expedition in his stead.

The mention of this general's name brings up a dismal story of political intrigue by which this whole series of military operations had been unfavourably affected. The part which he sustained toward Grant at this time reminds one of the part sustained by Gates toward Schuyler in the Revolutionary War. But McClernand was an abler man than Gates. Without any military training, he had nevertheless acquitted himself very creditably at Belmont, Fort

McClernand's schemes.

Donelson, and Shiloh, showing marked personal gallantry and some skill in handling troops. But his vanity was prodigious, while he had a very inadequate idea of military subordination, and seems to have regarded a military career chiefly as a means of political advancement. He was tired, he said, of furnishing brains for Grant's army, and he thought the time had come when his services entitled him to an independent command. In August preceding the operations above described he had obtained leave of absence and gone to Washington to give personal attention to his claims. As an Illinois politician he had long been known to Mr. Lincoln, whom he sought to persuade that the best method of capturing Vicksburg was by an independent expedition down the river. After much discussion he won over both Lincoln and Stanton to his views. Late in October Stanton gave to McClernand a paper secretly authorizing him to raise a volunteer force in the states of Indiana, Illinois, and Iowa, and when properly equipped and organized, to proceed with it against Vicksburg; and on the back of this paper, which McClernand was to show in confidence to the governors of the states in question, Mr. Lincoln endorsed his approval of the enterprise. The scheme, however, was not viewed with favour by Halleck. Though not endowed with great discernment, Halleck cherished a wholesome professional prejudice against amateur generalship, and he understood the viciousness of a plan which contemplated an advance by two mutually independent commanders against the same objective point. Such a plan was contrary to military principles, ruinous to discipline, and full of the seeds of disaster. With all his sagacity, Mr. Lincoln had not yet come to realize the force of such considerations. In the preceding spring much mischief had been wrought by thus carving out independent commands in Virginia; and it was now proposed to repeat this unwise policy in the case of Vicksburg. To crown all, Grant was not informed of it; and accordingly, not possessing the key to the brief enigmatical telegrams which kept coming from Washington during the month of November, he was so puzzled by them that his own movements were embarrassed. It was not until the 18th of December, two days before Sherman started from Memphis on the expedition against Vicksburg, that Grant was directed from Washington to put McClernand in charge of the expedition. It appears that Halleck's well-founded objections had been to some extent heeded by the President, for there was no intimation that McClernand was to be made independent of Grant; on the contrary, he was expressly placed under his direction. The order was at once sent by Grant to Sherman at Memphis and to McClernand, who was at Springfield in Illinois. Both telegrams had to go through Columbus, and as Forrest had just cut the wires, neither was ever received. Thus it was not until after the repulse at Vicksburg that Sherman learned that he was superseded, and that Grant had been obliged to abandon his advance through the interior of Mississippi.

On turning over his command to McClernand, Sherman proposed that, instead of lying idle until a new campaign could be planned, they should utilize their time by capturing a fortress known as Arkansas Post, which the Confederates had established on the Arkansas river about fifty miles from its mouth. This stronghold threatened the communications of a Union army operating against Vicksburg from the river, and it was highly desirable to get rid of it. The expedition was well-conducted and promptly successful, as might have been expected from the overwhelming force of the assailants, — 30,000 men, with 45 field-pieces, 7 gunboats mounting 66 heavy guns, and a powerful ram. The fort was defended by 3 heavy and 14 light guns, with a garrison of 5000 men. In spite of its strong position and the gallantry of its defend-

Capture of Arkansas Post.

ers, it could not hope to stand against such odds. On the 11th of January it was battered to pieces and its garrison captured, yet not until it had cost the Federals 1000 men killed and wounded, — a striking illustration of the difficulty of storming fortifications even under the most favourable circumstances. Elated beyond measure with this success, McClernand began talking about his "star" which was ever "in the ascendant," and announced to Sherman and Porter that he should now keep on to Little Rock and clear Arkansas of rebel troops. But in a letter to Grant a day or two before, explaining his reasons for moving against the Arkansas Post, he had mysteriously hinted at a campaign in the interior of the state; and Grant, aghast at the thought of thus wantonly diverting 30,000 men from the all-important work at Vicksburg, promptly signified to McClernand his disapproval of the whole movement. At the same time he informed Halleck by telegraph that McClernand had "gone on a wild-goose chase to the Post of Arkansas." In reply, Halleck authorized him to relieve McClernand from the command of the Vicksburg expedition, and either give it to the next in rank, or take command in person. Grant did not immediately act upon this permission, but peremptorily ordered McClernand back to the Mississippi.

McClernand and his "star."

That ambitious general sullenly obeyed, but took the occasion to empty the vials of his wrath in a confidential letter to Mr. Lincoln. "My success here," said he, "is gall and wormwood to the clique of West Pointers who have been persecuting me for months."

It was fortunate for the country that the "clique of West Pointers" were allowed to have their way. McClernand's case was only one among many which in the course of our Civil War illustrated the evils of amateur generalship. The old-fashioned American notion that a man who succeeds in one kind of work can succeed in any other by dint of native ability and without special training is not so commonly entertained now as it once was. It was a notion which, on the whole, did us credit; for it bore unconscious testimony to the quick wit and rare versatility of the American people. But the complicated conditions of modern life are beginning to show its fallaciousness, and the Civil War taught us some lessons in this regard. Of all the occupations of life, there is none in which the imperative need of professional training is so forcibly demonstrated as in warfare, where errors of judgment are visited with such prompt and terrible penalties. Among the commanders in our Civil War on either side, nearly all who achieved success on a large scale

Amateur generals.

were graduates of West Point, and most had served their apprenticeship in Mexico. On the other hand, our volunteer commanders who had had no special training seldom prospered in any higher position than that of general of division. There were one or two exceptions, but this was the rule, and McClernand was a conspicuous instance of it. Fortunately his power for mischief was short-lived. In superseding him, Grant waited only to make up his mind as to the best way of doing it. He seems to have been governed purely by unselfish motives. He would have been glad to restore Sherman to the command, and thus give him a chance to retrieve himself, for people at the North were clamorous with indignation over the failure at the Chickasaw bayou. But on mature reflection he concluded that he could best harmonize the jarring elements by assuming the immediate command in person, and on the 30th of January he did so.

Grant moves to the west bank of the Mississippi. He prepared to withdraw the forces from northern Mississippi and concentrate his whole army at Young's Point, opposite Vicksburg. The army was reorganized in four corps, respectively commanded by McClernand, Sherman, Hurlbut, and McPherson; and thus McClernand's dream of glory was abruptly ended. He protested bitterly, alleging that he had been the originator of the Vicksburg

The Vicksburg Problem

expedition, and had been entrusted with it by the President's express desire. Grant simply referred the protest to Lincoln and Halleck, and that was the last of it.

By this movement to the west bank of the Mississippi Grant's first plan for the capture of Vicksburg was definitely abandoned. It had resulted in complete failure, owing partly to the misconduct of the officer who surrendered Holly Springs, and partly to the unforeseen obstacles encountered by Sherman at the Chickasaw bayou. But behind these causes lay the McClernand affair, which diverted the attention of the authorities at Washington from Grant's requirements in November. Had he then been properly supported by the government, he might have established his base at Memphis, and, receiving his supplies by the railroad running thence through Grenada, might have moved upon Vicksburg from the rear, pursuing the same strategy which he had employed with such brilliant success in former campaigns. The occasion for dividing his army would not have come up, and united it was far more than a match for any force that Pemberton could oppose to it. This first plan of Grant's was no doubt the correct one, and could he have managed it in his own way, Vicksburg would probably have fallen before New

His first plan, thus abandoned, was the correct one.

Year's Day. The difficulties, though considerable, were nothing to those which Grant finally surmounted.

In order to understand the complicated operations to which Grant now devoted two weary months of fruitless and thankless labour, we must remember that Vicksburg was assailable only in the rear. Grant's first plan, which was now given up, had contemplated an approach upon the rear through the interior of Mississippi. When he captured the city, some months later, it was because he at last succeeded in approaching it from the rear. Now, with his army concentrated on the western side of the river, the difficult problem before him was how to take it across, and get into the rear of the city without sacrificing his line of communications. He could not do so by crossing below the city, for his supply ships came down the river from Memphis and could not be depended upon to pass by the guns of Vicksburg; while Port Hudson equally blocked the ascent of the river 250 miles below, so that supplies could not be sent up from New Orleans. On the other hand, Sherman's unsuccessful experiment had proved that he could not cross above the city unless he could get so far away to the north as to turn the extremity of the works at Haines Bluff, and this was impossible from the nature of the

Various alternatives.

ground. Grant's work during February and March consisted of a series of attempts to grasp first the one and then the other of the horns of this dilemma. His work may all be summed up under two plans, which we may call his second and third plans for capturing Vicksburg. The second plan was to find a passage, by canal or otherwise, whereby his supply ships might pass below Vicksburg without coming within range of its guns; it was like the problem which Pope had solved at Island Number Ten by cutting a channel through the submerged forest. Could this be accomplished, the army might cross below Vicksburg, and good hard fighting would do the rest. The third plan was to find a passage available for gunboats through the labyrinth of bayous to the north, so that with the aid of the fleet he might secure a foothold for the army beyond Haines Bluff, and thence come down upon the rear of the city. Both plans were Titan-like in their audacity; both contended with insuperable difficulties; and both were foredoomed to failure.

For the sake of convenience we may designate these plans as second and third, but they were prosecuted more or less simultaneously. Each of the plans comprised two experiments. The first was an attempt to dig a canal through the neck of the peninsula formed by the great bend of the river opposite Vicksburg. The distance was but little over a mile, but as the canal was designed to admit vessels of sixty feet beam and nine feet draught, the amount of excavation required was very considerable, and as much labour was necessary to keep the canal free from water while the digging was going on, the progress was very slow. A dam was built across the upper end, and dredging-machines were set to work, and at length, after six tedious weeks, success seemed near at hand, when all at once, on the 8th of March, a sudden rise in the river burst open the dam. If the torrent could have been confined between the levees of the canal, it might perhaps have helped the work by scouring the bottom, but its force was so great that it broke down these levees and submerged the surrounding country, sweeping away tents and tools, drowning horses, and driving off the men, who had to flee for their lives. The catastrophe was a godsend to the northern croakers, who all these weeks had been wagging their heads in scorn of "Grant's big ditch." The rebels saw in it the judgment of Heaven upon an impious attempt to disturb the order of nature. Many enthusiastic friends of the government, who had built great hopes upon the undertaking, were sadly disappointed. Not so Grant, who from the first had expected very little from it. He had observed that the lower end of

"Grant's big ditch."

the canal entered the river just opposite the bluffs at Warrenton, where the Confederates could easily plant batteries commanding it, and early in February he informed Halleck that he had lost all faith in the scheme. Indeed, before the catastrophe occurred, the enemy had already erected batteries at Warrenton which enfiladed the mouth of the canal, so that even if finished it would have been useless. Nevertheless, in deference to the public sentiment, which was shared by the government at Washington, Grant had given the project a fair trial, while looking out for some more feasible plan.

His other experiment for crossing below Vicksburg was begun the next day after his arrival upon the scene, and was carried on simultaneously with the canal experiment. About seventy miles above Vicksburg, on the opposite side of the river, is the crescent-shaped Lake Providence, a remnant of the old deserted bed of the stream. A muddy channel, more swamp than river, known as Bayou Baxter, imperfectly connected this lake with Bayou Macon, which flows into the Macon river, a tributary of the Tensas. The Tensas, in turn, flows into the Washita, which flows into the great Red river. This tortuous system of waters is navigable throughout its length, except in Bayou Baxter, which about midway between Lake Provi-

The Lake Providence experiment.

dence and Bayou Macon spreads out into a huge cypress swamp, in which for some distance the stream is quite lost. To clear a passage through this labyrinth, it was necessary to cut a channel through the swamp, dig up the stumps, and then break down the levees east of Lake Providence and let in the Mississippi river. It would thus be possible for ships coming down from Memphis to sail through this long detour without ever getting within forty miles of the guns of Vicksburg, and thus at length reëntering the Mississippi from the Red river, to ascend to the scene of operations. The supplies for the army would thus make a roundabout journey of 400 miles, but the route was quite safe from the enemy. McPherson's corps was at work upon Bayou Baxter through February and March, but the obstacles had not been all surmounted when Grant resolved upon the very different plan which finally proved successful.

While these experiments were going on, Grant was also endeavouring, with much more hope of success, to find a method of crossing his army to the north of Haines Bluff, so as to turn the right flank of the rebel line of works. The Yazoo Pass seemed to afford a promising opportunity for this. The line of steep bluffs which leaves the Mississippi

The Yazoo Pass experiment.

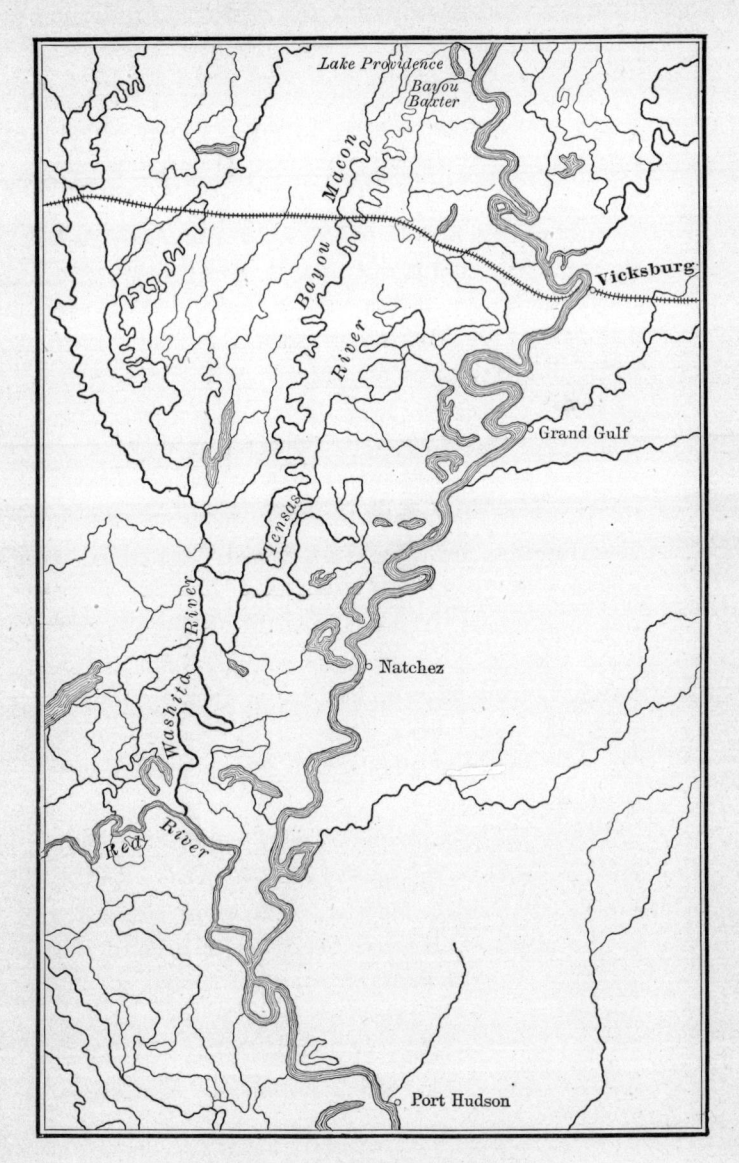

THE LAKE PROVIDENCE EXPERIMENT
FEBRUARY AND MARCH, 1863

at Memphis to meet it again at Vicksburg encloses with the river an elliptical area 200 miles long as the crow flies by 60 miles wide at its widest. Along the eastern portion of this ellipse, and near the base of the bluffs, run a series of rivers draining the elevated plains of the state of Mississippi. First the Coldwater at the north comes down to join the Tallahatchie, and presently their united volume, swelled by that of the Yallabusha, forms the Yazoo river, which empties into the Mississippi just above Vicksburg. All these streams were navigable for vessels of light draught. In the upper part of the ellipse, 150 miles due north from Vicksburg, the distance between the Coldwater and the Mississippi is only ten miles, and this is traversed by a winding bayou, some 80 feet wide by 30 feet deep, known as the Yazoo Pass. In former times this route, through the Yazoo Pass and along the rivers that flow under the bluffs, had been commonly taken by vessels plying between Vicksburg and Memphis. But the waters of the Mississippi, pouring into these narrow channels, had overflowed so much land that in order to abate the nuisance a powerful levee had been built, 100 feet thick and 18 feet in height, shutting up the Yazoo Pass and severing it from the great river. To break down this levee and restore the old state of things was easy;

and then it seemed as if the army might be conveyed in steamers all around the ellipse, from Milliken's Bend up to the Yazoo Pass, and then down the Coldwater, Tallahatchie, and Yazoo rivers to a point where it could land in the rear of Haines Bluff. It was perhaps the most gigantic flanking movement ever attempted in military history. The distance to be traversed along these serpentine streams was full 700 miles, — as far as from New York to Cincinnati, or from London to Marseilles, and as striking an illustration as one could wish of the inaccessibleness of this wonderful stronghold of Vicksburg.

This experiment, like the others, was begun immediately upon Grant's arrival. On the 2d of February a mine was exploded in the levee, and the waters rushing in completed its destruction. The Yazoo Pass was thus opened so that vessels could enter, but the enemy had been beforehand. Both the bayou and the system of rivers to which it gives access wind their way through dense forests of pecan-wood, sycamore, oak, and other hard woods, and it was easy by felling trees across the stream to make a formidable barricade. Several miles of the Yazoo Pass were thus obstructed. In one place eighty prostrate trees, reaching from bank to bank, and intertwining their huge branches with the dense and tangled growth on either side,

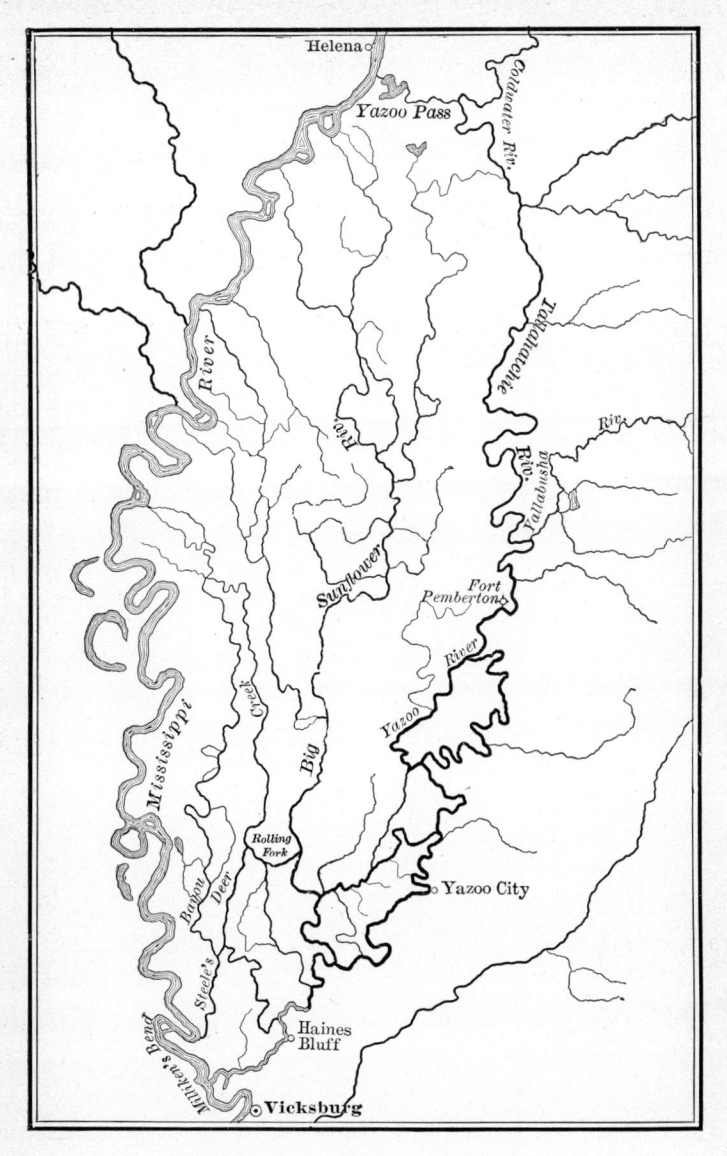

THE YAZOO PASS AND BIG SUNFLOWER EXPERIMENTS
FEBRUARY AND MARCH, 1863

formed a barrier more than a mile in length. It was necessary to chop the boughs and haul the great trunks, often weighing from twenty to thirty tons, quite out of the stream. The men, in parties of 500, worked like beavers, and in two weeks had cleared the way to the Tallahatchie river. Success now seemed assured in this direction. General Ross, with 4500 men, embarked on 22 steamers, and convoyed by a couple of ironclads, made his way 250 miles through the wilderness without losing a man, for there was so much of a freshet that the rebel sharpshooters could not reach the banks. By the 10th of March Ross was sailing upon the lower waters of the Tallahatchie, Quimby's division had been sent to support him, and General McPherson, with his whole corps, was preparing to follow as soon as steamers enough could be got together. But the Confederates had made good use of the time which their barricades had gained for them. Where the Tallahatchie and the Yallabusha unite to form the Yazoo river, there is a great looplike bend enclosing a peninsula, upon the neck of which the Confederates had now extemporized an earthwork and planted heavy guns. This work, which they called Fort Pemberton, completely barred the descent of the river, and as the peninsula was overflowed it could not be approached by infantry.

It remained to be seen whether the gunboats could silence its batteries. On the 11th and 13th of March attacks were made from a distance of 800 yards, but nothing was accomplished. The vessels suffered more damage than the fort. Another levee of the Mississippi, 300 miles distant, was by and by cut, in the hope that the increased volume of water flowing into the Tallahatchie might suffice to drown the fort; but the rise turned out to be insufficient for this. The Yazoo Pass experiment, therefore, auspiciously as it had begun, was now totally defeated. There was nothing for Ross to do but make his way back to the Mississippi river, and Grant had already begun to feel anxious lest the enemy might in some way contrive to surround and cut him off.

While reconnoitring to find some method of relieving Ross, another labyrinthine passage was discovered, through which it was hoped the army might cross far below Fort Pemberton to the rear of Haines Bluff. Through the middle of the long ellipse for nearly 200 miles flows a considerable stream known as the Big Sunflower river, emptying into the Yazoo 100 miles below Fort Pemberton and 20 miles above Haines Bluff. Were it only possible to get from the mouth of the Yazoo into the Big Sunflower without passing the batteries at Haines Bluff, such a route would be preferable to any as yet devised; and it seemed as if a way had at length been discovered through a network of narrow streams known as Steele's and Black bayous, Deer creek, and Rolling Fork. *The Big Sunflower experiment.* The chief obstacles here were the narrowness and sudden bends of the shallow streams, the cypress and willow trees growing in their very beds, and the dense mass of tangled branches and vines overhanging and blocking the way. On the 16th of March Sherman took one of his divisions up Steele's bayou in small steamers, preceded by Admiral Porter with five ironclads and four mortar-boats. The powerful ironclads slowly pushed their way through the bushes, and the transports followed still more slowly, while now and then a smokestack or a pilot-house was brushed away by the wild tangle overhead. Sharpshooters lurked in the thickets, and on the fifth day the admiral, having advanced thirty miles farther than Sherman and approached within a few hundred yards of the clear navigation of the Rolling Fork, found himself attacked by a considerable force. His position soon became perilous. The rebels brought squads of negroes, and compelled them at the point of the bayonet to fell great trees across the creek both in front and in rear of the ships. Presently Sherman, hearing of the danger, and finding a narrow path through the cane-brake, disembarked his troops by night and marched at their head to the rescue, lighting the way with candles. The skirmishers were dispersed, but it was found that the enemy had blockaded the entrance to the Rolling Fork, and occupied it in such force that he could not be dislodged. It was therefore necessary to retreat. There was not room enough to turn the ironclads around, and so their rudders were unshipped and they slowly backed out, bumping from side to side of the wretched creek, till on the 27th of March, after eleven days of toil and peril, the whole expedition floated again on the broad bosom of the Mississippi.

CHAPTER VI

THE FALL OF VICKSBURG

WHILE army and navy were using up the months of February and March in these combined experiments, the navy was also endeavouring to disturb the Confederate control over the river below Vicksburg. To this end, on the 2d of February before daybreak Porter sent the ram Queen of the West down past the dreaded batteries. She succeeded in running safely by, and immediately attacked and disabled the Confederate steamer Vicksburg, after which she cruised up and down the river for a fortnight, capturing and destroying Confederate vessels wherever found. At midnight of the 12th the powerful armoured gunboat Indianola ran swiftly past the batteries and escaped without a scratch, though under fire for twenty minutes. The admiral, in high spirits, now looked forward to the speedy conquest of the river between Vicksburg and Port Hudson, but events soon maliciously mocked him. On the 14th the Queen of the West, while running past a battery on the Red river,

Naval operations.

had her steam-pipe cut by a shot and became unmanageable. The crew escaped upon one of her prizes, but did not set fire to her, as there was a wounded officer on board whom it was impossible to remove. Thus she passed almost unharmed into the hands of the Confederates, and presently was ready to attack the Indianola, so lately her consort. In company with another rebel ram and a couple of light steamers, she chased the Indianola nearly up to Vicksburg, and on the night of the 24th, after a sharp fight, compelled her to surrender. The Indianola was much damaged, and while the Confederates a few days afterward were at work upon her, the astounding news was brought that a monitor was coming down upon them. Sure enough: there was the black and terrible little creature, already below the Vicksburg batteries, out of harm's way and coming swiftly down with the current. The Confederate ships did not stay to fight, but fled in a panic, and never slackened speed until they had reached the Red river. The men upon the Indianola set her on fire and hastened away. Yet the guns of the dreaded monitor sent forth neither sound nor flame. She was a dummy, a malicious ruse, a grim joke of Admiral Porter's. On the deck of an old coal barge he had built a wooden turret and painted it black. For a smokestack he had piled up some pork barrels emitting clouds of smoke from a mud furnace underneath, and this truly formidable craft was let loose with the current to scatter the Confederate vessels by the mere terror of her coming, — an excellent instance of the moral power of Ericsson's memorable invention!

So far as concerned the control of the water, however, the Confederates still had the laugh on their side. Porter saw that it was useless to dispute the case without bringing a great part of his fleet down, which was out of the question so long as the army entertained the thought of crossing the river above Vicksburg. When the news of these events reached New Orleans, it seemed to Admiral Farragut that the time had come to take his fleet upstream and pass Port Hudson. General Banks had reached New Orleans in December with a force intended to coöperate with the fleet in reducing this stronghold; but he had found it necessary first to make a campaign in the interior of Louisiana against a troublesome Confederate force under Richard Taylor, and it was long before he was ready to undertake his principal work. But Farragut felt that his ships were needed above Port Hudson, and on the night of March 14, with seven stout vessels, he set out to pass the batteries. This time it was a fierce fight for an hour and a half. Four ships retreated downstream disabled, and one was destroyed, but the gallant admiral in his flagship, the Hartford, with one consort, succeeded in passing. From this time forth the Federal ships were able to patrol the Mississippi below Vicksburg, and to close the mouth of the Red river, which was a serious blow to the Confederates. But so long as Port Hudson remained defiant, the problem of sending supplies by water to a Union army below Vicksburg remained unsolved.

In these various enterprises two weary months had been consumed, and Grant seemed as far as ever from taking Vicksburg. He had not yet been able to secure a foothold on dry land whereby to get near it. He had apparently tried every available method of approach, he had shown great boldness and ingenuity of conception and rare perseverance, yet now, at the end of March, he had accomplished absolutely nothing. Loud complaints were heard at the North. People were getting impatient. It was long since a Federal army had tasted the sweets of a decisive victory. Burnside had been terribly defeated at Fredericksburg. Rosecrans's great struggle at Stone river had apparently been fruitless, and Grant seemed to be wasting the precious moments in digging ditches. There were but few who as yet cordially recognized his ability. His victory

A gloomy outlook.

at Fort Donelson was indeed the most brilliant success yet achieved by a northern general, but it was thought that he might have blundered into one great success, and in proof of this theory, it was asked, had he not soon after been *nearly* defeated at Shiloh? People were clamorous for his removal. The President's office at the White House was beset with politicians urging Mr. Lincoln to supersede him. As generals capable of doing what Grant could not, one frequently heard mentioned the names (Heaven save the mark!) of Fremont, or Hunter, or McClernand. The intrigues of the last-named general seemed at one time almost likely to succeed. But Lincoln showed himself wiser than those who were so ready with their advice. He said, "I rather like the man ; I think we 'll try him a little longer."

Lincoln's patience was well rewarded. It was this " trying him a little longer " that saved the country. Grant seemed to have exhausted all possible schemes, but his lexicon con- <small>Grant's determination.</small> tained no such word as "fail," and he was getting ready to attempt the impossible, — to defy Fortune and subdue her. It was proved that he could not cross with his army to the north of Haines Bluff, nor could he preserve a secure line of communications if he were to cross to the south of Vicksburg. To put such a fortress as Vicksburg between him·

self and his base of supplies was not to be thought of; it would be putting himself just where the enemy wanted him. Nevertheless, Grant did think of it.

There were just three new alternatives before him. *First*, he might cross in front of Haines Bluff and try to carry it by storm; but that meant almost inevitable defeat. *Secondly*, he might take his whole army back to Memphis and resume his first plan of approach through the interior of Mississippi. That was a perfectly sound course, and was earnestly recommended by General Sherman; but it would look so much like retreat that the moral effect upon the country would be disheartening. *Thirdly*, he might descend below Vicksburg, detach a force to coöperate with Banks at Port Hudson, and after the fall of that fortress move upon Vicksburg, with a sure base of supplies at New Orleans.

<small>Fresh alternatives.</small>

This was not yet defying Fortune, but Grant was rising to the occasion. Every one of his generals thought it sheer madness to put the army south of the city. Grant, however, was not wont to hamper himself with councils of war. He used to listen in silence to the opinions of his generals, and then do as he thought best. He had now made up his mind what to do, and accordingly on the 29th of March, having concentrated his army

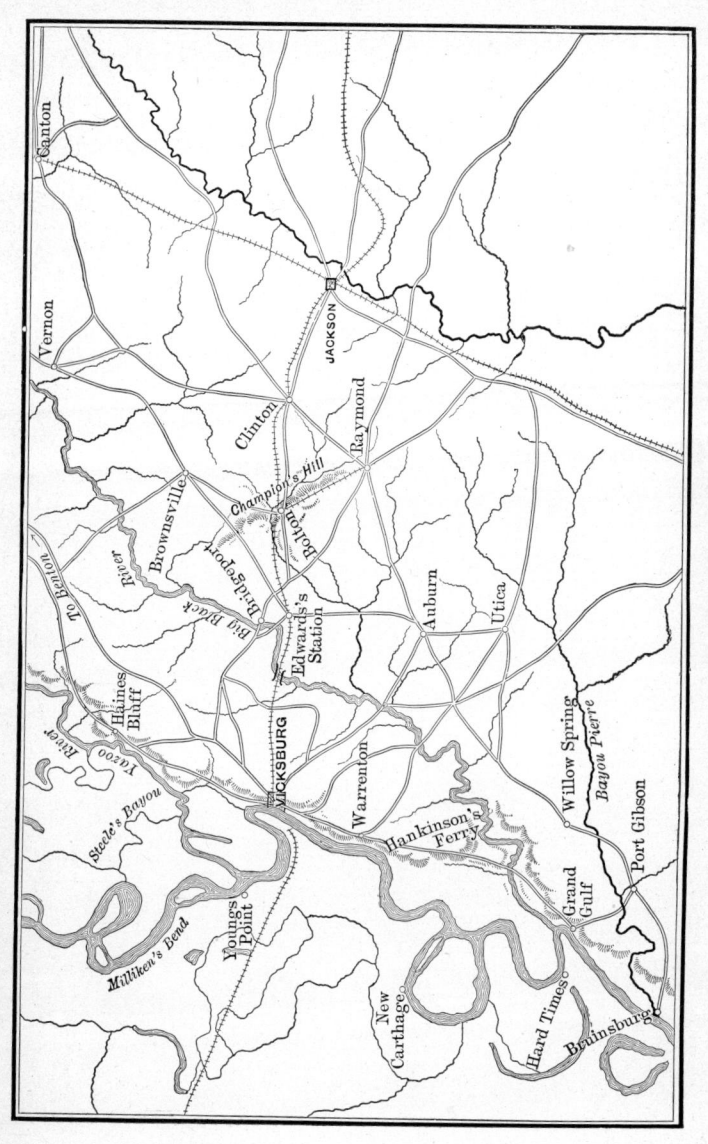

VICKSBURG AND ITS APPROACHES, MAY, 1863

The Fall of Vicksburg

at Milliken's Bend, McClernand's corps was ordered to lead the way to New Carthage, twenty-seven miles below. To this point Grant still thought it possible to bring supplies by cutting little canals to connect a network of bayous, and work of this sort was still kept up until the advancing season, which dried the channels so as to make them useless, dried also the roads in that wilderness of swamps, and began to afford ground upon which corduroy roads could be built fit for men and wagons. As the movement to the north of Vicksburg had been finally abandoned, it was desirable to bring the greater part of Porter's fleet below the city; and Grant seized the occasion to risk the passage of ten shiploads of rations and forage under cover of the gunboats. This enterprise was completely successful. Eight gunboats were left at the mouth of the Yazoo, and on the night of April 16 all the rest of the fleet passed down. *The movement southward.* The Confederates set a few houses on fire to light up the scene, and rained heavy shot upon the river, while Porter's ships in reply sent shell after shell into the streets of Vicksburg. Every ship was struck and many were damaged, but only two were disabled, and after three hours the whole fleet, including the supply ships, was safe below the city. Ten days later another squadron, consisting of transports and barges laden with rations, succeeded in running the gauntlet; and now at last Grant was ready to cross the Mississippi. The labour of moving the army through the Louisiana swamps had been enormous, and it was only on the 29th of April, one month from the beginning of the movement, that the advance corps had reached the hamlet of Hard Times, opposite the fortress of Grand Gulf, the extreme left or southernmost of the defences of Vicksburg, on a bluff twenty-five miles south of the city and just below the mouth of Big Black river.

The next thing in order was to cross the river and take Grand Gulf. On the 29th of April the works were briskly bombarded for more than five hours by Porter's fleet, but they were too high overhead to be seriously damaged. Not a single rebel gun was dismounted, and accordingly the army could not cross here. During the night the fleet ran down past the batteries, convoying the transports and supply ships, while the army marched still farther down upon the west bank. A negro brought word that there was a good road from Bruinsburg, six miles below Grand Gulf, to *Grant crosses the Mississippi.* Port Gibson on the high ground twelve miles inland. Nothing better could be desired. Next morning McClernand's corps embarked, and before sunset they

The Fall of Vicksburg 229

had reached the summit of the bluffs on the east side of the river, while McPherson's corps pushed on behind them. During the whole of these two days Sherman, assisted by the eight gunboats which had been left above Vicksburg, completely absorbed the enemy's attention by moving his forces up the Yazoo and landing them as if to attack Haines Bluff. On the 1st of May he received orders from Grant to move down the west side of the Mississippi, cross to Bruinsburg, and follow McPherson as rapidly as possible. Grant had immediately sent McClernand forward to Port Gibson, as a place which it was important to seize at once. Port Gibson stands at the junction of roads from Bruinsburg and Grand Gulf, with roads leading directly to Vicksburg and to Jackson, the state capital. By seizing it, Grant would compel the enemy to evacuate Grand Gulf. On the evening of April 30 General Bowen, the Confederate commander at Grand Gulf, discovering McClernand's presence on the road to Port Gibson, marched out to attack him; and early next morning the two forces encountered each other about four miles from that town, and a battle began which lasted all day. The enemy, with his reinforcements arriving from Vicksburg, numbered 8500 men. Grant came upon the scene early in the

First victory; at Port Gibson.

battle, and with a portion of McPherson's corps which arrived at noon, he had over 20,000 men. The Confederates fought with their usual gallantry, but by nightfall their right flank had been turned, and they were swept from the field with a loss of 1000 killed and wounded and 650 captured. The Union loss in killed and wounded was 850. Next morning our army entered Port Gibson in triumph, and spent the day pursuing the routed enemy for fifteen miles, as far as Hankinson's ferry, on the Big Black river, and capturing 1000 prisoners. That evening the Confederates hastily evacuated Grand Gulf, and retreated across the Big Black; so hurried were their movements that they left five heavy guns as spoils for the victors. Next day, the 3d of May, Grant occupied this stronghold and established his base of supplies there, while the troops remained three days in bivouac at Willow Springs and Hankinson's ferry, awaiting the arrival of Sherman's corps and fresh ammunition and rations.

Confederates evacuate Grand Gulf.

The critical moment in Grant's career had now come. During the long weary weeks of struggle with creeks and swamps, his mind had been gradually rising to a great resolve, which the turn of events was now about to make perfectly definite and clear. He had at last secured a footing on

the high ground east of the river, and was in possession of one of the strongest of the rebel fortresses. At this season supplies could be brought, though liable to tedious delays, over the rough roads on the west side. In case of emergency it had been shown that they could do such a thing as run down the river under the Vicksburg batteries. Yet his situation was not a desirable one to remain in. It was precarious at best, and delay would increase the danger. *The critical moment.*
His first intention had been to establish himself here, and detach a corps to coöperate with Banks in reducing Port Hudson. After the removal of that formidable obstacle, supplies could be regularly and safely brought up from New Orleans. If it were not for this vexed question of supply, there was everything to tempt him to an immediate movement upon Vicksburg. The enemy had been surprised, defeated, and somewhat demoralized; now was the time to follow up this initial success with blow after blow. At this crisis there came a letter from Banks in the interior of Louisiana, stating that he could not reach Port Hudson before the 10th of May. This was all that Grant needed to decide his movements. It was still a week to the 10th of May, and after that it might very well take a month to reduce Port Hudson. Meanwhile the enemy, realizing the danger of

Vicksburg, would send troops from every quarter to reinforce it. Delay would be ruinous, and Grant instantly made up his mind to move upon the rear of Vicksburg.

To face the difficulties in the way of such a movement required the stoutest of hearts and the coolest of heads. Grant's force, consisting of the three corps of Sherman, McPherson, and McClernand, numbered 45,000 men. In Vicksburg and its neighbourhood Pemberton had an army of about 50,000; but Grant, unlike many Union commanders, was apt to underrate the enemy's strength, and he supposed it to be only 30,000. Another Confederate army was gathering to the east and north of Jackson. Its strength was unknown, but likely to be considerable, for the rebels were weakening their garrisons at Charleston and Mobile and every point from which troops could be spared to reinforce it; and Grant knew that Joseph Johnston was on his way from Chattanooga to take the command in person. It was necessary for Grant to interpose his forces between these two armies and beat them in detail, first driving Johnston eastward, then turning upon Pemberton, crushing him in battle and pushing him back upon Vicksburg. In order to do this, it was necessary to keep his army together; if he should detach forces to guard his line of communication

A difficult situation.

The Fall of Vicksburg 233

with Grand Gulf, he could not bring men enough into battle to ensure him the victory. But nothing could be more certain than that Pemberton would fall upon his line of communications the moment he should move eastward against Johnston. Grant therefore came to the startling decision to cut loose from his base altogether, to feed his troops on what they could carry in their haversacks and what they could pick up on the way, and moving with all possible speed, unencumbered by heavy wagons, to vanquish the enemy and gain a new base of supplies on the Mississippi north of Vicksburg before famine should have time to overtake him. This was defying Fortune outright. No general ever conceived a more daring scheme. There was no precedent for it in the history of modern warfare. Napoleon and other European generals who had "lived upon the country" had done so through a regularly organized system of requisitions. No one had ever undertaken an elaborate campaign in an enemy's country with no more provisions than could be carried in haversacks or got by foraging. Doubtless all would go well if everything should turn out as Grant had planned, but campaigns are seldom carried out precisely as they are conceived, and in the event of defeat the total destruction of the

Grant's sublime audacity.

army could scarcely be averted. Accordingly none of Grant's generals approved of the movement; even the daring Sherman had little faith in its success. As for Halleck, he was not informed of the scheme until too late to prevent it. As soon as the news of it reached Washington, on the 11th of May, Halleck ordered Grant to retrace his steps and move toward Port Hudson to coöperate with Banks. But by that time Grant was fortunately beyond the reach of the telegraph, and the order did not find him until victory had been achieved. With sublime self-reliance he took the destinies of the army and the nation upon his shoulders, and wrought out a triumph that could have been obtained in no other way.

In making this bold decision, Grant knew that Johnston laboured under difficulties. He knew that a concentration of rebel troops near the state capital could not be speedily effected. Some weeks ago Van Dorn, with his great force of cavalry, had been imprudently taken from Mississippi and sent to assist Bragg at Tullahoma; and soon afterward Grant had despatched Colonel Grierson on a cavalry raid which turned out to be one of the most brilliant and useful of the war. From Grierson's the 17th of April to the 2d of May, cavalry raid. with a force of little more than 1000 men, Grierson had made a tour of 600 miles

The Fall of Vicksburg

through the state of Mississippi, effectually cutting three different lines of railroad, destroying 60 miles of telegraph, and isolating the city of Jackson on the north, south, and east, besides thoroughly confusing the enemy and distracting his attention. Nothing, however, could so completely bewilder the enemy and throw him off upon a false scent as the unprecedented move which Grant was about to make.

With these elements of success duly considered, Grant started on the 7th of May, as soon as Sherman had crossed the river. The men were furnished with rations for five days, and foraging parties were sent out each night to scour the country and bring in everything eatable they could lay hands on. Grant's march was admirably adapted to mask his purpose. He sent small detachments west of the Big Black to threaten Vicksburg and keep Pemberton in the neighbourhood of the city. The left wing under McClernand marched up the eastern bank of the Big Black toward Edwards's station on the Vicksburg and Jackson railroad, about midway between the two cities. The centre under Sherman was headed for Bolton station, a few miles farther east on the same road. The right wing under McPherson was directed toward Jackson by way of Raymond. On the 12th McPherson's advance encountered

5000 Confederates in a strong position at Raymond and routed them in a sharp fight of two hours, each side losing about 400 in killed and wounded. The enemy also lost 400 in prisoners, and thus discomfited withdrew to Jackson.

Second victory; at Raymond.

Meanwhile Pemberton, supposing Grant's immediate goal to be Edwards's station, advanced in that direction, intending to offer battle; but Grant was not quite ready to dispose of him. He rightly interpreted the affair at Raymond as indicating a concentration of rebel forces about Jackson, and his first business was to nip it in the bud. Accordingly he turned McClernand and Sherman eastward upon Clinton to support McPherson in his advance upon Jackson. On the evening of the 13th General Johnston arrived at Jackson and took command, but could muster only 6000 men, mostly consisting of those who had been defeated the day before at Raymond. Reinforcements were on the way, however, and in a few days Johnston would have had over 20,000 men; but Grant's celerity spoiled all this. On the 14th, while the other two corps were within supporting distance, McPherson came up and overwhelmed Johnston, capturing 800 prisoners and all his artillery. McPherson's loss was about 250. The stars and stripes were

Third victory; at Jackson.

hoisted over the capitol, and Grant slept in the house where Johnston had slept the night before. The one useful thing that Pemberton might have done on this day would have been to come up to Clinton and attack Grant in the rear, and indeed Johnston had sent word to him to do so; but Pemberton thought he knew better. Seeing Grant carelessly moving so far away from his base at Grand Gulf, Pemberton naturally thought that sound strategy required him to lay hold of Grant's line of communications; and accordingly he wasted the day in marching down toward Raymond. Of course it never entered his head that Grant had divested himself of all such encumbrances as lines of communication!

Thus did Grant's very audacity, by fooling the enemy, contribute to its own success. Had Pemberton pressed him in the rear, it might have detained him till Johnston could be reinforced. But that chance was lost, and Grant now took care that Johnston should not speedily gather his forces. Leaving Sherman to burn the bridges, factories, and arsenals at Jackson, and tear up the railroads in every direction *Grant turns westward.* for twenty miles, he now faced his army to westward and started for Vicksburg. Johnston had retreated to Canton, thirty miles north of the capital, and had now no means of getting back save by marching. Early on the morning of the 16th Pemberton received a peremptory order to march to Clinton, it being Johnston's intention to join him there, and with their united masses head Grant off and prevent his ever getting back to the Mississippi. But when this despatch reached Pemberton, two thirds of Grant's army were already passing Bolton, ten miles west of Clinton, and out of Johnston's reach by quite two days' march.

Hearing of Pemberton's approach, Grant hastened to the front, sending word to Sherman to bring up his corps. Pemberton was found strongly posted a little south of the railroad about three miles west of Bolton. His left wing occupied the bald crest of a wooded hill some seventy feet in height, known as Champion's Hill, and this crest was well-crowned with artillery. His whole line, stretching a couple of miles south from the hill, consisted of about 18,000 men. It took eight hours of severe fighting to dislodge this force. On the Union side the work was almost entirely done by McPherson's corps and Hovey's division of McClernand's, directed by Grant in person, and constituting the right wing. The Confederates were defeated, losing 1400 in killed and wounded, 2500 prisoners, and all their artillery; while one division of 4000 men, cut asunder from the rest of the

Fourth victory; at Champion's Hill.

army and unable to rejoin it, fled southeasterly many miles beyond Jackson.

Half of Pemberton's force had thus crumbled away; the rest retreated in disorder toward Vicksburg. To deal this shattering blow cost Grant 2500 men. It was the decisive stroke of the campaign. The Confederates were now scattered to all points of the compass; there was no more chance of uniting under Johnston; while the Federals, in solid column and elated with victory, were fast nearing the goal of all their labours. That evening Grant received Halleck's order, dated five days before, telling him on no account whatever to undertake such a campaign as this, but to go down and unite with Banks. He could read this order now with equanimity. He had staked everything, but he had won. Unless something extraordinary should happen, Vicksburg was doomed.

The march thither next morning was attended by a brief but notable passage at arms. At eight o'clock McClernand's corps had reached the bridge over the Big Black river. Pemberton had placed 5000 men there in a position precarious unless reinforced, and yesterday's defeat had prevented this. In less than an hour one third of this force was captured, with 18 pieces of artillery and 1400 stand of arms; the rest had fled in a panic, not forgetting, how

Fifth victory; at Big Black river.

ever, to set fire to the bridge, which had been smeared with turpentine and was soon in a blaze. This delayed the Federals for a whole day while they were building a rude bridge, and it may perhaps have prevented their entering Vicksburg with the fleeing enemy. During that day Johnston advanced fifteen miles from Canton in search of Pemberton, who now, twice beaten, was taking refuge behind the stout works of Vicksburg. Next day, the 18th, while McClernand and McPherson marched straight toward the city, Sherman moved northwesterly and occupied the Benton road about half way between Vicksburg and Haines Bluff, thus rendering the latter stronghold untenable. The garrison abandoned it in too much haste to destroy anything; and so the great fortress, with all its guns and stores, and with its command of the Yazoo river and all the northern approaches to Vicksburg, fell into Union hands in good condition and ready to be used against the enemy. The right wing of the Union army now rested on the long-coveted bluffs above the city, and looked down upon the Mississippi with feelings like those which surged in the bosoms of the Ten Thousand Greeks when from a peak in Asia Minor they caught sight of the friendly sea. Grant was with Sherman this morning, and the two rode out together upon the very bluff which five

Fall of Haines Bluff.

The Fall of Vicksburg

months before the latter had vainly tried to storm. "Until this moment," exclaimed Sherman, "I never thought your movement a success. But this *is* a campaign! this is a success, if we never take the town." Grant took out a fresh cigar and lighted it, smiled, and said never a word.

Vicksburg was no longer the unapproachable Gibraltar of America. This wonderful campaign had made her like any other fortress. Grant's lines were drawn about her, and the bluffs which so long had baffled him now guarded his new base of supplies. The soldiers had contrived to live fairly well off the country and had not suffered from hunger, though they had eaten so much poultry with so little bread that the sight of a chicken disgusted them. Never, perhaps, was a campaign carried out so precisely in accordance with its plan. It was just eighteen days since Grant had crossed the Mississippi, eleven since he had cut loose from his base at Grand Gulf. In those eighteen days he had marched 200 miles, and by the novelty of his movements disconcerted and separated forces much larger than his own. With a loss of not more than 5000 men he had defeated two armies in five battles, taking nearly 100 cannon, and destroying or capturing more than 12,000 of the enemy. And to crown all, he had solved the apparently insoluble problem

An amazing campaign.

of investing Vicksburg. To find a parallel in military history to the deeds of those eighteen days, we must go back to the first Italian campaign of Napoleon in 1796.

When Johnston, on the night of the 17th, heard of the decisive overthrow at Champion's Hill, he instantly sent word to Pemberton to abandon Vicksburg if not too late, and march northeastward to join him at Vernon. He saw that Haines Bluff must fall, that Vicksburg would then become untenable, and that Pemberton's only remaining chance was to save his army. It was noon of the 18th when Pemberton received this message, and it nearly drove him frantic. He had not realized the full significance of his defeat, and could not bring himself to admit that the case was as bad as the sagacious Johnston saw it to be. While he was discussing the matter with his generals, Sherman had occupied the road leading northeast in such force that it was decided the order could not be carried out. So Pemberton waited his doom. The city was well provided with food, but in course of time it must succumb to starvation, unless relieved.

Vicksburg invested.

Grant, however, did not at first contemplate a siege. The Confederates were so disheartened by their defeats that he doubted their ability to resist an assault. On the 19th an attempt was

The Fall of Vicksburg

made to storm their works, but it was unsuccessful, though it secured more advanced and sheltered positions for the Federal troops. The failure was disappointing, for time was precious. Reinforcements were on the way to Johnston, and it was feared that he might approach in sufficient strength to relieve the city. Accordingly on the 22d another and desperate assault was made. The Federals pressed up close to the works under a murderous fire. In several places brave men succeeded in climbing the parapets and planting their flags, where they waved several hours, while the rebels were shot down as fast as they stepped up to remove them; but the works were not carried. Two of these cases occurred in McClernand's corps, just as Grant was about to give orders to stop the assault. In an altogether too sanguine and heated mood McClernand sent word that he was "partly in possession of two forts" and with a vigorous push hoped to carry everything in front of him. This naturally led Grant to renew the fruitless assault. Similar incidents occurred in Sherman's and McPherson's commands, but their military eyes read the situation more correctly. If McClernand had sent word that his men had reached the ditch but could not get into the forts, he would have described just what he saw before him, and much useless

Two unsuccessful assaults.

bloodshed would have been avoided. In these two assaults of the 19th and 22d the Union army lost 4000 men, and made up its mind to settle down to a regular siege. Shortly after this McClernand issued a congratulatory address to his corps, full of insinuations against the other troops and their commanders. The address was evidently intended for a political constituency in Illinois. It was published in the newspapers, but, in flat defiance of army regulations, no copy of it had been sent to headquarters. This was a plain act of insubordination. During all these months Grant had been extremely patient with McClernand, for, as he said, " he could not afford to quarrel with a man whom he had to command." Now, however, he sent him home to Illinois, and gave the command of his corps to a trained and well-tried soldier, General Edward Ord. This was virtually the end of McClernand's military career, though he afterward held some obscure position in Texas.

<small>McClernand dismissed.</small>

As soon as a siege was decided on, provision had to be made against the contingency of Johnston's arrival. Grant's army was reinforced from various quarters till it numbered 70,000 men, so that he was enabled to detach a strong force under Sherman to hold the line of the Big Black river in his rear. Defensive works were raised along

The Fall of Vicksburg

this line and as far as Haines Bluff, so strong that when Johnston, after collecting with much difficulty 30,000 men, arrived in the neighbourhood, he prudently refrained from making an attack. Under such circumstances the fall of Vicksburg was only a question of time. There was no more fighting worthy of mention. Mining, countermining, and sapping went on as usual in sieges. Shells were thrown into the city as they had been for months, only now more constantly, the army's siege guns aiding the mortars of the fleet. To escape this perpetual storm of deadly missiles, the inhabitants had reverted to the custom of earlier ages and learned to dwell in caves. The bluff on which the city stood was honeycombed with subterranean vaults and passages, like the Roman catacombs, and caves favourably situated brought high rents. Food grew scarcer and scarcer. Flour sold at ten dollars a pound and bacon at five dollars a pound. Mule meat[1] was in demand. "Mule tongue cold, à la Bray," it was jocosely said, was a favourite side dish. On the 28th of June Pemberton received a curious letter from an unknown number of soldiers, which said, among other things, "If you can't feed us you had better surrender us, hor-

Vicksburg besieged.

---

[1] Which if well fatted is a great delicacy, as French cooks know; but doubtless the mule meat of sieges is lean and tough.

rible as the idea is. . . . I tell you plainly, men are not going to lie here and perish; if they do love their country, self-preservation is the first law of nature, and hunger will compel a man to do almost anything. You had better heed a warning voice, though it is the voice of a private soldier. This army is now ripe for mutiny unless it can be fed." The newspapers — which are not given to looking facts in the face — tried to take a more hopeful view. On July 2 one of them said: "The great Ulysses has expressed his intention of celebrating the Fourth of July in Vicksburg by a grand dinner. . . . Ulysses must get into the city before he dines in it. The way to cook a rabbit is first catch the rabbit," etc.

But Ulysses had caught his rabbit. On that same day Pemberton had abandoned all hope, and next morning he sent out a flag of truce. The day was spent in arranging terms. Grant did not give up his principle of "unconditional surrender," but allowed some merely formal privileges, such as marching out with colours flying to stack arms. <small>Surrender of Vicksburg.</small> The prisoners were all paroled, thus saving the time and expense of transporting and feeding so great a number of men. At ten o'clock in the morning of the Fourth of July the Union army occupied the city, and before evening Sherman had started with 50,000 men in pursuit of Johnston, whom he chased beyond the state capital, and left too hopelessly demoralized to threaten any more mischief in that part of the world.

The capture of Pemberton's army was the largest that up to that time had been made in modern warfare. The nearest approach to it had been Napoleon's capture of the Austrian army at Ulm in 1805, when he took 30,000 men and 60 cannon. At Vicksburg Grant took 37,000 men and 172 cannon. Sedan and Metz were still in the future. There was no longer any question as to Grant's military capacity. The northern people were wild with delight, while the first chills of despair began to creep over the Southern Confederacy. The capture of Vicksburg, with the victory just won at Gettysburg, marked the turning-point of the Civil War. *The turning-point of the Civil War.* Five days later Port Hudson, which had withstood a six weeks' siege and two assaults, surrendered to General Banks on hearing of the fall of Vicksburg. On the 16th of July the merchant steamer Imperial, which had started from St. Louis on the 8th, drew up to the wharf at New Orleans, and in President Lincoln's vigorous language, "the Father of Waters rolled unvexed to the sea."

CHAPTER VII

CHICKAMAUGA

NEXT after Richmond and Vicksburg, the mountain fastness of Chattanooga was the most important strategic point in the Southern Confederacy. It was the centre of great lines of railroad radiating in every direction to the Mississippi, the Ohio, the Atlantic Ocean, and the Gulf of Mexico. Situated at the lower end of that huge mountain defile known as East Tennessee, in the heart of a region which some have called an American Switzerland, it guards the only avenue by which Virginia can be approached directly from the southwestern states. Its possession by a Federal army would practically isolate Virginia and North Carolina on the one hand, and lop off Mississippi and Alabama on the other; and by opening the way into the interior of Georgia would throw what was left of the war entirely into the Atlantic region. Its possession by the Confederates gave them control of eastern Tennessee, enabled them easily to move reinforcements between Virginia

Importance of Chattanooga.

and the West, and was a perpetual menace to middle Tennessee and Kentucky.

Besides this great strategic importance, Chattanooga had its peculiar political value. It was situated in the midst of a population which from the beginning of the war had suffered persecution for their enthusiastic and uncompromising love of the Union. Still nearer to the heart of the Confederacy, indeed, there was a considerable area where sentiments of loyalty to the Union were strong, but ineffective because of their isolation. The hardy mountaineers of western North Carolina and northern Georgia and Alabama were not associated by any bonds of interest with the slaveholders of the lowlands, and had no sympathy with their scheme of secession. When two of Foote's gunboats, after the fall of Fort Henry, ascended the Tennessee river into northern Alabama, they found, in some places, the shores crowded with people loudly cheering their arrival and throwing up their hats with glee at sight of the Union flag. Even in South Carolina, in the upland region which in the Revolutionary War had witnessed the victories of King's Mountain and the Cowpens, it is said that not one person in ten was a secessionist. This whole area of the Alleghanies was a loyal area, and to clear it of Confederate armies,

The loyal mountaineers of the Alleghanies.

250 *The Mississippi Valley in the Civil War*

as had already been done in West Virginia, was to set it free.

Thus political and military reasons combined to make Chattanooga the great objective point of the Army of the Cumberland, as Vicksburg was the goal of the Army of the Tennessee, and as Richmond was the goal of the Army of the Potomac. But the progress of the Federals toward Chattanooga was slower and less steady than their progress toward Vicksburg, and this was due mainly to their different relations to the great rivers. In advancing from Cairo toward Vicksburg, we have seen how the Federals were powerfully assisted as far as Corinth by their control of the Tennessee river as a highway for supplies. Proceeding up the Tennessee, which in that part of its course runs parallel to the Mississippi, the Federals were at the same time conquering the latter river downward, simply by taking its great fortresses one after another in flank. When they left the Tennessee and had to support themselves by railroads, their progress became much more difficult, as was illustrated by the failure of Grant's first movement against Vicksburg. Now the Tennessee river is not navigable for ships of war above the Muscle Shoals near Florence in Alabama, some 400 miles from its mouth and more than 200

The upper Tennessee river not a good line of communication.

miles below Chattanooga. Even if it were navigable in that part of its course, its value as a line of communication was greatly diminished by the fact of its running parallel instead of perpendicular to the enemy's front. In approaching Chattanooga, therefore, the Federals were obliged to depend for their supplies on the long line of railway running from Louisville through Nashville; and at least half their energies were consumed in watching this line.

We have seen that there was a moment in the summer of 1862 when Chattanooga might have been seized and held. As the Federals had that spring concentrated all their forces west of the Alleghanies for the great movement upon Corinth, so the Confederates had gathered together all their strength to oppose them, and Chattanooga was left well-nigh defenceless, so that a single Federal brigade was able to begin bombarding it. After the fall of Corinth, the prize of Chattanooga was for him that should move quickest. Buell might have taken it, had not Halleck insisted upon his employing the precious hours in mending a railroad that was of no use to any one but the rebels when mended. This lamentable delay allowed Bragg to get there first, and within six weeks he had illustrated its use as a sally-port from which to invade Kentucky, throw

A lost opportunity.

Cincinnati into a panic, and threaten the destruction of Buell's fine army.

The most that was accomplished by the tremendous battle at Stone river was to keep Bragg upon the defensive. Had Rosecrans's plan of attack succeeded that day, the total defeat of Bragg would have uncovered Chattanooga. As it was, Rosecrans just got off with a whole skin, and the two armies lay sullenly facing each other, their fronts about thirty miles apart, Rosecrans at Murfreesboro, Bragg at Shelbyville and Tullahoma, for nearly six months. Things were not so quiet, however, as would seem from this immobility of the armies. It was a busy half year. Each general was trying with his cavalry to reach out a long arm behind the other and cut his communications. They had tried hard pounding at Stone river without much profit to either; now it remained to be seen which could trip the other up. The cavalry expeditions on either side came almost to assume the proportions of campaigns. At the end of January Bragg sent a cavalry force to surprise and capture Fort Donelson, but it was repulsed, and came back after losing 1000 men. In April Rosecrans sent out a troop which penetrated far into Georgia, cutting railroads, defeating the brilliant raider Forrest, and burning the Round Mountain ironworks, one of

Chickamauga

the principal manufactories of war material in the South; until at length Forrest attacked again and captured the whole troop, 1500 in number.

In warfare of this kind the Confederates had the advantage, as their cavalry was more numerous and better trained; and when Rosecrans at length began to rival them in this arm of the service, the inequality was restored by the arrival of Van Dorn from Mississippi. In May, 1863, Van Dorn was murdered in a private quarrel, and the loss was a grievous one to Bragg, as he had set his heart upon starving his antagonist into retreating. How diligently the Confederates worked may *Diligence in destruction.* be seen from the report of the superintendent of the Louisville and Nashville railroad for the year ending July 1, 1863. During that year there were but seven months and twelve days when trains could run over the whole length of the road. Every bridge and trestlework of any consequence, on the main road and all its branches, had been destroyed and rebuilt within the year; many had been destroyed and rebuilt three or four times. Stations and cars were burned and engines demolished; and in one place a tunnel had been choked with rubbish to a distance of 800 feet. Under such circumstances it was not strange that Rosecrans's army should often have had to subsist on half rations. The country was scoured for forage till it was stripped bare. Vegetables could not be had in quantity sufficient to keep off scurvy. In early summer a regiment passing over a field newly planted with potatoes would pull them up and eagerly devour them raw without waiting to wipe off the dirt.

In contending with such difficulties, and with the horrible spring roads, the months wore away, while people at home censured Rosecrans as they censured Grant, and wondered whether anything was ever going to be done, and what the government was spending three million dollars a day for. The government responded to these expressions of feeling, and early in the spring Halleck hit upon a curious device for hastening matters. He wrote letters to Rosecrans and Grant, offering the rank of major-general in the regular army to the general who should soonest win an important victory. Grant never took any notice of the letter, but Rosecrans treated it as an insult, and replied to Halleck that he felt "degraded at such an auctioneering of honours," and that if we had a general who would fight for his own personal benefit when he would not for the sake of his country, he ought to be despised by all honourable men. The incident is interesting, and strongly characteristic of the men concerned. Rosecrans's feelings were those of a

Rosecrans snubs Halleck.

high-spirited gentleman, but it was impolitic thus to show his contempt for his superior officer; it set not only Halleck, but the despotic and passionate Stanton against him.[1] Perhaps Grant's cold silence was not less eloquent, but he presently won such a triumph at Vicksburg as made it of little account how Halleck felt.

In May, when Johnston was straining every nerve to raise a force to relieve Vicksburg, the question arose whether Rosecrans ought not at once to move against Bragg, to keep him from sparing any of his men for such a purpose. Hal-

[1] If Stanton and Halleck had expected to find in Rosecrans a more docile and submissive general than Buell, they were greatly mistaken. Of course I am not here speaking of military subordination, but of the abdication of individual judgment, which is a very different thing. Perhaps they may now have been able, by the comparative method, to get some light on the subject of Buell's alleged "slowness." During the first eight months under Rosecrans, from October, 1862, to June, 1863, the Army of the Cumberland marched about 32 miles and fought the battle of Stone river. In the preceding eight months under Buell the same army had marched

from Louisville to Nashville	185 miles
from Nashville to Corinth	217 "
from Corinth to Battle Creek	217 "
thence *via* Nashville to Louisville	336 "
thence circuitously in pursuit of Bragg, and back to Nashville	485 "

In all, 1440 miles, besides fighting the battles of Shiloh and Perryville. See Fry, *The Army under Buell*, p. 76.

256 *The Mississippi Valley in the Civil War*

leck urged such a movement, and Grant took the same view, but Rosecrans ingeniously argued that if Bragg were to be defeated so as to lose Chattanooga, his troops would be all the more likely to be sent to Mississippi, just as after the fall of Corinth they had hastened from Mississippi to Chattanooga. However, as the siege of Vicksburg progressed *Rosecrans decides to move.* toward its close, Rosecrans decided to move in full force, and on the 24th of June his army started from Murfreesboro. About the same time Burnside, who had been in command at Cincinnati, moved into eastern Tennessee with 25,000 men, to take Knoxville and put an end to the distresses there.

Rosecrans's advance was well-planned and skilfully executed. He hoped to manœuvre Bragg back upon Chattanooga and out of it *A preliminary campaign of manœuvres.* without a battle, and his first steps toward this end were well taken. Making a false movement upon Bragg's advanced position at Shelbyville, and thus absorbing the enemy's attention, he rapidly concentrated his forces at Manchester, threatening Bragg's line of retreat. The Confederate general then fell back behind his fortifications at Tullahoma. But now, by a second turning movement, Rosecrans obliged him to abandon this strong position and fall back across the mountains and the river into

Chattanooga. This preliminary campaign ended on the 3d of July, the same day which witnessed Meade's victory at Gettysburg and the hoisting of the white flag by the rebel commander at Vicksburg. In nine days Rosecrans had driven the enemy from middle Tennessee without a battle. He had one great advantage in a superiority of numbers which enabled him to extend his left wing toward the enemy's rear, while still retaining force enough on his right to make serious demonstrations there. He had now nearly 70,000 men, while Bragg had but 43,000. Accordingly on reaching Chattanooga, Bragg felt it necessary to call in Buckner's force from eastern Tennessee, thus giving up Knoxville, which Burnside immediately occupied. Much good had thus been accomplished by Rosecrans at small cost. The people, elated with the recent victories as much as they had before been depressed, looked on with eager expectation. Grant, Rosecrans, and Meade were at that moment the three conspicuous figures whose every movement occupied the attention of the whole country.

The second stage of the campaign so well begun was devoted to driving the enemy out of Chattanooga. The place was excessively difficult to approach from the north side of the Tennessee river in any direction. The Union army lay in a northeast and southwest line from McMinnville to Winchester. The most direct approach to Chattanooga was by the left through Therman and over Waldron's Ridge, a spur of the Cumberland Mountains named after a hardy pioneer of a century ago. But Rosecrans had two good objections to that road. One was that it would carry him far from the railway, with a long wagon-haul over steep and dangerous roads; the other was that Bragg fully expected him to come that way in spite of its difficulty. The alternative route was by the right through Bridgeport and Stevenson and over the mountains of northern Alabama and Georgia. This would keep Rosecrans near to the railway and to his depot of supplies which he was just establishing at Stevenson, but it necessitated his moving through a country so difficult that Bragg did not believe he would dare to attempt it. A series of parallel mountain ranges, hard to climb and penetrable only through narrow defiles, stood in his way.

The approaches to Chattanooga.

The first of these steep ranges, parallel to the Tennessee river and very near its bank, was known as Raccoon Mountain. Next came Lookout Mountain, a name destined to be famous in song and story, and more descriptive than such names sometimes are. The mountain, 100 miles in length, rears its bold crest at its northern end nearly 3000 feet above sea level and more than 1400 over the great river whose strong swift current rushes along below on its journey of 600 miles to its junction with the Ohio. It is here crowned with steep palisades, from the summit of which parts of seven states may be seen, spread out in a magnificent panorama. Toward the lofty peaks of North Carolina — the highest this side of the Rocky Mountains — it bears a similar relation to that held by the Rigi-Kulm in presence of its neighbour Alps. Between Raccoon and Lookout lies the wild valley drained of its waters by Lookout creek. Eastward from Lookout comes Missionary Ridge, some forty miles in length and running also up to the river. It encloses with Lookout Mountain the Chattanooga valley, through which flows Chattanooga creek; and near the mouth of the creek stands the town of Chattanooga, superbly situated in the midst of a great amphitheatre of hills. Its position may well suggest the name of "Hawk's Nest," which the Indian word has been supposed to mean; but, heartless as it seems to disturb so pretty a fancy, we have the testimony of the famous chief, John Ross, that in his native Cherokee the name "Chattanooga" means "a good fishing-place."

Eastward again from Missionary Ridge we come upon Pigeon Mountain, a sickle-shaped range

A difficult country.

enclosing the Chickamauga valley, drained by West Chickamauga creek. In the lower part of this valley the wide space contained within the curved blade of the sickle was presently to become the scene of the most dreadful act of the tragic drama now unfolding. At their southern or upper ends the Chattanooga and Chickamauga valleys unite in a single valley known as McLemore's Cove. Still eastward of Pigeon Mountain we find Chickamauga Hill and Taylor's Ridge, drained by the middle and eastern branches of Chickamauga creek. Crossing these ranges we come to Chattanooga Mountain, the last of the series, beyond which the streams all flow in the opposite direction toward the Gulf of Mexico. East of the whole series, and on the southern watershed, stand the towns of Dalton and Resaca, stations on the railroad from Chattanooga to Atlanta, where Bragg had his base of supplies.

Mountains after mountains.

Now, obviously by moving his army directly across these formidable mountain barriers and aiming straight at Dalton, Rosecrans would keep his own base at Stevenson well-covered, while he would threaten the enemy's line of communications and compel him to evacuate Chattanooga. In spite of its natural difficulties, therefore, Rosecrans chose this route, more especially as he perceived that

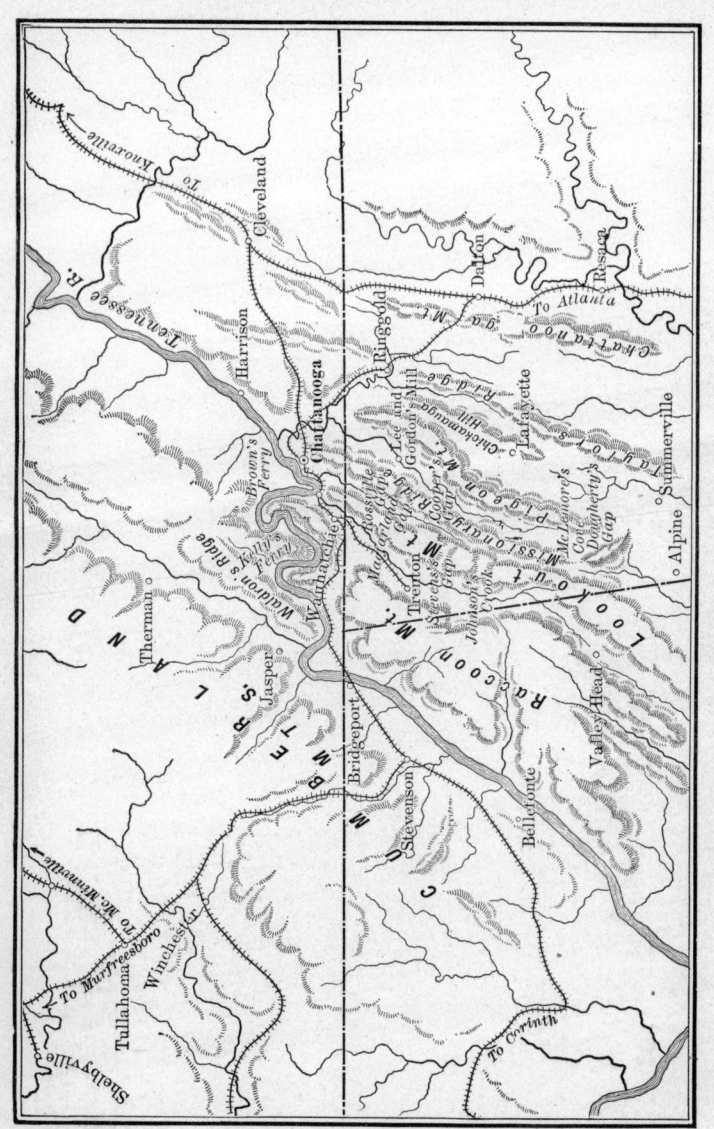

CHATTANOOGA AND ITS APPROACHES, SEPTEMBER, 1863

Bragg's attention was absorbed in the opposite direction. Accordingly, as soon as the railroad to Stevenson was in thorough repair, and a sufficiency of supplies accumulated there, Rosecrans crossed the Cumberland Mountains and descended into the valley of the Tennessee river.

In moving over the mountains Rosecrans greatly extends his front.

The more effectually to hoodwink Bragg, he kept his left wing thrown out so as to menace Chattanooga from the north; and on the 20th of August he began shelling the town from across the river. His front extended from opposite Harrison, ten miles above Chattanooga, to Bellefonte, fifty miles below, too great a distance for his numbers to cover. Between the 29th of August and the 4th of September, still keeping up his demonstrations on the left, Rosecrans moved the great bulk of his army across the river and began his march over Raccoon Mountain. The left wing, under Crittenden, took position at Wauhatchie, a railway station in Lookout valley; the centre, under Thomas, crossed to Trenton; the right wing, under McCook, crossed from Stevenson and Bellefonte to Valley Head, whence cavalry demonstrations were made as far as Alpine. These movements were completed by the 8th of September. When Bragg first began to hear of them he was incredulous, but at length, on the 7th and 8th of September, taking in the situation and seeing his communications threatened, he evacuated Chattanooga and moved twenty-five miles south to Lafayette, where he covered the railroad and hoped to fall heavily upon the Federal columns as they debouched from the mountain passes. On the 9th Crittenden's corps marched from Wauhatchie into Chattanooga and took possession of that long-coveted town.

<small>Bragg evacuates Chattanooga.</small>

This capture (as it seemed) of the prize by sheer manœuvring, without a battle, was hailed by the northern people with an outburst of joy. It seemed as if everything were going right at last. But dire disaster was soon to follow on the heels of this premature rejoicing. The seeds of calamity were sown in the enormous extension of the Federal lines. Two alternatives were open to Rosecrans. On the one hand he might draw the forces of Thomas and McCook down Lookout valley behind the friendly shelter of the great mountain, and, passing around its northern point in Crittenden's footsteps, concentrate his army upon Chattanooga. The northern crests of Lookout Mountain and Missionary Ridge, which command the amphitheatre in which the town is situated, would require to be held in force. Then Chattanooga could be held against all comers and made the starting-point for a new

<small>Seeds of disaster.</small>

movement for the overthrow of Bragg and his army. This would have been practicable and prudent, whereas in that difficult and dangerous country, any other course was needlessly venturesome. In one of those wild glens it was not always easy to learn what mischief might be brewing in another, and in issuing from the steep and narrow passes one might come upon ruin unawares. But Rosecrans in an evil hour chose the alternative of pushing through the mountains, in the hope of cutting off Bragg's southward retreat and annihilating his army on the spot.

<small>Two alternatives.</small>

In adopting this hazardous course Rosecrans was duped by appearances and by treacherous information. Bragg in evacuating Chattanooga had not the slightest intention of retreating. He had come out full of the spirit of fight, to cover his communications and to find his antagonist. But he sent scores of pretended deserters through the mountains and into Chattanooga, telling sad stories of the headlong flight and utter demoralization of the Confederate army. This notion was even, in some unknown way, disseminated in Washington, and Rosecrans received telegrams from that city which confirmed him in his false impressions. Accordingly he ordered Crittenden to leave one brigade in Chat-

<small>Rosecrans chooses the wrong one.</small>

tanooga, and with all the rest of his corps pursue the enemy along the railroad to Ringgold and Dalton. He sent Thomas's corps through two rugged gaps in Lookout Mountain into McLemore's Cove; and he pushed forward McCook from Valley Head to Alpine and Summerville. Such movements were hardly justifiable except against a beaten and demoralized enemy. The orders were issued on the 9th of September, and it was not until the 12th that Rosecrans discovered his frightful mistake. No wonder if the suddenness of the discovery somewhat shook his nerves. The situation was appalling. The Union army was separated into three parts over a distance of fifty-seven miles from Ringgold to Alpine, for McCook had luckily taken the alarm and gone no farther. These three corps numbered each scarcely 20,000 men; and between them at Lafayette, close in front of the Union centre, was Bragg's whole army in excellent condition and reinforced by troops from Mississippi, so that it numbered full 55,000! It looked as if Rosecrans were going to end his brilliant campaign by seeing his army annihilated corps by corps, for he could not possibly draw it together in less than three or four days.

Things, however, did not come to such a pass as that. If Lee or Stonewall Jackson had been in Bragg's place, the worst might have happened, but Bragg was too slow in making up his mind.[1] Crittenden moved from Ringgold into Chickamauga valley, near Lee and Gordon's Mill, and Thomas, skilfully withdrawing from the enemy's front and moving along the west side of Missionary Ridge, passed through Cooper's Gap and joined him. But there was woeful delay in making this junction, and the delay was due to the necessity which Thomas was under of waiting for McCook. The latter general was ordered by Rosecrans to march from Alpine through Dougherty's Gap, straight into McLemore's Cove, but being assured by people in the neighbourhood that there was no practicable road that way, he retraced his steps over Lookout Mountain to Valley Head, and marched through Johnson's Crook and Stevens's and Cooper's Gaps

Bragg loses the golden opportunity.

---

[1] A few days before, in a conversation with General Daniel Hill, Bragg had petulantly exclaimed: "It is said to be easy to defend a mountainous country, but mountains hide your foe from you, while they are full of gaps through which he can pounce upon you at any time. A mountain is like the wall of a house full of rat-holes. The rat lies hidden in his hole, ready to pop out when no one is watching. Who can tell what lies behind yonder wall?" The truth is, says General Hill, that Bragg "was bewildered by the popping out of the rats from so many holes. The wide dispersion of the Federal forces, and their confrontal of him at so many points, perplexed him, instead of being a source of congratulation that such grand opportunities were offered for crushing them one by one." *Battles and Leaders,* iii. 641, 644.

into Chickamauga valley. This roundabout route took him five days to traverse, and it was not until the night of the 18th that his corps was entirely closed up on Thomas's right.

Meanwhile the anxiety of Rosecrans had scarcely allowed him to sleep, — and with good reason. Even as it was, with all the enemy's slowness in seizing his advantage, this delay in McCook's movements came near destroying the army. But for this delay no battle need have been fought in Chickamauga valley. If McCook could have come up two days sooner, the army would probably have been concentrated at Chattanooga, holding the crests of Lookout Mountain and Missionary Ridge. Then Rosecrans's mistake would have been retrieved, and Bragg could not have attacked him save at great disadvantage. The delay worked mischief to Rosecrans in two ways. It detained him in Chickamauga valley at least two days longer than there would otherwise have been any need for, and it also allowed time for Bragg to receive a heavy reinforcement from Virginia. Rosecrans was thus not only obliged to fight in the wrong place, but he was obliged to fight against heavy odds. No sooner had the news of the evacuation of Chattanooga reached Richmond than the Confederate government put forth its utmost energies in support of

Evil results of McCook's delay.

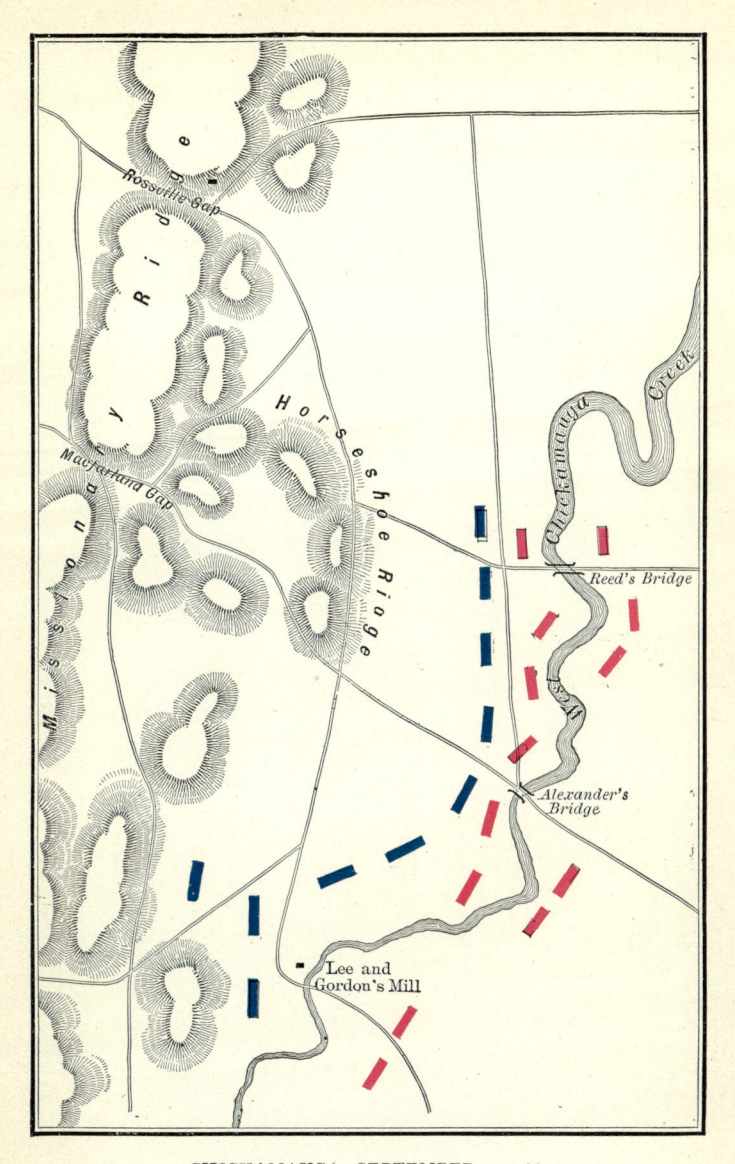

CHICKAMAUGA, SEPTEMBER 19, 1863

Jefferson Davis's favourite commander. General James Longstreet — a host in himself — was detached from Lee's army, with the two fine divisions of Hood and McLaws, and sent in all possible haste to reinforce General Bragg. Under ordinary circumstances this reinforcement would have come directly by rail through eastern Tennessee, but the free use of that road was a privilege which the rebels were never again to enjoy. The Federal occupation of Knoxville and Chattanooga already blocked the way, so that Longstreet was obliged to go around by rail through the Carolinas and Georgia, and come up from At- *Arrival of* lanta to Bragg's assistance. This delay *Longstreet.* was probably our salvation. If Longstreet had been present two or three days earlier, it is not likely that Rosecrans would have been allowed to concentrate his forces without preliminary fighting. Three brigades of Longstreet's corps under General Hood arrived on the 18th, — the same day on which the Federal concentration was completed, — and Bragg, knowing that the rest would soon arrive, made his arrangements for an attack on the following day.

The details of the battle of Chickamauga are somewhat complicated, but its salient points are easy to understand. Both armies were in Chickamauga valley, Rosecrans on the west side of the

creek, Bragg on the east side. It would have been
desirable for Rosecrans, if he could
have done so, to reach Chattanooga
without a battle, and then choose his
own time and place for fighting. His roads
thither lay through McFarland and Rossville Gaps
in Missionary Ridge. If attacked now, he must
hold these roads at whatever cost, and accordingly
he placed Thomas on the left, opposite Reed's and
Alexander's bridges, with McCook on the right
and Crittenden in reserve. He told Thomas that
he should be properly reinforced if it took all the
rest of the army to do it. On the other hand,
Bragg's object was to attack the Federal left in
flank, drive it back in confusion on the centre, and
seize the roads through Rossville and McFarland
Gaps, thus interposing his victorious army between
Chattanooga and the defeated Federals. His plan
of battle was much the same as at Stone river,
except that now he was to pivot on his left wing
and press forward with his right. But its issue
was very different from what it had been at Stone
river. The attack which he had planned was a
failure from the outset, but a sudden catastrophe
in a different part of the field — an accident which
was not down on anybody's programme — threw
victory into his hands. He did not open the battle
clearly and vigorously, as at Stone river. Before

The problem at Chickamauga.

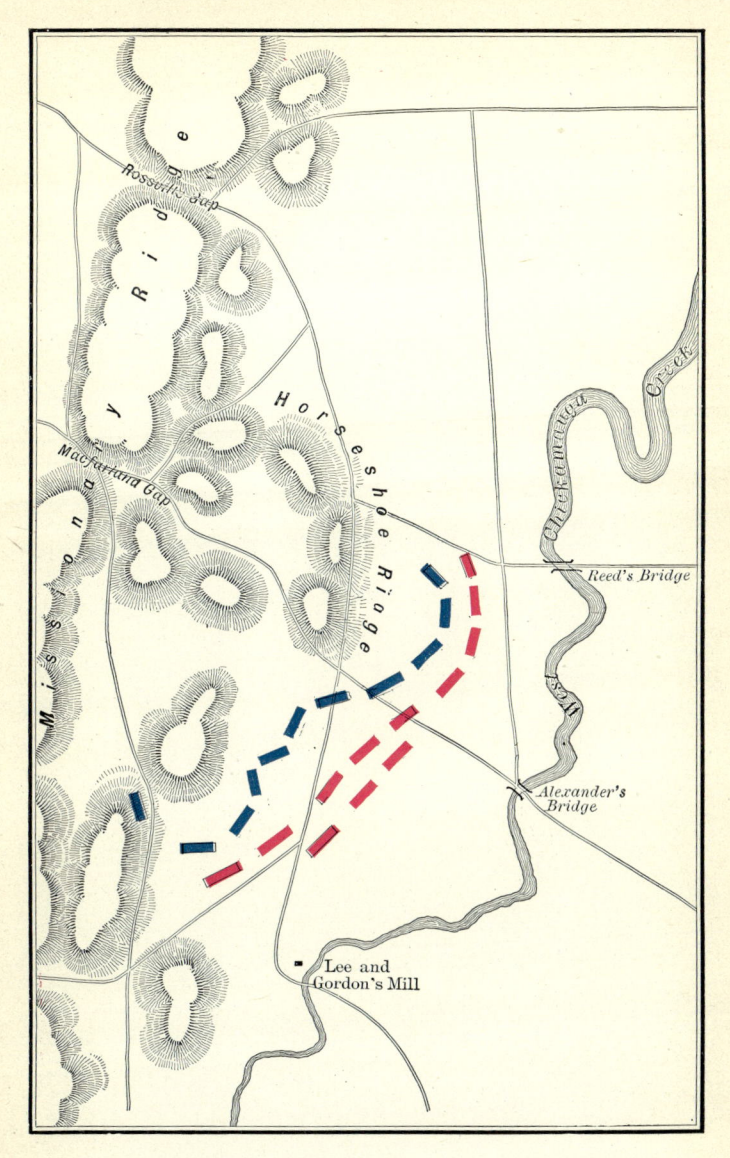

CHICKAMAUGA, SEPTEMBER 20, 1863, MORNING

his preparations were completed, he discovered that the Federal lines extended much farther to the north than he had supposed, so that he was himself obliged to draw northward. While he was accomplishing this movement, on the morning of the 19th, one of his brigades got entangled with one of Thomas's brigades, and rein- *First day of* forcements coming up first from one *the battle.* side and then from the other, the skirmish quickly grew into a battle, which raged till nightfall. It was a series of desperate charges and countercharges, the prelude to a still more deadly fight on the morrow. At the close of the day Thomas's grasp upon the Rossville road was even firmer than at the beginning, so that the advantage was, on the whole, with the Federals.

During the night Longstreet arrived with the remainder of his corps, and Bragg somewhat improved the arrangement of his troops, bringing all his infantry across the creek, and placing Polk in command on his right and Longstreet on his left. His plan was the same as the day before — to wheel on his left as a pivot and turn the Federal left. Polk attacked vigorously between nine and ten o'clock. Thomas held his own as sturdily as before, but was obliged to call for reinforcements, and Rosecrans began weakening his right in order to support him. While this was going on, the catastrophe occurred which gave away the battle to the enemy. Near the centre of the Federal line, where the shock of battle had not yet arrived, three divisions were posted in zigzag fashion. The first of these was Reynolds's division; next on the right was Brannan's, considerably refused to the right and hidden among trees; next was Wood's division, nearly at right angles to Brannan's. About noon an aide of General Thomas, riding along the line and not seeing Brannan's men in their screened position, too hastily translated his first crude impression into a fact and, on reaching Thomas, informed him that there was an empty space between Reynolds and Wood. Thomas instantly transmitted the false information to Rosecrans. Now Rosecrans would have known better, had it not been for one thing. Some time before, the place now occupied by Wood had been occupied by Negley; but Negley had been sent to the left to reinforce Thomas, and Rosecrans had ordered Wood to take his place. This had all been done, and the line was all as it should be. But when Rosecrans heard that there was a gap in the line, he naturally supposed that Wood had not yet quite got into position, and he sent an aide to hasten his movements. The aide thus gave the order in writing: "The General Commanding directs that

The fatal order.

"The General commanding directs that you close up on Reynolds as fast as possible and support him"

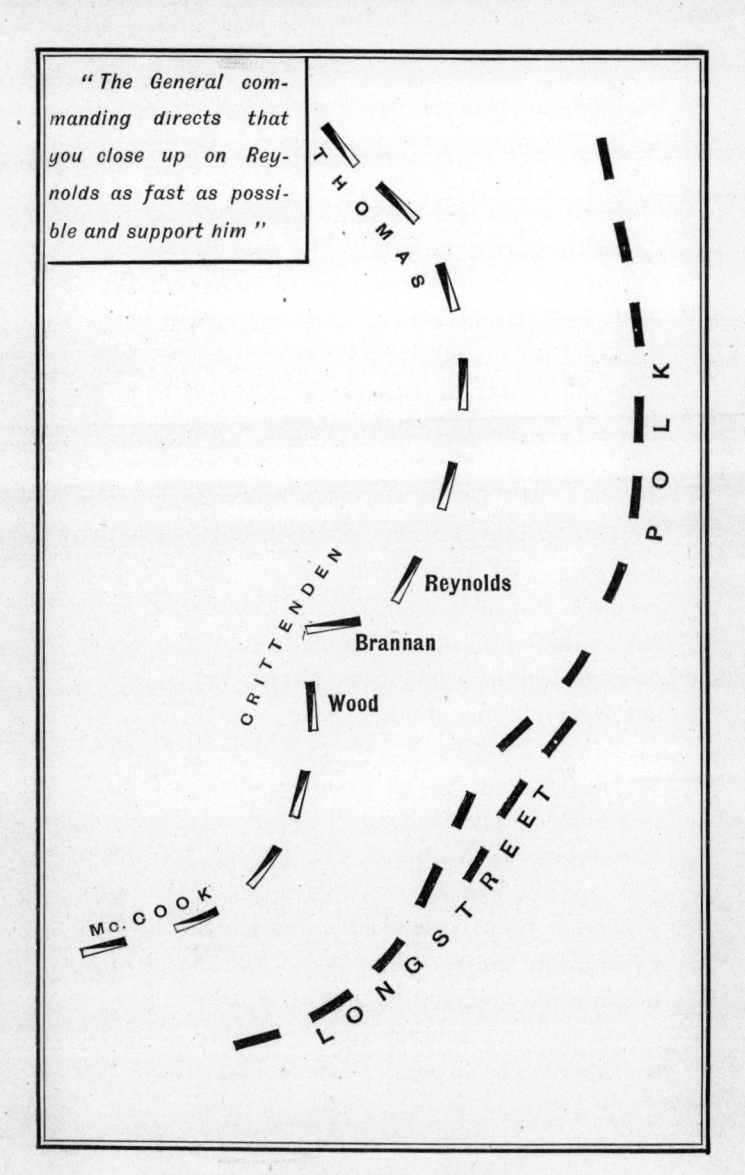

CHICKAMAUGA: THE FATAL ORDER TO WOOD

you close up on Reynolds as fast as possible, and support him." He should have said " close up on Brannan." General Wood was naturally bewildered by such a mysterious order. How could he close up on Reynolds, when there was Brannan's whole division in line between them? He could not close up on him, but he might support him by passing around Brannan's rear. This, thought Wood, must be what Rosecrans meant, and so with all promptness he moved his division accordingly, leaving a great empty space in the very middle of the battle-front. Thus in the endeavour to fill up an imaginary gap there was created a real gap. It was just such a sort of misunderstanding as is perpetually happening in the little ordinary affairs of life. How often do we witness innocent but awkward blunders arising from hasty observation and lack of precision in the use of language! But war has no pity for innocent blunders. General Longstreet would have willingly sacrificed ten thousand men to make such a hole in the Federal line as General Wood had just left there. For some little time the battle had been surging along down the line toward the centre, and just at this moment *The dire catastrophe.* Longstreet received Bragg's order to attack. Into the dreadful opening which Wood's movement had left, Longstreet poured eight brigades, one after another, in an overwhelming mass. The Federal divisions on either side were slammed out of place "like doors swung back on their hinges and shattered by the blow." The whole right wing was taken on its left flank, completely torn away from the rest of the army, and swept off the field in utter and hopeless rout. The heroic exertions of division and brigade commanders were all in vain. Nothing human could stand when struck in such a fashion. Rallying was out of the question; there was nothing to be done but get out of the way. Rosecrans was caught in the throng and whirled off the field, and so were McCook and Crittenden. The cannon were all in the enemy's hands. The road to McFarland Gap was crowded with fugitives. More than half the Federal army was in full flight. Not an officer above a division-commander was left on this part of the field.

Happily, however, it was not the Federal right wing that held the key of the position. That key was the Rossville road, which Thomas had been holding like a vise ever since yesterday morning. If the enemy were to gain that road and interpose between Thomas and Missionary Ridge, they could force him to surrender on the spot. The Army of the Cumberland would be annihilated. Chattanooga would be lost, and the rebel army, flushed with a victory far

A critical moment.

greater than any they had yet won, a victory compared to which even Chancellorsville was nothing, would in a few weeks plant their batteries before Nashville, perhaps before Cincinnati. Such mighty issues rested that afternoon upon the shoulders of one great man. It was a crisis scarcely less terrible than that of Gettysburg. But the occasion was never found to which Thomas proved unequal. The more disasters thickened about him, the more grandly did that noble Virginian defy them. Calm and imperturbable at all times, his clear head was never at a loss for resources. The extent of the disaster upon the right was first revealed to him by the appalling sight of huge masses of the enemy coming toward his flank instead of the reinforcements for which he was so earnestly looking, — a sight fit to shake the stoutest nerves! Retreat was inevitable, but nothing was allowed to loosen his hold upon the position he had undertaken to defend. Less than a mile in his rear there was a curved ridge known as the Horseshoe, convex toward the enemy's front, and over this horseshoe ran the Rossville road, that goal of the enemy's efforts. To this ridge Thomas retreated, and on its most favourable points skilfully planted his artillery; and gathering there some 25,000 men, stood like a rock, which the angry waves of war might buffet in vain. Long afterward men

spoke of him as the "Rock of Chickamauga."
For six weary hours those 25,000 men — their
numbers lessening moment by moment
till nearly 10,000 were stretched upon
the ground — stood at bay and hurled back again
and again the furious onset of 60,000 rebels mad
with desire to clutch the prize they had so nearly
won. Riding to and fro among his men as quietly
as if on parade, infusing them all with his own
great spirit, quick to see each emergency as it
came and to meet it with some fresh device, the
hero held his ground. At one moment early in
the afternoon, the rebel lines were extended so
far beyond our left as to threaten the Rossville
road, when their advance was suddenly checked
by the arrival of that superb soldier, the rough
and ready Gordon Granger, with 4000 men. He
had marched without orders to the sound of the
cannon, and the tremendous energy with which he
supported Thomas is shown by the fact that nearly
half his men were killed or wounded before dusk.
As evening approached it was discovered that the
last cartridge had been fired. In the wild turmoil
which attended the rout of the right wing some-
body had ordered the removal of all the ammunition trains, and powder and ball were no more to
be had save by searching among the dead bodies
of friend and foe. Then with grim determination

Marginal note: Terrific fighting.

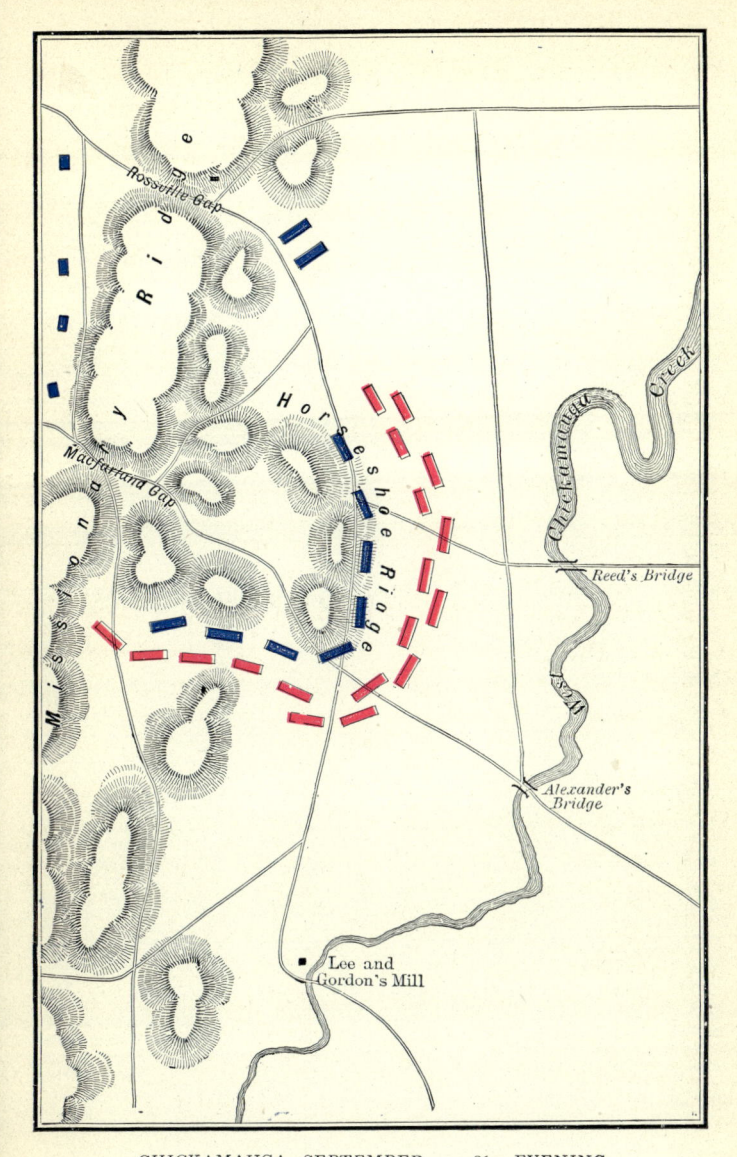

CHICKAMAUGA, SEPTEMBER 20, 1863, EVENING

bayonets were fixed. Longstreet, loath to own himself baffled, had sent to Bragg for reinforcements, but none were forthcoming. "He told me," says Longstreet, "that the men had been beaten back so badly that they could be of no service to me." With such portions of his corps as still retained some freshness, Longstreet attempted a last assault, but his men were driven down the hillside with cold steel and with muskets used as clubs. Their strength was exhausted; they were baulked of their prey; and night found Thomas still master of the Rossville road, and the Union army saved from destruction. The annals of warfare may be searched in vain for a grander spectacle; and in the years to come, so long as American children are born to love and serve their country, rescued at such dreadful cost from anarchy and dishonour, may they be taught to revere the glorious name of Thomas, the Rock of Chickamauga!

The Rock of Chickamauga.

When Rosecrans was swept away in the tide of fugitives, he at first made every effort to turn down a road which led through the valley straight to Thomas's position. But learning that this road was occupied by the enemy, he kept on through McFarland Gap, attended by General Garfield, his chief of staff, hoping to return by the Rossville road and thus make his way to Thomas. They found Rossville Gap choked with stragglers and teamsters fleeing toward Chattanooga, and were told that Thomas was killed, and the whole army knocked to pieces. Some soldiers from Negley's division told Rosecrans that their comrades were all coming close upon their heels in disorderly flight. Now as Negley's was one of the last fresh divisions he had sent to the left in support of Thomas, Rosecrans was convinced that the worst must be true. While they were talking there came one of those lulls which every now and then interrupt the din of battle. Leaping from their horses, Rosecrans and Garfield laid their ears to the ground to detect, if possible, the meaning of the distant murmur. There was no boom of cannon, only a faint and fitful crackle of musketry from different quarters of the field. It was one of the moments when Thomas had hurled back the rebel masses in disorder, and they were waiting to reform their lines for a fresh onset. But to the anxious listeners the scattered sounds seemed only to confirm the stories, but too probable, which had just been told them. If these stories were true, the fragments of the army — all save such as must have surrendered — would soon be pouring through the passes to Chattanooga, and the best thing to be done was to get there as soon as possible and

Chickamauga 277

begin preparations for withstanding a siege. So Garfield advised, and so Rosecrans did, while Garfield rode to the front to learn how things were faring.

About four o'clock Rosecrans rode up to the door of the adjutant-general's office in Chattanooga, faint and ill. During this week that he had been drawing together his scattered forces, he had slept but little; and on this second day of battle he had been in the saddle since early dawn, with nothing to eat. The officers who helped him into the house did not soon forget the terrible look of the brave man stunned by sudden calamity.[1] Presently McCook and Crittenden came in, and not long after a despatch from Garfield telling how he had found Thomas. Rosecrans read it aloud, and waving it in the air shouted, "Thank God! the day is not lost; gentlemen, go at once to the front." But it was too

---

[1] In later years I used occasionally to meet Rosecrans, and always felt that I could see the shadow of Chickamauga upon his noble face. The first time that I was introduced to him I was reminded of the strange look that haunted the face of the mother of Barnaby Rudge; a look that remained amid all changes of expression, the dim but abiding shadow of a look to which an instant of terrible and overwhelming experience only could have given birth. Afterward I always noticed this look, and am sure that it was not merely in my fancy. (See *Barnaby Rudge*, chap. v.)

late now to turn defeat into victory. It was Garfield that should have gone to Chattanooga, and Rosecrans that should have gone to the front. On the roads about Missionary Ridge there were brigades and divisions moving aimlessly for want of a chief, and Thomas had so drawn upon himself the whole fury of the rebel attack that these scattered fragments of the army were but feebly molested. Could Rosecrans have stayed on the field and exerted himself, as he had done so gallantly at Stone river, in forming a new line of battle, perhaps the issue might have been similar to the issue of that memorable contest. For there was a moment when the three divisions of Negley, Sheridan, and Davis, thrown against the left of the enemy assailing Thomas, might perhaps have restored the battle; but each general, following his own judgment, chose a different route, and neither arrived at a position where he could effect the result. The only commander who succeeded in rendering valuable assistance to Thomas was Gordon Granger, as we have seen, who was guided simply by the din of battle and his common sense. At night, in pursuance of an order from Rosecrans, Thomas moved quietly away from Horseshoe Ridge, and the whole army was drawn up at Rossville Gap and on the heights

Chickamauga

adjoining, where it remained all the next day unmolested. On the morning of the 22d it had all been retired to Chattanooga.

The name "Chickamauga" has been said to mean "Valley of Death," in allusion, perhaps, to some wholesale Indian slaughter of long ago. However that may have been, the place had now fairly earned such a sombre epithet. In its dimensions and in its murderousness the battle of Chickamauga was the greatest battle fought by our western armies, and one of the greatest of modern times. In our Civil War it was exceeded only by Gettysburg and the Wilderness; in European history one may compare with it such battles as Neerwinden, or Malplaquet, or Waterloo. At Shiloh and Stone river there were about 80,000 men engaged, and in each the total losses in killed and wounded were about 20,000, the opposing armies and their losses being in each case nearly equal. At Chickamauga there were not less than 130,000 men engaged, and the total losses in killed, wounded, and missing amounted to nearly 37,000; but the figures on the two sides were not evenly matched. Rosecrans had begun the campaign with about 70,000 men, but had to leave detachments to guard his stores at Stevenson and to occupy other important points, so that he brought about 62,000 men

Awful slaughter.

into the field. Bragg, after his reinforcements from Virginia arrived, must have had about 70,000 men. The Union loss was nearly 17,000, while that of the Confederates was not far from 20,000, a large proportion of which was incurred in the furious and futile assaults at Horseshoe Ridge.

CHAPTER VIII

CHATTANOOGA

IN retiring into Chattanooga, Rosecrans felt obliged to take a step which soon threatened to imperil the army even more than the ordeal through which it had passed. He withdrew a small force which had been stationed on the point of Lookout Mountain. With the forces then at his disposal this step was doubtless necessary, but its consequences were lamentable. The railroad from Stevenson, crossing the Tennessee river at Bridgeport, passes over a depression in Raccoon Mountain into Lookout valley and runs thence over a narrow ledge, with the river on one hand and the precipitous end of Lookout Mountain on the other, into Chattanooga. This was the only line of railroad by which supplies could be brought to the beleaguered army, and the only way to hold it was to hold Lookout Mountain. But Rosecrans did not think it practicable to keep up communication between his army in and about the town and the detachment on the mountain, and accordingly he

Rosecrans in Chattanooga is besieged by Bragg.

withdrew the latter. In doing this, of course, he did not abandon his only method of getting supplies. He retained one avenue for that purpose, but it was a very poor one, and the immediate consequences of loosening his hold upon the railroad were alarming. Bragg instantly occupied the mountain, and placed batteries there commanding railroad and river. On the east his forces occupied the crest of Missionary Ridge, about 400 feet above the level of the town, and patrolled the bank of the river for some miles. From water to water he held the Union army invested in a semicircle. The only route by which food could come was a narrow and crooked wagon-road over Waldron's Ridge from Bridgeport through Jasper, a distance of sixty miles. Such a line of supply was a sorry dependence for 40,000 men with their animals, added to the population of the little town; and Bragg, well knowing how precarious it was, sat down to compass the starvation of the Federal army.

Longstreet advocated a bolder method. He recommended crossing the river in full force above Chattanooga and threatening the Nashville railroad so as to cut off Rosecrans's retreat and compel him to come out and fight at a disadvantage; after which the Confederates might move up through eastern Tennessee, crush Burnside, and invade Kentucky. But Bragg's mood was not sufficiently sanguine for such an enterprise, and he felt that he made much surer of his prey by simply wait- *Wheeler attacks the supply trains.* ing. For some days the wagons, wearily jolting over the rough mountain road, brought food and blankets and ammunition with some degree of promptness. Then came General Joseph Wheeler, on the 1st of October, with four or five brigades of rebel cavalry, and burned 300 well-stocked wagons and slew their 1800 mules. To stop this dangerous work a strong force of Union cavalry from Bridgeport spent a week in fighting Wheeler and driving him back across the river.

Then heavy rains came on, and proved a worse foe than the rebel troopers. The poor mules could scarcely tug their wagons through the deep mud, and as the delay shortened their forage, they grew weak from hunger and dropped by the way till all passing was blocked. The trips to Bridgeport took longer and longer, each new trip brought back fewer wagons, and every day the rations for man and beast grew smaller. The artillery horses, being least needed at the mo- *The peril from rains.* ment, fared worse in the scanty allotment of forage, and died by hundreds. On the road and within the Union lines more than 10,000 mules and horses perished. Thus the army, unable to haul its artillery, soon became practically immovable. It could not retreat without inviting destruction, and remaining where it was, gaunt famine stared it in the face. Bragg might well believe that all he had to do was to wait.

But the United States government was awakening to the needs of the occasion. If Lee's army could be temporarily weakened in behalf of Bragg, it was safe to take from Meade in order to give to Rosecrans. It had not at first been thought necessary to do this, because Burnside was in eastern Tennessee with 25,000 men, only 100 miles from Chattanooga, and almost daily since the 11th of September Lincoln and Halleck had been telegraphing him to go to Rosecrans without a moment's delay. If he had moved when first notified, his corps would have been present at Chickamauga, and the story of that battle might have been different. But there were difficulties in the way which to a man of Burnside's make-up seemed insuperable; and he never got quite ready to start. As the dangers thickened, the Eleventh and Twelfth corps, numbering 23,000 men, were detached from the Army of the Potomac, and sent, under command of General Hooker, to the rescue. They went by rail around through Ohio and thence southward, with all their baggage and artillery, making the circuit of 1200

Arrival of Hooker with two corps.

miles from the Rapidan to Stevenson in about a week. On October 3 Hooker established his headquarters at Stevenson. Once arrived on the scene, his first business was to assist in opening communications with the beleaguered army.

On the 19th of October, before this work had begun, Rosecrans was removed from command. President Lincoln had made up his mind that at this critical juncture of affairs the presence of the conqueror of Vicksburg was needed. Grant was called north from Mississippi, and met the Secretary of War at Indianapolis. He then learned that he was placed in command of all the forces between the Mississippi and the Alleghanies, and two orders were shown him, the one retaining Rosecrans in command of the Army of the Cumberland, the other removing Rosecrans and putting Thomas in his place. It was left for Grant to choose which he would have, and without a moment's hesitation he selected Thomas. Sherman succeeded Grant in command of the Army of the Tennessee. Rosecrans was sent to command the department of Missouri. McCook and Crittenden went home to await an investigation of the disaster at Chickamauga;[1] and their two depleted corps, consolidated into one, were given to Gordon Granger.

Rosecrans superseded by Thomas.

[1] "McCook . . . seemed at Perryville, Stone river, and Chick-

Grant's first telegram to Thomas was, "Hold Chattanooga at all hazards; I will be there as soon as possible." Thomas replied, "We will hold the town till we starve." To some that time seemed not far off. There were officers who had nothing to eat but rancid pork and mouldy bread, and kernels of parched corn had come to be reckoned a luxury. A week ago Jefferson Davis had visited Bragg at his headquarters. Ascending Lookout Mountain and climbing to the top of a jagged rock on its summit, known as Pulpit Rock, the President of the Confederacy surveyed the

amauga, pursued by a strange fatality. He assumed a kind of boastful over-confidence that in war always presages failure, because it takes the place of the careful preparation that secures success. . . . He possessed a peculiar open frankness of manner and *bonhomie* that made him many friends, and he had many admirable traits of character. . . . Crittenden was greatly beloved by his men. He was always genial, kind, just, and brave to a fault; and as he came to my brigade, which was drawn up to bid him farewell, mounted on his beautiful gray horse, . . . and made us an admirable, almost electrical, little speech, if it had been in my power I would have made him commander-in-chief of the armies. . . . Now came the new régime. But already, before their arrival, and with the assumption of command by Thomas, our hopes went up with a great bound. . . . Grant and Sherman were different from the commanders we had known before. They wore vests and coats unbuttoned; and as to military bearing, old Frederick would not have had them in his camp. . . . But they had from the start, and always retained, the perfect confidence of the army; and that faith was not misplaced." Hazen's *Narrative of Military Service*, pp. 152. 153, 164.

scene before him with exultation, and prophesied the speedy surrender of the Federal army. But the tables were soon and most unexpectedly to be turned. When Grant arrived at Chattanooga, on the evening of the 23d, he found that Thomas had already ordered Hooker to concentrate his forces at Bridgeport with a view to opening a new line of communications.

Grant arrives at Chattanooga.

An admirable plan had been conceived by General William Farrar Smith, — familiarly known to the soldiers as "Baldy" Smith, — chief engineer of the Army of the Cumberland. On the 19th of October, the day on which Rosecrans was superseded, General Smith was reconnoitring the banks of the Tennessee river in the neighbourhood of Brown's Ferry, when this beautiful scheme occurred to him. Next day, on his return to Chattanooga, finding General Thomas in command of the army, Smith imparted to him his plan. On the 22d Thomas issued the needful orders for putting it into operation; and when Grant arrived, a day later, he gave it his hearty approval. It was an indispensable preliminary to the brilliant operations which followed, and some writers have shown a disposition to claim the credit of it for Grant. It was certainly creditable to Grant's military judgment that he

General "Baldy" Smith.

instantly recognized the merit of the plan, as Thomas had already done. But there can be no doubt that the plan originated with Smith, and would have been carried out exactly as it was, even if Grant had remained in Mississippi. Let us now observe the features of this famous scheme.

Opposite the point of Lookout Mountain the river makes a great bend, enclosing a peninsula some three miles in length by less than a mile in width, known as Moccasin Point. Opposite the lower side of this peninsula a narrow range of hills runs along close by the water's edge, with a gap at Brown's Ferry. A road from opposite Chattanooga runs across the neck of the peninsula to Brown's Ferry, and thence continues nearly southward along a deep gorge between the narrow range of hills and the base of Raccoon Mountain until, as it enters Lookout valley, it curves westward and passes over a depression in Raccoon Mountain to Kelly's Ferry. Over this same depression runs the wagon-road from Bridgeport to Wauhatchie in Lookout valley, and also the railroad from Bridgeport to Chattanooga. Now the railroad, passing close under the point of Lookout Mountain and through the rebel lines, could not of course be wrested from the enemy without storming the mountain. But the banks of the river below Kelly's Ferry to

The Brown's Ferry scheme.

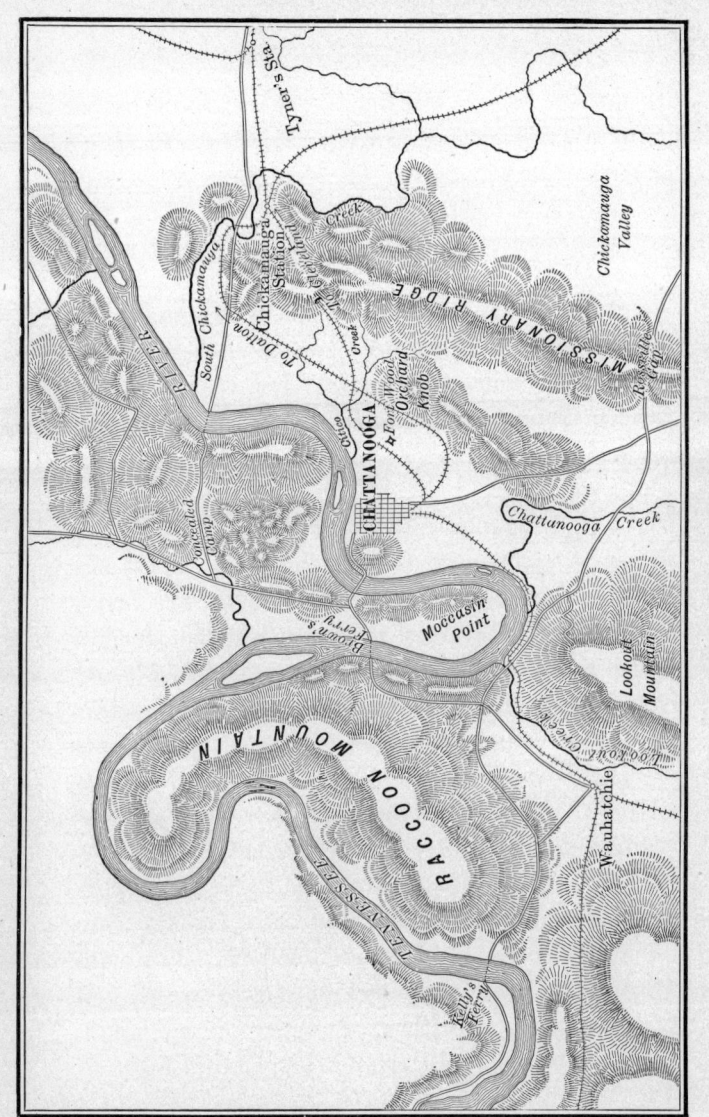

ENVIRONS OF CHATTANOOGA, OCTOBER-NOVEMBER, 1863

Bridgeport were entirely free from rebels, and obviously, if the wagon-road through the gorge could be secured, it would make an excellent line of communications. Supplies to any amount could be brought up the river in steamboats to Kelly's Ferry, and from that point hauled in wagons through the gorge to Brown's Ferry, and thence across the neck of the peninsula to Chattanooga, twice crossing the river by pontoon bridges. By this route the distance to be traversed by wagons was only eight miles. In order to get possession of this route it was necessary to secure the narrow range of hills and place a strong force in Lookout valley. Such a scheme needed such an auxiliary force as Hooker's to carry it into operation. Now under General Smith's personal supervision it was executed with complete success. Although a staff-officer, he was entrusted with the requisite command over troops to make the enterprise completely his own; a point in which Thomas and Grant showed true wisdom.

In order to secure the narrow range of hills profound secrecy was required, for if the Confederates were to divine the scheme and occupy the hills in force, they could not be dislodged without a desperate and doubtful fight. The north end of Lookout valley was occupied by a Confederate brigade, which could be reinforced to any extent by the short road around the point of Lookout Mountain. The problem was to seize the narrow range of hills by stealth, lodge Hooker with a strong force in Lookout valley, and establish a route by which he could be reinforced at pleasure from Chattanooga. At the end of three days the pontoon bridges were ready, the ground had been duly reconnoitred, and everybody had his instructions. At three o'clock on the foggy morning of the 27th fifty-two pontoon boats, each containing twenty-five picked men, 1300 in all, commanded by General William Hazen,[1] were started from Chattanooga and glided noiselessly down with the swift current, with no tell-tale plash of oars. In two hours' time they had landed at Brown's Ferry, driven away a rebel picket force, and taken possession of the narrow range of hills. While this was going on, General Smith, with a force of 2700 men, and three batteries, marched across the neck of Moccasin Point to Brown's Ferry, where they crossed in the pontoon boats and ascended the hills. The range was thus held throughout its whole length by 4000 men, who speedily felled trees and made a formidable abattis, while they planted their three batteries on the end toward Lookout valley in such wise as to sweep the narrow road around the point of

Its complete success.

[1] For the numbers, see Hazen's *Narrative*, pp. 154, 161.

Lookout Mountain, by which alone the Confederates could send troops into the valley without climbing over the mountain. These 4000 men could defend such a position against three or four times their own number. As soon as they had crossed the river the work on the pontoon bridge was vigorously begun, so that by ten o'clock in the forenoon an excellent and secure road was in Grant's possession, direct from Chattanooga to the mouth of Lookout valley, and over this road he could send troops into the valley much faster than the Confederates could send them around the point of the mountain.

The next morning Hooker started from Bridgeport, with part of the Eleventh corps, under Howard, and one division of the Twelfth, under Geary, something over 10,000 men in all, and marched along the railroad to Wauhatchie, where he arrived late in the afternoon and took possession of all the roads in the valley. The single Confederate brigade there could do nothing but get out of his way, and a few shells from the batteries at the top of Lookout Mountain did little harm. But by midnight Longstreet had brought the greater part of his corps into the valley and assaulted Hooker in force. It was a wild scene under the uncertain light of the moon, with the cannon reverberating

Hooker occupies Lookout valley.

among the mountains. By four in the morning Hooker was master of the field, and Longstreet had retreated into his camp in Chattanooga valley. To complete the whole scheme, Palmer's division had been sent some days before around by the road over Waldron's Ridge and through Jasper, to hold the road by which Hooker had advanced, and this movement was duly executed.

The enemy made no further attempt to dislodge Hooker, and by the bridge at Brown's Ferry Grant could quickly reinforce him to any extent required. The new line of communications, through Brown's and Kelly's ferries, was now completely secured, *The siege of Chattanooga is raised.* wagons loaded with rations came rumbling into Chattanooga every few hours, and all danger of famine was at an end. Still more, by Hooker's new position the Army of the Cumberland was joined to its reinforcements from the Army of the Potomac, and its effective strength thus became equal to the enemy's. The siege of Chattanooga was virtually raised, and the situation in Lookout valley boded no good to Braxton Bragg. It is such beautiful operations as this that make military history a fascinating study. In all its details we perceive the touch of a master hand. Grant showed his appreciation by recommending Smith for promotion to the rank of major-general, saying, "No man in the service is better qualified than he for our largest commands."[1]

Bragg was sorely chagrined at this collapse of his hopes of starving the Union army, but he did not begin to imagine what his adversary had in store for him. He did not see what the Brown's Ferry affair foreboded. So little did he dream that the Federals would soon be ready to resume the offensive, that on the 3d of November he sent Longstreet with 20,000 men and 80 guns to annihilate Burnside, or chase him out of eastern Tennessee. After having accomplished this task, Longstreet was to return.

Bragg sends away Longstreet.

Bragg has been severely criticised for thus weakening his army at such a crisis. It was a grave mistake and hardly excusable. Bragg must have known that the fate of Chattanooga would have to be settled by a battle; and it ought to have been clear to him that if he won that battle, Knoxville would be at his mercy, while if he lost it, Knoxville would be relieved. To risk the loss of the battle at Chattanooga, in order to pick from

---

[1] It was also appreciated by the enemy, as witness the following, from the Richmond *Press:* "The admirably conceived and perfectly executed *coup* at Brown's Ferry . . . has robbed the Confederacy of all its dearly earned advantages gained at Chickamauga." Hazen's *Narrative*, p. 164.

the bough an apple that was sure to drop into his lap if he won it, would seem the height of imbecility. Yet Bragg was no fool. Though he had not the divine spark of genius, he was an adversary whom it was creditable to beat. It was reported and believed by some people that Jefferson Davis, on his visit to Bragg, devised the Knoxville expedition for Longstreet because he and Bragg did not get on well together. General Grant, while mentioning this report, humorously suggests an alternative explanation : " It may be that Longstreet was not sent to Knoxville for the reason stated, but because Mr. Davis had an exalted opinion of his own military genius, and thought he saw a chance of 'killing two birds with one stone.' On several occasions during the war he came to the relief of the Union army by means of his *superior military genius*." [1]

Why did he do so?

But supposing that Bragg himself originated or approved the sending away of Longstreet, although the blunder does not admit of excuse, we can nevertheless perhaps understand how it may have happened. Bragg knew that the Federal army was at that moment in no fit condition to attack him in his strong positions. The best illustration of this was what happened immediately upon Longstreet's departure. No sooner had Grant

[1] Grant's *Memoirs*, ii. 87. The italicizing is Grant's.

observed this weakening of the enemy's force than he proposed to Thomas an assault upon Missionary Ridge, in the hope of recalling Longstreet and relieving Burnside, in accordance with the frantic telegrams which kept coming from Washington. From the tone of some of the despatches one would gather that neither Lincoln, Stanton, nor Halleck had a particle of confidence in Burnside's ability to take care of himself, and the question is forcibly suggested, why was he kept so persistently in important commands? To return to Grant, when he proposed the assault upon Missionary Ridge, Thomas reminded him that the artillery horses were all dead, and so long as cannon could not be hauled, the mobility of the army was like that of a man with his legs cut off.

A possible explanation.

Bragg knew, indeed, that the Union army was expecting further reinforcements. He knew that Sherman was coming from Mississippi with part of the army which had captured Vicksburg. Halleck had ordered this movement soon after the defeat at Chickamauga. Sherman had started from Vicksburg on September 27, and in steamboats accomplished the 400 miles to Memphis by October 2. He had then before him 400 miles of marching in order to get within reach of Chattanooga; and Halleck, true to his snail-like traditions, had ordered him to repair the railroad yard by yard as he advanced; that same blessed old railroad, for the sake of which Halleck had once sacrificed Buell's hopes of success, and God knows how many thousand lives! Thus hampered, Sherman plodded along at such a rate that the 27th of October — a whole month from the time of his leaving Vicksburg — found him only at Iuka, still 200 miles distant from Chattanooga. Thus Sherman, when weighted with Halleck, could move as slowly as Buell, under like circumstances. At this rate Bragg might well reckon that Longstreet could proceed 100 miles to Knoxville, crush the feeble Burnside, and get back in time to counteract any movements that might be awaiting the arrival of Sherman. At all events, he knew that a mere demonstration against Burnside would throw Mr. Lincoln and the northern states into a wild panic, and be likely to divert to Knoxville any Union reinforcements that might otherwise be sent to Chattanooga. From this point of view there may have been a grain of sense in Bragg's plan. What ruined it was the unforeseen appointment of Grant to the command of all the western armies. It instantly wrought a combination of energies quite new to Bragg's experience. Since the fall of Vicksburg, Halleck no longer overruled and hampered Grant, but deferred to his judgment. Accordingly the movements in the western theatre of war began to keep time to Grant's ideas and not to Halleck's, and there was an end of that slowness upon which Bragg had counted. On the 24th of October, the morning after his arrival at Chattanooga, Grant sent word to Sherman to "drop everything" and hurry to Stevenson with his entire force. The result was that, in spite of broken bridges and long detours thereby necessitated, Sherman got his army up to Stevenson and Bridgeport by the 14th of November, and next day reported in person to Grant at Chattanooga. At this moment Longstreet, who had encountered unforeseen obstacles to a rapid progress, had got scarcely half way on his march to Knoxville. Throughout the northern states, the anxiety for Burnside was intense, but Sherman's arrival at Chattanooga put a new face upon things, and enabled Grant to strike a blow so tremendous that among its far-reaching consequences the rescue of Burnside and the relief of eastern Tennessee appear but as minor incidents.

Arrival of Sherman at Chattanooga.

The wagon-road from Bridgeport through Lookout valley and the narrow gorge to Brown's Ferry was now to become a channel for reinforcements as well as supplies. Sherman's whole army was to be moved through it to the north of the river, with a view to crossing again far above, and seizing the extremity of Missionary Ridge. Less than a mile behind Missionary Ridge, at the junction of the railroads to Cleveland in eastern Tennessee and to Dalton in Georgia, was Chickamauga station, where Bragg had his depot of supplies. To get possession of this station, and of the road between Cleveland and Dalton, would by a happy coincidence cut off all supplies not only for Bragg, but also for Longstreet. A point of such vital importance could not be gained without a battle, and it was possible to plan the battle so that in the effort to save this position the enemy should incur shattering defeat. While Hooker was to divert the attention of the Confederates by a vigorous demonstration against Lookout Mountain, Sherman was to attack their right wing near the north end of Missionary Ridge and cut them off from Chickamauga station.

Chickamauga station.

But the task of getting Sherman's force into the neighbourhood of the Confederate right wing was one that called for very delicate management. It was beautifully done. The enemy, looking down from his lofty eminences upon the whole vast field, and seeing the Union army gathered for so long a time before his left and centre, in Lookout

Sherman's stealthy advance toward Chickamauga station.

valley and the plain before Chattanooga, felt little fear for his right, and so the northern end of Missionary Ridge was inadequately guarded. It was of the first importance that Sherman's movement to this point should be hidden. One of his divisions was therefore first moved from Bridgeport into Lookout valley near Trenton, to draw Bragg's attention thither. The remaining divisions were taken along the wagon-road to Brown's Ferry, where they crossed on the pontoon bridge, and then diverged into a road leading due northward quite away from Chattanooga, and losing itself to sight among densely wooded hills. Here, a couple of miles north of the river, Sherman had a concealed camp. The enemy, seeing the troops cross at Brown's Ferry, but observing no further indications of their presence north of the river, very naturally concluded that they were going to Knoxville to relieve Burnside. So completely was Bragg hoodwinked that on the very eve of battle he sent away two divisions to reinforce Longstreet, and was able to get only one of them back again in time to be of service. At the same time he seems to have thought it possible to scare Grant by declaring his intention of attacking him, and thus prevent his sending any more forces in the same direction. This was perhaps the weakest thing Bragg ever did. He sent Grant a letter, saying,

"As there may still be some non-combatants in Chattanooga, I deem it proper to notify you that prudence would dictate their early withdrawal."

Grant was not the bird to be caught with such chaff. He was inclined to regard the letter as designed to cover an intention of retreat, and was confirmed in this impression by the story of a deserter. He did not wish Bragg to get away unpunished, and accordingly on the 23d of November Thomas was ordered to make a demonstration in force. Thomas's line was in front of Chattanooga, facing Missionary Ridge. It consisted of the three corps of Granger, Palmer, and Howard, the latter having been detached from Hooker. In all Thomas had about 30,000 men. At two in the afternoon they advanced with such deliberate precision that for a while the rebels supposed them to be on parade, but presently they made a sudden rush forward and captured a mound known as Orchard Knob and a low range of hills forming the enemy's front line of entrenchments. This demonstration showed the Confederates in full force on Missionary Ridge, but it accomplished much more. During the night this advanced line was fortified and crowned with artillery, for dragging which horses were borrowed from Sherman. Two days later, in the closing scene of the battle, this artillery played

Capture of Orchard Knob and adjacent line of hills.

an important part in protecting the assault upon the Confederate centre. Still another effect was produced. This preliminary attack in front caused Bragg that night to weaken his left wing on Lookout Mountain by withdrawing one strong division in order to transfer it to his extreme right. The observed presence of Howard's corps on Thomas's left, near Citico creek, made him think it wise to guard that all-important quarter somewhat more strongly.

This strengthening of the Confederate right was destined to work an important change in Grant's plan of battle. Sherman's march on the 24th was delayed by many obstacles, and at last he was separated from his rear division by a sudden rise of the river, which broke down the pontoon bridge at Brown's Ferry. To replace this loss, Thomas sent him Davis's division, and thus he went on in full strength. Following the route through his concealed camp, Sherman threw a pontoon bridge across the river, a little below the mouth of the South Chickamauga creek, and above the extreme right of the Confederate army. Having completed his crossing about noon, he moved on three divisions *en échelon*, his left leading up the left bank of the creek, until all arrived at the terminal slopes of Missionary Ridge, where the Dalton railroad runs along their base.

Breaking of a bridge.

By four o'clock Sherman had secured the adjacent summits, and began massing the three divisions there, while Davis's division was left to guard the rear as far back as the pontoon bridge.

But now this brilliant general was rudely reminded that there is many a slip betwixt the cup and the lip. Up to this moment the crest of Missionary Ridge, as viewed from below and from a distance, had appeared to be continuous, so that Sherman had expected, after ascending it, to march without hindrance southward past the tunnel of the Cleveland railroad, and thus to reach a point where he could cut off the Confederate army from Chickamauga station. Grant had not only looked for this, but he had expected Sherman to get into position on the ridge at such an early hour on the 24th that the great battle might take place on that day. But now it was near sunset when Sherman, looking southward from his new vantage ground, saw before him not a continuous crest, but a yawning valley, with another frowning crest beyond. He had no good topographical map, and hitherto his eye had been deceived because of a crest which lies just to the east of that depression, and viewed from a distance looks continuous with the crests to the north and south of it. Sherman, therefore, had not reached his goal. Neither had he taken

Sherman's disappointment.

the enemy by surprise. For on that frowning crest northward of the tunnel he sees the rebels in force. There were two divisions of them, one of which Bragg had taken from Lookout Mountain the night before. They had hastily fortified themselves upon the knob north of the tunnel, and upon the two tines of the fork to the south of it; and with them were those fine old war-dogs, Hardee and Cleburne! These positions must be carried by storm, and the hour of sunset is too late for such an experiment. So Sherman fortifies himself on his isolated heights and waits for morning. A message from Grant orders him to make his attack at daybreak, and tells him that Thomas will soon support him by an attack on the rebel centre.

Meanwhile, during all this short winter day, most picturesque and stirring events were going on at the extreme right of the Union position. The rear division of Sherman's army, which had been prevented from crossing at Brown's Ferry, remained at Hooker's disposal, considerably increasing his strength. This circumstance led Grant to convert the intended demonstration against Lookout Mountain into an assault sufficiently vigorous to detain the rebel force upon the mountain and prevent Bragg from withdrawing it in order

An effect of the breaking of a bridge; new orders to Hooker.

to strengthen his right wing against Sherman. Hooker was evidently inspired that morning with the ardour of battle that had won for him the sobriquet of " Fighting Joe ; " he sought permission to interpret his orders with sufficient liberality to allow him to storm the summit of the mountain if he should find it feasible, and he received from Thomas instructions to go ahead and do his best. So Hooker began his adventurous movement before daybreak of the 24th. He had three divisions, one from the Army of the Potomac, one from the Army of the Cumberland, one from the Army of the Tennessee, in all about 10,000 men. These divisions had never fought side by side before. The ascent of the mountain was difficult, even if there had been no foe there. On the west side there was no way of getting up save by narrow paths which could be traversed only in single file. An ascent here was impracticable, as the men could be shot down faster than they could advance. But on the other side, near the point of the mountain, there was a good wagon-road winding zigzag to the very top. This road connected the rebels on the mountain with the centre of their army, and to take it would turn their position and put them to flight.

Hooker's troops were in the valley west of Lookout creek which was swollen so that it could not be forded. With two of his divisions he set about building a rude bridge near the mouth of the creek, while the other division, under the dauntless John Geary, marched up to Wauhatchie and, crossing there, began to move diagonally up the steep side of the mountain, always bearing northward so as to reach and round the point, and ultimately gain the wagon-road. The movement was favoured by the absence of the division which Bragg had felt obliged to withdraw in the night; there were still, however, 7000 Confederates in position on the mountain,—quite enough to give them odds against Hooker with his 10,000 lower down. Every available point was entrenched and commanded by artillery, but the Confederate force was not quite sufficient to enable them to make the best use of all these advantages. In many places their guns could not be depressed so as to bear upon Geary's column, which pertinaciously crept along under their muzzles, climbing over boulders, bursting through the tangled underbrush, keeping up a skirmishing fire, and always making progress, while its route was marked by the prostrate bodies of men dying and dead. By noon Geary had reached the point of the mountain, and come out upon the smoother ascent which was traversed by the wagon-road.

Geary's ascent of Lookout Mountain.

Meanwhile Hooker, with his other two divisions,

had finished their bridge and crossed it; and then, pushing straight up toward the peak, connected with Geary's left. As the whole solid force approached the wagon-road, the fight became fiercer. Up and up they went into the clouds, which were settling down upon the lofty summit, until they were lost from sight, and their comrades anxiously watching in Chattanooga valley could hear only the booming of cannon and rattle of musketry far overhead, and catch glimpses of fire flashing from moment to moment through the dark clouds, as if the old mythmaker's notion of the thunderstorm were realized, and elemental spirits were engaged in a deadly struggle for the dominion of the upper air. At four o'clock a messenger came to Thomas with the news that the summit was carried. Well done, "Fighting Joe!" In days to come, whensoever Chancellorsville is mentioned, something will also have to be said of the "battle above the clouds."

The "battle above the clouds."

Next morning, the 25th of November, the air was clear and frosty. The clouds had vanished, and the sun rose bright and dazzling, while thousands of eager eyes were turned towards the top of Lookout Mountain. And over its sharp outline, visible for miles and miles, on the very summit of Pulpit Rock, where Jefferson Davis had stood a few weeks ago and

Presage of victory.

uttered his audacious prophecy, there floated on the morning breeze the lordly stars and stripes. Loud shouts of victory, cheer after cheer, rose up melodiously together from the army below,[1] in earnest of the crowning triumph whereof the air was full of presage.

Victory came, but not in the way that Grant had expected. According to his plan, Hooker was to keep the enemy occupied on Lookout Mountain, while Sherman was to turn his right flank and sever his communications with Chickamauga station, and all this was to be accomplished on the 24th. Now Hooker had done more and Sherman less than was on the programme. Sherman had met with unforeseen obstacles, while Hooker had captured the mountain, so that the Confederates driven thence were at liberty to be transferred to Bragg's right, there to strengthen the resistance to Sherman. At daybreak the movement of troops northward along Missionary Ridge could plainly be detected from the Union lines.

An unexpected situation.

I am particular in emphasizing these points, because a few years ago there was a visible tendency toward the growth of a "Grant legend," in which that general's reputation was made to

[1] Cist, *The Army of the Cumberland*, p. 251; Hazen, *Narrative of Military Service*, p. 172.

suffer from misplaced and undiscriminating praise. Among other things it was asserted by Grant's injudicious admirers that among the world's great fights, the battle of Chattanooga was well-nigh unique in having been fought from beginning to end exactly as it was first planned in the superb brain of the Union commander. Now if anything in this world can be said to be clear, it is that the battle of Chattanooga was not fought as Grant had planned it; while at the same time a correct history of it shows us that one mark of a great general is the ability to modify his plans on the spur of the moment, and to turn the unexpected incidents to his own advantage.

Need for further changes of plan.

We have seen how the breaking of a bridge turned the demonstration against Lookout Mountain into a movement which resulted in its capture. Since a small garrison would now suffice to hold it, Grant ordered Hooker to bring down the bulk of his force into Chattanooga valley and connect with the right wing of Thomas's army, which occupied the low range of hills in front of Missionary Ridge. Early in the morning Sherman began his assault upon the north end of the ridge, but he encountered desperate resistance and made but little progress; insomuch that as Grant scrutinized

Sherman's attack upon Bragg's right.

the situation from Orchard Knob, the thought crossed his mind that if the Confederate right wing could maintain its ground against Sherman till nightfall, what was to hinder Bragg from evacuating his positions during the night and retreating upon Cleveland to effect a junction with Longstreet?[1] Matters must be pressed more vigorously, and to this end Grant sent a new order to Hooker, telling him to advance to Rossville Gap, and then, turning northward along Missionary Ridge, to assail Bragg's left flank. A front attack by Thomas *Hooker moves against Bragg's left.* had been in Grant's mind since yesterday, and had been mentioned in his evening order to Sherman, but the difficulties attending such a movement so impressed Grant that he was inclined to withhold it until Bragg's line should be more or less shaken by one or both of the flank attacks. The crest of Missionary Ridge rose 400 feet above its foot-hills, and the irregularities in the ground made the ascent so difficult that Bragg declared that a single cordon of skirmishers ought to hold it against the whole Federal army. Confident in this view of the case, Bragg sent brigade after brigade to his right to withstand Sherman, until his centre grew so thin as to invite attack, even in its strong position. From Orchard Knob, where Grant and

[1] Comte de Paris, *The Civil War in America*, iv. 289.

Thomas were standing side by side, every feature of these movements could be plainly seen, and as the day wore on Grant's anxiety for Sherman increased. Inequalities of ground prevented his seeing what was happening on the extreme Union right, and he looked long in vain for the appearance of Hooker's men on Missionary Ridge north of Rossville Gap. The Confederates, in their retreat from Lookout Mountain, had destroyed the bridge over Chattanooga creek, so that Hooker's progress was seriously delayed.

Bragg weakens his centre to strengthen his right.

At last Grant decided to make a demonstration with his centre, hoping thus to alarm Bragg into recalling some of the troops that were contending against Sherman. Should Hooker appear at a favourable moment above Rossville Gap, this demonstration could easily be converted into an assault upon the rebel centre. It was for Thomas's army to make this important movement. At Stone river and at Chickamauga Bragg had tried Thomas as anvil; he was now to feel him as hammer.

Grant decides to threaten Bragg's centre.

Baird's division occupied the left of Thomas's line, as Howard had been sent, with the Eleventh corps, to the aid of Sherman. To the right of Baird came Wood, then Sheridan, then Johnson; four divisions, numbering 20,000 men. The enemy's force in front was now much smaller than this, probably 13,000 infantry, with 2000 artillerists; but it was strongly entrenched near the base of the ridge, and again near the summit. The instructions to the division-commanders were to carry the first line of works, and then halt in the rifle-pits to reform their lines. Further instructions were withheld until the effect of this first charge could be seen, and also in the hope of Hooker's timely appearance on the scene.

The orders to the storming line.

At half past three o'clock the signal was given by six guns fired in quick succession from Orchard Knob, and two strong lines of skirmishers moved forward, soon followed by 20,000 men with levelled bayonets, and all on the double quick. A heavy fire was opened on them from sixty rebel guns, which were vigorously answered by the Union batteries. The long lines of bayonets gleaming in the wintry sunshine were a magnificent and formidable sight. The four divisions reached the first line of entrenchments almost at the same moment and instantly poured over them, scattering their defenders, of whom at least 1000 were captured. Then came a marvellous moment. These brave assailants were thrilling in every nerve with victory, but the position into which they had rushed was scarcely tenable.

A magnificent charge.

Swept by a fierce artillery fire, exacerbated by the rifles of hidden skirmishers, it was a veritable hornet's nest, from which escape must quickly be sought in retreat or advance. But the exultant mood of these men was not the mood for retreat; an uncontrollable impulse carried them straight onward up the slope, without tarrying a moment for orders. To adopt a happy phrase of the Count of Paris, they "fled forward" in a contagious fury of aggressiveness which nothing could quell.

It was with grave concern that Grant and Thomas saw this magnificent charge continue be-
<small>An anxious moment.</small> yond its prescribed goal. If successful, it meant speedy victory, but if repulsed, it would leave the victorious enemy between the isolated forces of Sherman on the one hand and Hooker on the other; and the probable result would be, — Sherman driven across the Tennessee, Thomas pushed back into Chattanooga, and Hooker badly mauled. Grant exclaimed, "Thomas, who ordered those men up the ridge?" "I don't know," replied Thomas, "I did not; Granger, did you?" "No," said Gordon Granger, "they are going without orders; when those fellows get started, all hell can't stop them!" Grant muttered that somebody would suffer if the movement failed.[1]

---

[1] See the account of General Fullerton, Granger's chief of staff, in *Battles and Leaders*, iii. 725.

No such calamity, however, was forthcoming. The 20,000 bayonets pushed their way up the hill under a storm of shells and musketry. Sheridan lost 1300 men out of his division of 6000; in other quarters the loss was not so heavy. In some places, to avoid the fire, men went on all fours, but nothing stopped their advance. In less than an hour from the signal to start, the crest was carried almost simultaneously at six different places. Wood's and Sheridan's divisions were the first to clear the summit, and among these General Hazen contends that his brigade, of Wood's division, was foremost.[1] The gunners were slain at their posts, and the cannon turned upon the enemy. The whole Confederate centre was routed. Men threw down their arms and fled, or were captured in crowds. Bragg himself narrowly escaped capture.

Bragg's centre crushed.

While this was going on, Hooker arrived at Rossville Gap, pushed up the ridge, and routing the rebel left sent it tumbling in upon the routed centre. One division, fleeing before Hooker, was thus thrown directly in front of Johnson's division, by which it was captured. The pursuit was kept up, mainly by Sheridan, as far as Chickamauga creek, and many prisoners were taken. At Baird's end of the as-

Total defeat of the Confederates.

[1] See his *Narrative*, pp. 173–235.

sailing line, where the enemy had been massing to move against Sherman, a sturdy resistance was encountered. The rebel right wing held its ground till toward nightfall, when seeing the rest of the army crumbled to fragments it gave way and abandoned the field. The pursuit was continued for two days, while Sherman, with 25,000 men, started for Knoxville to relieve Burnside; but the defeat of Bragg cut Longstreet's line of supply, and on learning of Sherman's approach he got out of the way as speedily as possible. Thus the siege of Knoxville was raised by the same stroke that freed Chattanooga from the presence of the foe. It was a double victory.

The next day after the storming of Missionary Ridge was Thanksgiving Day; the completeness of the victory had begun to be realized throughout the country by the time people sat down to dinner; and, as Halleck said in his congratulatory telegram, Grant had made it indeed a day of thanksgiving. It was in some respects the most brilliant victory of the war. For a battle of such dimensions, the losses in killed and wounded were remarkably small, — some 6000 on the Federal side, something less on the side of the Confederates, who fought mostly behind entrenchments. Grant captured more than 6000 prisoners, 40 pieces of artillery, and 7000 stand of

<small>Greatness of the victory.</small>

arms. That the destruction of life was so much less than at Shiloh, or Stone river, or Chickamauga, was largely due to the adroit manœuvring which made the enemy's almost impregnable positions avail him so little. In this respect the battle of Chattanooga is one of the most interesting in modern history.

It is also one of the most picturesque. The immense length of battle-front, thirteen miles from Sherman's left to Hooker's right, the extraordinary difficulty of the ground, the dizzy heights scaled, the grandeur of the scenery, all combined to make it a wonderful spectacle. Unlike most of our battles, in which the movements were mostly hidden from sight in the forest, here the fighting went on to a great extent in the full view of both armies. "Many a time," General Sherman tells us, "in the midst of the carnage and noise," he "could not help stopping to look across that vast field of battle, to admire its sublimity."[1] On that field were arrayed portions of our three great armies of the Potomac, the Cumberland, and the Tennessee, thus for the first time brought together under one leader; and of all the battles of the war, this was the only one in which our four most famous Union generals — Grant, Sherman, Thomas, and Sheridan — hap-

Grandeur of the battle-field.

[1] Sherman's *Memoirs*, i. 362.

pened all to be engaged. No wonder there was so little left of Braxton Bragg!

But it was not only for its picturesque features or its interesting tactics, but still more for its strategic importance, that the battle of Chattanooga was so brilliant. The victory gave us henceforth undisputed possession of Chattanooga, with all that this implied. As the capture of Vicksburg cut the Confederacy in two on the line of the Mississippi, so the victory at Chattanooga cut in two the remainder of it on the line of the Alleghanies. The great campaigns of the following spring and summer were conducted entirely upon soil which formed part of the original thirteen Atlantic states. The Mississippi valley was now recovered for the Union.

The Mississippi valley recovered.

Once again, indeed, toward the end of the following year, the Confederacy ventured to invade this region, and threw a great army as far north as Nashville, where dire catastrophe awaited it. Our next chapter will give some account of this important episode in the conclusion of the Civil War.

CHAPTER IX

NASHVILLE

IT is worth while to note that each of the four cardinal victories which restored the supremacy of the United States government in the West was won under the leadership of Grant. Fort Donelson, Shiloh, Vicksburg, Chattanooga, — these names are the landmarks in that mighty story. If we may liken the whole war to one stupendous battle of four years' duration, it is evident that the United States was gradually defeating the Confederacy by turning its left flank. At the beginning of the year 1864 the Confederate right in Virginia still held its ground. There three years of warfare had apparently accomplished nothing. Lee was still midway between Richmond and Washington, defiant and apparently unconquerable. It was not strange that to the general who had done so much this last and most difficult problem should be entrusted. It was fitting that to Grant should be assigned the task of overthrowing Lee. It was also right that in undertaking this task Grant should have unlimited control of the whole field of operations. Thus only could unity of purpose in the movements of the different armies be ensured. For want of such well-defined unity of purpose the conduct of the war had hitherto languished. A good instance was furnished by the series of campaigns just passed in review for the possession of Chattanooga. Immediately after the fall of Vicksburg Grant had wished to take his army to Mobile, and in concert with the fleet under Farragut capture that important city. He understood the peril to which Rosecrans's army must necessarily be exposed in advancing into the difficult mountain region of northern Georgia. He knew that Mobile, threatened at once by land and by sea, must fall unless troops should speedily be sent to its defence; and he knew that those troops were most likely to be taken from Bragg. His advice was not heeded. If it had been followed, the disaster of Chickamauga might have been averted. The glorious victory at Chattanooga, which had ensued upon giving him unhampered command in the West, pointed clearly to the next step which ought to be taken. In March, 1864, a bill was passed through Congress reviving the grade of Lieutenant-General, which heretofore had been held only by Washington and Scott.[1] Grant was promoted to this rank,

[1] Scott's, which was conferred in 1855, was only a brevet rank.

and made general-in-chief of all the armies of the United States. Thus he was enabled not only to begin operation in Virginia with hands untrammelled, but also to control the whole field of war, so that a victory in Tennessee or Georgia should exert its full effect upon the situation in Virginia. In another twelve-month the fruits of this sound policy were gathered, and the conqueror of Vicksburg and Chattanooga became also the conqueror of Richmond.

Grant made general-in-chief.

The true character of this final epoch of the war, however, cannot be understood without keeping clearly before our minds the mutual relations between the grand operations in the eastern and western theatres of war. The work of overthrowing Lee called into play other agencies besides the campaigns in Virginia which Grant superintended in person. Moreover, with regard to that frightful tale of bloodshed, from the Wilderness to Petersburg, it may be doubted whether it really added anything to Grant's just reputation as a soldier.

After the end of the war the full grade of General was created by Congress, and conferred successively upon Grant, Sherman, and Sheridan. At a much later date Schofield, on becoming general-in-chief, was made Lieutenant-General. During the Civil War the Confederate government usually gave the full rank of General to the commanders of armies, and that of Lieutenant-General to the commanders of corps, which would limit the grade of Major-General to the commanders of divisions.

To start with an army twice as large as the enemy's, and then to throw away 60,000 men in killed and wounded without either inflicting a proportionate loss or advancing perceptibly toward the goal of the campaign, is hardly a record of great generalship, and it is not the kind of record which Grant had made for himself at Vicksburg and Chattanooga.[1] When Grant, after three weeks of slaughter, arrived at the North Anna river, there could be no doubt that he had been outgeneralled, or — to use Colonel Dodge's happy expression — had received a complete stalemate.[2] Then came the horror of Cold Harbor, which Grant himself, with manly candour, afterward deplored;[3] and then the change of base to James river, a point which might have been directly reached with small loss!

Grant's first Virginia campaign.

In truth, when Grant first came to Virginia he evidently underrated his antagonist, and was pos-

[1] General Sherman once told me that that fearful amount of slaughter was after all necessary, because the South would never give up so long as it had an army of any size worth mentioning; it was therefore a melancholy necessity to pound the life out of Lee's army, even at the cost of half a dozen lives for one, a price which the more populous North could afford. But to admit that Grant could not avoid paying such a price is to concede the superior generalship of Lee.

[2] Dodge, *A Bird's-Eye View of our Civil War*, new ed., 1897, p. 214.

[3] Grant's *Memoirs*, ii. 276.

sessed with the notion that the Army of the Potomac had never had its full fighting power drawn out. Perhaps he may have shared to some extent in the feeling to which another western general, of much smaller calibre, John Pope, gave such objectionable expression two years before, when he declared his contempt for "certain expressions he found much in vogue, such as bases of supplies and lines of retreat." In somewhat similar mood Grant is said to have spoken slightingly of grand tactics. *Manœuvring vs. hammering.* We are told that shortly before the battle of the Wilderness, when Meade was saying that he proposed to manœuvre thus and so, Grant interrupted him with the exclamation, "Oh, I never manœuvre!"[1] This anecdote harmonizes with the popular conception of Grant as a general who achieved success by "continuous hammering" rather than by strategical or tactical devices.

Yet if Grant really said that he never manœuvred, he must have been speaking very carelessly, for he certainly did manœuvre a great deal, and to very good purpose. His campaign in the rear of Vicksburg was a series of splendid strategic manœuvres, and it showed how military skill can achieve a vast result without great loss of life. So, too, with the Chattanooga campaign, it abounded

[1] Swinton's *Army of the Potomac*, p. 440.

in beautiful manœuvres, helped by the skill which
<small>Grant's ma-</small> took advantage of accidents and thus
<small>nœuvres.</small> made them "lucky accidents." Smith's
operation at Brown's Ferry, which Grant adopted,
was a masterpiece of manœuvring; the moving of
Sherman's forces to the northern end of Missionary Ridge was another; the storming of Lookout
Mountain was developed from a manœuvre intended to assist Sherman. The sending of Hooker
to Rossville Gap, and the order to Thomas's four
divisions to advance upon Missionary Ridge, were
both manœuvres designed to make Bragg weaken
his right wing; and as for the sublime spontaneous
rush of Thomas's men, which crushed the enemy's
centre, its success was prepared by the previous
manœuvres. Again, in Virginia, after the experiments at the Wilderness and Spottsylvania had
shown that "continuous hammering" was exhausting our own strength much quicker than the enemy's, Grant's movements by the left flank were
manœuvres, and very skilful ones.

In truth, a thorough trial of the pounding policy
made it clear that the obstacle to Federal success
in Virginia did not consist in the fancy that the
Army of the Potomac had not had its full fighting
capacity drawn out, but in the fact that its antagonist's movements were guided by superior genius.
At the west Grant had been opposed by generals

of varying degrees of ability, — Buckner, Sidney Johnston, Beauregard, Van Dorn, Pemberton, Bragg, — for the most part good soldiers, but none of them a *demonstrated* genius. In Virginia he found himself opposed by a general of the calibre of Turenne or Marlborough, and his eyes were gradually opened to the difference. By the end of July, 1864, after three months of alternate manœuvring and hammering against an army scarcely half the size of his own, his policy was practically reduced to detaining Lee at Petersburg until the whole of the Confederacy should be knocked away from behind him, leaving him in the air without a prop.

The only way to dispose of Lee.

This business of knocking away the Confederacy from Lee was performed by the splendid army with which Sherman, in May, 1864, started from Chattanooga toward Atlanta. It was work which would never have been performed under the old régime, with the marplot Halleck at the head of things; for we know that some of Sherman's most important movements were strongly disapproved by that personage. What was needed was the unity of design secured by having all great operations controlled by a master intelligence, like Grant's, which could appreciate and assist the brilliant conceptions of Sherman. We must devote a very few words to

Unity of operations secured.

the operations of the latter, before we go on to the decisive part that was finally played within the limits of the Mississippi valley.

When Grant was made general-in-chief of the armies of the United States, Sherman succeeded him in the chief command at the West, and under Sherman were three armies with three superb commanders: the Army of the Tennessee, under McPherson; the Army of the Cumberland, under Thomas; and the Army of the Ohio, formerly under Burnside, but now commanded by Schofield. At the beginning of May, 1864, this triple army covered a line about twenty miles in length, a little south of Chattanooga: McPherson on the right, with 25,000 men, Thomas in the centre, with 60,000, and Schofield on the left, with 15,000; in all 100,000 men, with 260 guns. Opposed to this force was a Confederate army of 65,000 men strongly fortified at Dalton, under command of Joseph Johnston, who among the southern generals ranked next in ability to Lee. Johnston had superseded Braxton Bragg, whom Mr. Davis had called to Richmond to be chief of his general staff.

The armies of Sherman and Johnston.

It was generally understood by the public that Sherman's grand object in this campaign was the capture of Atlanta, the principal city of Georgia between the mountains and the sea-coast. But Grant and Sherman well knew that a far more important object was the destruction or capture of Johnston's army,[1] and this was likely to be no light task. Johnston was a master of Fabian strategy, whom it was next to impossible to bring to battle unless he saw a good chance of winning.

At the very outset, indeed, Sherman seems to have had an opportunity of forcing Johnston to fight at a great disadvantage, or to retreat upon dangerous roads. Johnston expected to be attacked at Dalton, but Sherman sent McPherson, with his 25,000 men, through Snake Creek Gap, to seize Resaca and there in full force oppose Johnston's inevitably consequent retreat from Dalton. If this movement succeeded, it was hoped that Johnston's southward retreat would be deflected eastward to Spring Place, in which event we might have captured half of his army. "Such an opportunity," says Sherman, "does not occur twice in a single life, but at the critical moment McPherson seems to have been a little timid."[2] Sherman thought that McPherson ought to have put his whole force astride of the railroad at Resaca; but

How Sherman lost a golden opportunity.

[1] "Neither Atlanta, nor Augusta, nor Savannah, was the objective, but the 'army of Jos. Johnston,' go where it might." Sherman's *Memoirs*, ii. 26.

[2] Sherman's *Memoirs*, ii. 34.

Johnston asserts that if this had been done, he would himself, on letting go his hold upon Dalton, have thrown his entire army upon McPherson and crushed him.[1] This seems probable. For the purpose which Sherman had in view, McPherson's force was much too small, and its commander did wisely in taking up a strong defensive position west of Resaca. Sherman's mistake lay in not following Thomas's advice and sending Thomas himself, with his 60,000 men, through Snake Creek Gap, instead of McPherson. It would then have been difficult for Johnston to avoid a fight with Thomas, in the course of which McPherson and Schofield, with 40,000 men, might have been thrown upon his rear, achieving his destruction.

Such a chance, as Sherman truly says, does not occur twice in a lifetime, and the wily Johnston took good care that it should not again be offered to Sherman. It remained for the latter to avail himself of his numerical superiority to outflank his antagonist and push him back by turning his strong positions one after another. This work was done in masterly fashion until by slow stages Johnston was driven back upon Atlanta. During all this time, from May 5 to July 17, the two armies were almost in contact with each other, and there

Johnston pushed back upon Atlanta.

[1] *Battles and Leaders,* iv. 266.

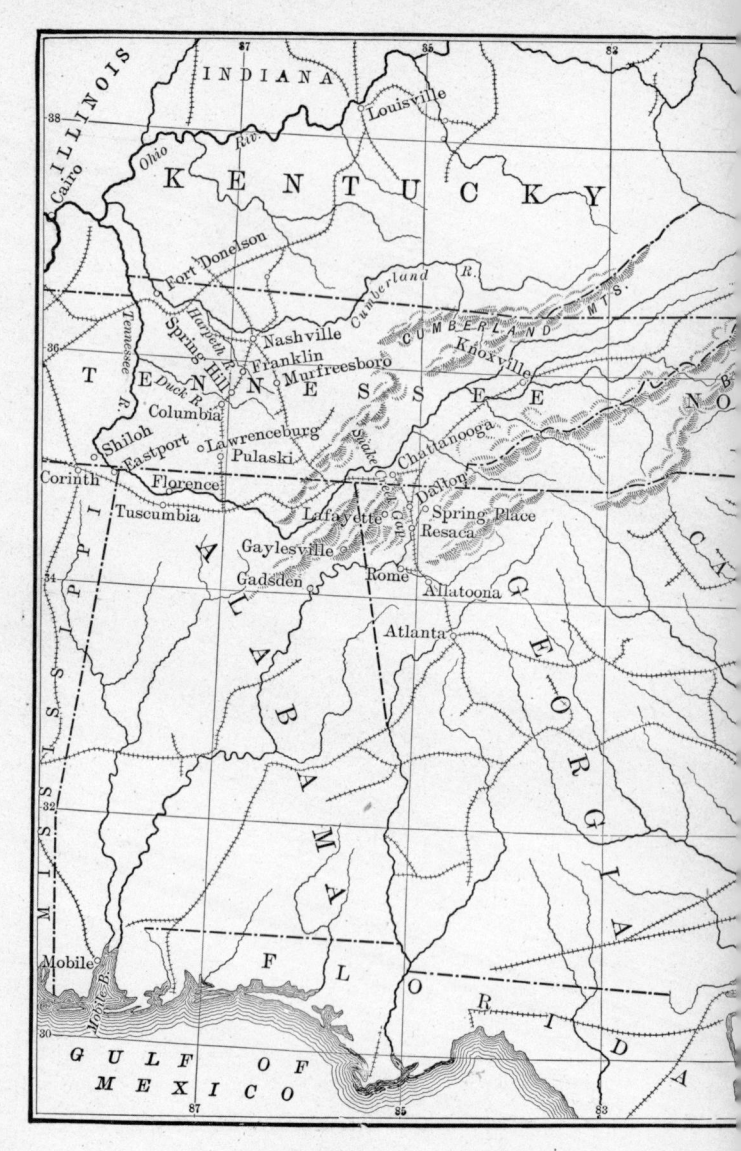

CAMPAIGNS OF SHERMAN

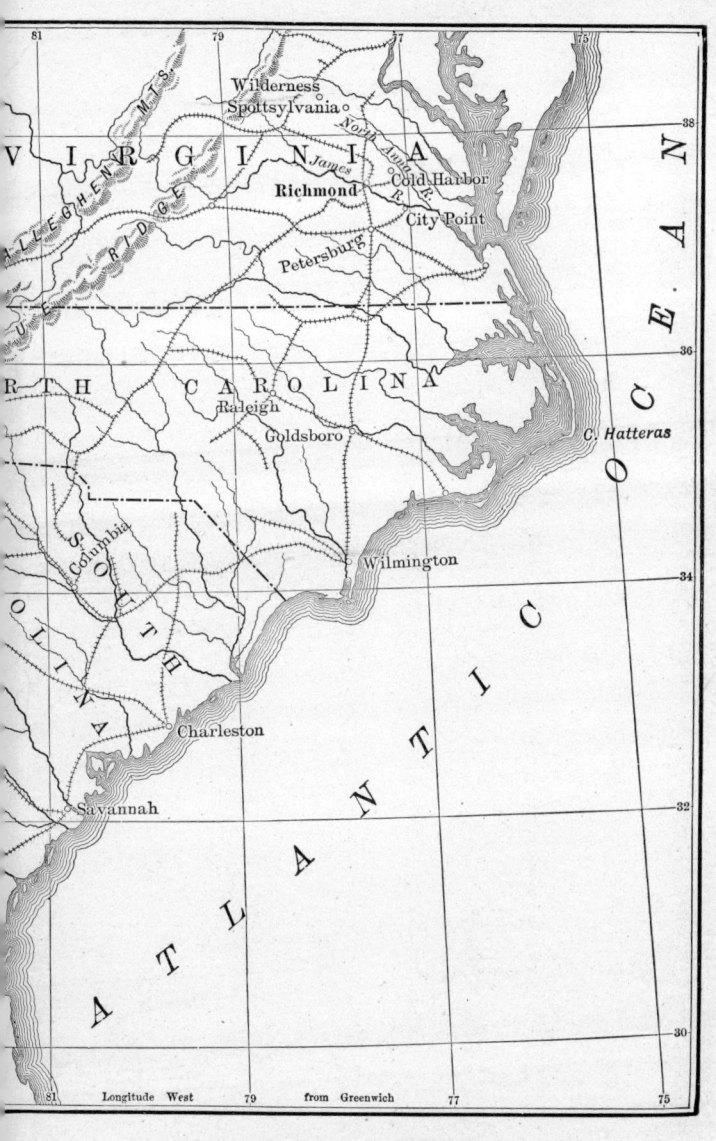

AND THOMAS IN 1864

was frequent skirmishing, but little waste of life, except at Kenesaw Mountain, June 27. On that occasion, mindful of his primary object, Sherman tried the effect of an assault, but desisted when he saw that he was losing faster than the enemy. The Union army lost 3000 men, the Confederates scarcely 500.

In this sort of campaign, despite Sherman's rare skill and resourcefulness, the element of time was working against him and in favour of Johnston. The victorious advance southward was daily lengthening Sherman's line of communications and shortening Johnston's; and as the former was weakened by the necessity of detaching men to guard the long line, so the latter was more and more relieved from such a necessity. Apparently, then, the time was approaching when the Confederate general might no longer think it worth while to decline battle. The experience of Fair Oaks, in May, 1862, showed that Johnston could strike quickly and heavily when the occasion offered itself. But as the armies drew near to Atlanta, the patience of Jefferson Davis was exhausted. His feelings toward Joseph Johnston were unfriendly and unfair, *Johnston superseded by Hood.* and appearances now seemed to justify the blame which he was ready to visit upon him. On the 17th of July he removed Johnston from command,

and appointed in his place one of his corps-commanders, John Bell Hood.

This general, a native of Kentucky, was just entering upon his thirty-fourth year. He had been graduated at West Point in 1853, and had then seen some rough service fighting the Comanche Indians, after which he was for some time a cavalry instructor at West Point. At the beginning of the Civil War he entered the Confederate service, and soon attained the rank of brigadier-general. At Gaines's Mill, where he was severely wounded, his brigade lost more than half its number, and he was brevetted major-general on the field. He was in most of the Virginia battles of 1862. At Gettysburg he lost the use of an arm; afterward, going west with Longstreet, he was in the thick of the fighting at Chickamauga, where he lost a leg. From Dalton to Atlanta he commanded a corps with the rank of lieutenant-general, and now, on his promotion to the command of an army, he was made a full general.

<small>Hood's previous career.</small>

When the news of Hood's appointment reached the Union army, it formed the subject of some conversation between Sherman and McPherson, as they sat on the steps of the porch of a country house. " McPherson had been of the same class at West Point with Hood, Schofield, and Sheridan.

Nashville 329

We agreed that we ought to be unusually cautious and prepared for hard fighting, because Hood, though not deemed much of a scholar, or of great mental capacity, was undoubtedly a brave, determined, and rash man."[1] This opinion is not discordant with that of General Howard, who writes, "Just at this time, much to our comfort and to his surprise, Johnston was removed and Hood placed in command of the Confederate army."[2] In truth, Hood's valour outran his discretion, and he had one of the gravest faults in a commander, impatience. His reputation was that of a hard fighter, who was put in command in order to fight, and may be said to have held his command on condition of plentiful fighting. Mr. Davis was tired of Fabius, and preferred to try his luck with Terentius Varro.

What the Union generals thought of his appointment.

On July 20 Hood attacked the Federal army at Peach Tree creek, near Atlanta, and a week of desultory fighting ensued, in which he lost perhaps 8000 men without accomplishing anything.[3] The

[1] Sherman's *Memoirs*, ii. 75.

[2] *Battles and Leaders*, iv. 313.

[3] In one of these fights, on July 22, the noble McPherson, one of the best generals in the service of the United States, was killed. Howard was appointed by Sherman to succeed McPherson in command of the Army of the Tennessee, much to the disgust of Hooker, who resigned and went home. Sherman

superior skill of Sherman became more and more apparent, until at the beginning of September, when Hood was on the point of being cooped up in Atlanta, he saved his army by evacuating it.

Hood evacuates Atlanta.

With this result Sherman had small reason to feel pleased. At last Hood had really scored one against him. Of course it was desirable that the Federals should possess Atlanta. At the North its capture was regarded as a great victory, and it came at a very opportune moment, just in the heat of the presidential canvass. It opened the eyes of many people to the silliness of the Democratic platform in pronouncing the war a failure. There can be no doubt that the acquisition of Atlanta was a very useful achievement, which reflected great credit upon Sherman. Nevertheless, the escape of Hood's army was a serious disappointment; it contained the seeds of possible disaster to the Union cause, and it instantly made Sherman's situation more or less awkward. The only hope of the Confederates, at this late date, was in prolonging the agony until the patience of the North should be exhausted. Should General McClellan, the Democratic candidate for the presidency, be elected over Mr. Lincoln in November,

was surely right, for Hooker, with all his dash, had abundantly proved himself unfit for any high command involving great responsibility.

it would strongly indicate that such a moment was approaching. In Virginia Lee's power of resistance seemed interminable, and more than once the idea of marching to Grant's assistance, after Atlanta should have fallen, had crossed Sherman's mind; but how could such a feat be attempted without first destroying Hood's army? On the other hand, it would not do to keep the victorious Union army inactive in Atlanta; that would be acknowledging a stalemate. *Difficult problems for Sherman.*

While Sherman was considering the situation, Hood helped to simplify it by assuming the offensive and threatening his long line of communications. To meet the exigency Sherman sent Thomas back to Nashville, and left one corps, under Slocum, to hold Atlanta, while he moved in pursuit of Hood. On the 5th of October a detachment of Hood's army attacked Allatoona, which had been made a depot of supplies for the Federals; but the Union commander at that point, General Corse, made a superb defence, and the rebels were repulsed with heavy loss. A week later Sherman was at Rome, while Hood moved from Resaca to Dalton, which he captured with its garrison of 1000 men. By October 15 Hood was a few miles south of Lafayette, and Sherman had arrived at Snake Creek Gap, where he had been operating five months *Hood assumes the offensive* before. These retrograde movements caused some anxiety at the North, for it looked as if Sherman's grip on Georgia might be loosening. But he never let go Atlanta, nor did he relinquish his scheme for marching to the coast and dealing a blow at Virginia. After much discussion he had prevailed upon Grant to sanction such a movement, provided that Hood's army could first be disposed of. There was always a reasonable hope of entrapping the fiery Hood into a combat. Indeed, on October 16 he came very near offering himself as a prey to Sherman, but all his officers agreed that it was not safe to risk a battle. Against this unanimous opposition Hood did not feel like contending, and thus the existence of his army was prolonged for two months more.

Still, Hood could accomplish nothing by entrenching himself and waiting upon events. Action was as necessary for him as for his adversary. So he conceived the plan of striking northward into Tennessee, in the hope of drawing Sherman after him. In this case the Union general would have to

and makes up his mind to invade Tennessee.
let go Atlanta, and virtually surrender all the advantages he had gained by his summer's work. But if Sherman should not follow him, then Hood felt able to demolish any force that might oppose him in Tennessee. He believed that he could capture

and hold Nashville, and make it a base from which to invade Kentucky. In the latter state he hoped to find many recruits and to threaten Cincinnati, as Kirby Smith had done two years before. After a victorious campaign of this sort, he might take his army eastward through some of the gaps in the Cumberland Mountains and fall upon Grant at Petersburg. Then after defeating Grant, the combined armies of Lee and Hood might either turn and rend Sherman, in case of his being within reach, or else might face to the north and march with irresistible majesty upon the city of Washington. Such were the far-reaching thoughts which Hood entertained on two October nights in bivouac in a beautiful valley near Lafayette.[1]

From that point Hood moved to Gadsden, in Alabama, while Sherman followed as far as Gaylesville. Hood felt it necessary to leave his cavalry, commanded by Wheeler, in Georgia, to watch and harass Sherman; and this force he expected to replace by the cavalry of Forrest, who was then in the western part of Tennessee. On the last day of October Hood arrived at Tuscumbia, where he expected to find abundant supplies for his northward march upon Nashville. But the supplies had been woefully delayed, and the railroad from Corinth was

Hood's fatal delay at Tuscumbia.

[1] See his own account in *Battles and Leaders*, iv. 426, 427.

broken in places, so that Hood was compelled to wait three weeks at Tuscumbia; and that delay worked his ruin.

By this time Sherman had made up his mind what to do. He would reinforce Thomas and leave him in Tennessee to deal with Hood, while he himself would return to Atlanta, and thence move in force upon Virginia. But as the distance from Atlanta to Petersburg is 500 miles as the crow flies, and the whole intervening space was a difficult country possessed by the enemy, it was desirable first to march to the sea-coast, and there establish a secure base for the northward march to Virginia. On the 2d of November Sherman received Grant's permission to undertake this great movement at once, on the understanding that Thomas was to be left strong enough to keep Hood from doing mischief. On the 15th Sherman started, taking with him four infantry corps, numbering 63,000 men, besides Kilpatrick's cavalry, 5000 in number. The march through Georgia met with little serious opposition. It ended on December 23 with the capture of Savannah, including 150 heavy guns and 25,000 bales of cotton, as a Christmas present for Uncle Sam. From this point the far more arduous northward march through the Carolinas was to begin.

Sherman leaves Hood and marches to the seacoast.

We have now to see how Thomas fared during the critical weeks after Sherman's departure, and the question at once arises, Was he left with sufficient strength for the task assigned him? It was a task of supreme importance. If Hood should defeat Thomas, or elude him and capture Nashville, the whole country would condemn Sherman's movement as foolhardy, involving an immense immediate risk for an ultimate gain that was problematical until the immediate risk should be eliminated. *Ought not Sherman to have left more men with Thomas?* Sherman's success was really wrapped up in that of Thomas. Considering this fact, would it not have been more prudent in Sherman to have taken only three corps, say 50,000 men, along with him, and thus have spared an additional 13,000 for Thomas? In the light of the ensuing events, it certainly seems that it would have been wiser.[1]

The force which Sherman left behind for Thomas consisted of the Fourth corps, under Stanley, 12,000 men, the Twenty-third corps of 10,000 men, commanded by Schofield, and about 5000 cavalry, now to be commanded by General James Harrison Wilson, whom Grant sent from Virginia with the mes- *Thomas's forces, present and prospective.*

[1] See Ropes's masterly paper on General Sherman, in *Papers of the Military Historical Society of Massachusetts*, x. 144.

sage, "I believe he will add fifty per cent. to the effectiveness of your cavalry." Altogether, this force of 27,000 was inadequate to cope with Hood's 40,000 infantry and 10,000 cavalry led by the redoubtable Forrest. But Sherman sent to Missouri for an additional force of 14,000 men, commanded by Andrew Jackson Smith, of the regular army, an able general. In September the irrepressible Sterling Price had bounced up once more in Missouri, and Smith had been busy in driving him out of the state. So important was it to get Smith and his men into Tennessee without delay that Grant sent his chief of staff all the way to St. Louis to urge the business forward. It was hoped that they would be ready to leave St. Louis on November 10, but the march across the whole state of Missouri consumed many days. Smith did not arrive in St. Louis until the 24th, and then it was not until the last day of the month that he arrived at Nashville and effected a junction with Thomas. At the same time a crowd of some 5000 belated men, returning from various parts of the country to their commands, were sent up to Nashville from Chattanooga and organized into a provisional division, under General Steedman. Other floating molecules, aggregating into a mass of 4000 or so, and including several regiments of coloured troops, came in early in December, and likewise the cavalry was doubled. So that at last General Thomas found himself at the head of a motley host, numbering from 50,000 to 55,000 men.

Until the end of November, however, he had only about 27,000, so that it was necessary to avoid a battle. Hood's long delay at Tuscumbia — an accident upon which no one could have reckoned — allowed the Union army time for concentration; but the incidents of the anxious fortnight after Sherman's departure abundantly prove that there was an element of rashness in not leaving one more army corps behind. Thomas could have placed such a force at Eastport on the Tennessee river, which would probably have spoiled Hood's plans for crossing.

In the absence of any such obstacle the Confederate general, having obtained his supplies and been joined by the larger part of his cavalry, crossed the great river at Florence, and began his northward march November 19. Thomas was at Nashville, intent upon gathering troops, and the bulk of his little army — the Fourth and Twenty-third corps, with Schofield in command — was at Pulaski. By the 22d Hood's advance had reached Lawrenceburg, on the Federal flank, so that Schofield was obliged to retreat upon Columbia. After brisk marching he reached that place on the 24th, barely in time

Hood's northward march.

to anticipate Forrest in securing the bridges and fords of Duck river. Had the rebel cavalry arrived first upon the scene, they might have cut Schofield asunder from Thomas, and thus have brought swift ruin upon the Federals. On the 27th Schofield's army crossed the river and destroyed the bridges, while Wilson's cavalry undertook to hold the fords.

In spite of Wilson's utmost efforts Forrest got his horsemen across the river on the 28th, and pushed the Union cavalry northward, leaving the way clear for the Confederate infantry to cross. This made it necessary for Schofield to retreat upon the little town of Franklin, on the Harpeth river. On the way thither was situated the village of Spring Hill, a centre of wagon-roads which it was all-important to secure. On the 29th Stanley was sent ahead with two divisions, one of which he found it necessary to leave on the road to guard an exposed point, while with the other he pressed on and occupied Spring Hill. The sun went down that evening upon a most anxious and critical situation. The Union cavalry found its energies absorbed in preventing Forrest from closing the way to Franklin; while at various points were caught glimpses of Confederate infantry. There was even some slight skirmishing with the

Schofield's retreat through Spring Hill to Franklin.

division of Patrick Cleburne, one of the ablest
and boldest officers in the Confederate service.
By two hours after sunset Hood had at least
20,000 infantry close by Spring Hill, and why
Stanley's solitary division was not overwhelmed
before daybreak is one of the mysteries that may
perhaps never be explained.[1] Had the enemy been
led by hesitating men of the McClellan type, or
by puzzle-headed men like Burnside or Pope, the
loss of such an opportunity would not have been
strange; but when we consider Hood's well-nigh
reckless audacity and the rare combination of skill
and energy in Cleburne and Forrest, the escape of
Schofield's little army that night seems marvellous
indeed.

Its march next morning, in spite of an occasional
brush with the enemy's cavalry, was not seriously
molested. By noon the whole force was in position
in front of the town of Franklin, excepting Colonel Opdycke's rear-guard, which was still feeling

[1] Colonel Henry Stone, of Thomas's staff, declares that "a
single Confederate brigade, like Adams's or Cockrell's or Maney's,
— veterans since Shiloh, — planted squarely across the pike, either
south or north of Spring Hill, would have effectually prevented
Schofield's retreat, and daylight would have found his whole
force cut off from every avenue of escape by more than twice its
numbers, to assault whom would have been madness, and to avoid
whom would have been impossible." *Battles and Leaders*, iv.
446.

the enemy. The Federal line, entrenched upon rising ground, was convex in shape, resting both flanks upon the Harpeth river. About half a mile from its extreme left this line of battle crossed the turnpike from Columbia. The space between river and turnpike was occupied by Jacob Cox's division of the Twenty-third corps, while beyond the pike for another half mile stretched Ruger's division of the same; the remaining space on the right was filled by Kimball's division of the Fourth corps, while Wood's division had advanced beyond the river with the long wagon-trains. On a bluff beyond the river Federal batteries were planted, commanding the space in front of the Federal line. Wilson's cavalry were also north and east of the river, to check any turning movement on the part of the rebel cavalry.

Position of the Federal army at Franklin.

In the Federal line of works, just west of the turnpike, were two regiments of Andrew Smith's long-wished-for corps from Missouri. These veterans had just arrived, and with them was a raw regiment from Ohio, which had not yet had its "baptism of fire." There were about forty pieces of artillery in the works.

While these admirable arrangements had been quickly made to receive the enemy's attack, it was hoped that he might defer it until the morrow.

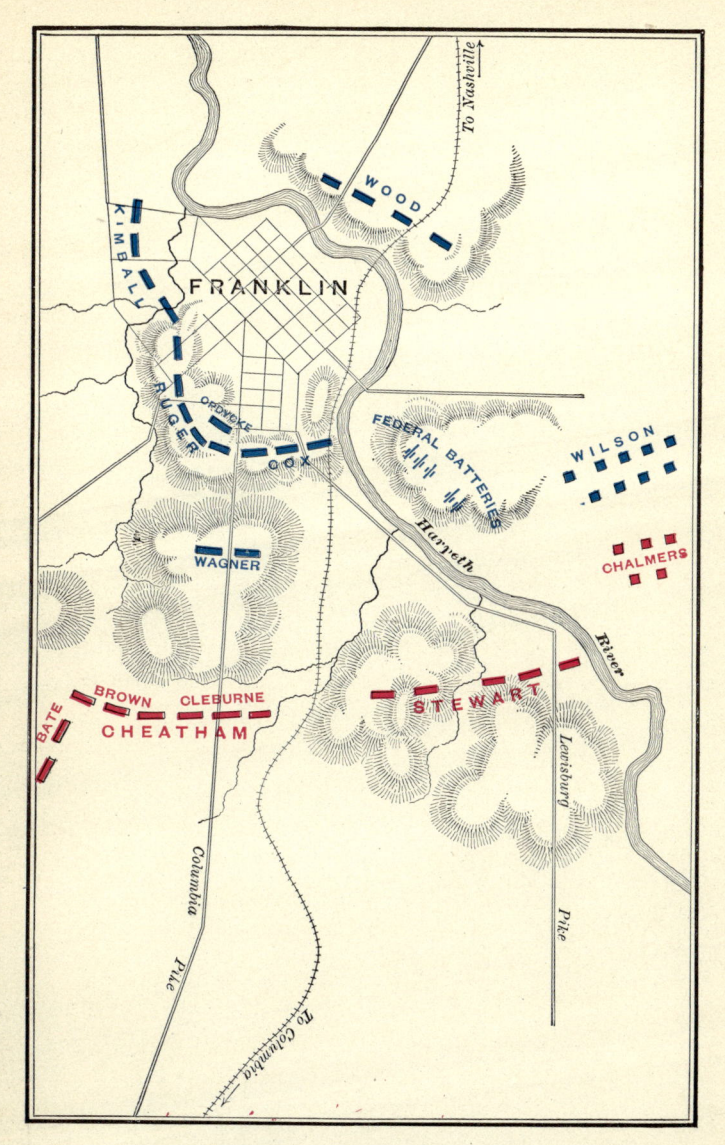

FRANKLIN, NOVEMBER 30, 1864

Early in the afternoon a telegram from Thomas asked Schofield if he could detain Hood at Franklin for three days. Schofield replied that he thought not, whereupon Thomas ordered him to retreat that night as far as the Brentwood Hills, in front of Nashville. *Retreat upon Nashville ordered.* While these messages were going over the wires, the impetuous Hood, who had fully awakened to the magnitude of the opportunity which he had lost the previous night, was preparing his charge — the desperate and mighty rush of two army corps — against the strong Federal line.

Excellent as the Federal position was in nearly all respects, it had in it one element of weakness which came well-nigh proving fatal. Of Wagner's division of the Fourth corps, which had been serving very efficiently as rear-guard, the first brigade — Colonel Opdycke's — had taken *An alarming blunder.* position within the lines, as a reserve just west of the turnpike. The other two brigades — Lane's and Conrad's — had made a temporary halt upon a knoll rather more than a quarter of a mile to the front of the lines. They were not entrenched, as it was of course not intended to leave them there, but in the hurry of the day's proceedings they had not yet been withdrawn, when Cleburne and Brown, with 10,000 men on the double-quick, came upon them like an avalanche. There was nothing to do but to run for the Federal lines, and (as the Koran would say) it was an evil quarter of a mile thither. The Federal soldiers in line for some distance each side of the turnpike were obliged to withhold their fire for fear of killing their comrades, and so the onward rush of Cleburne's and Brown's divisions was virtually unopposed. In wild enthusiasm, while the welkin rang with the "rebel yell," the Confederates swarmed into the Union entrenchments along with Lane's and Conrad's fugitives, of whom they captured nearly 1000. In a twinkling they scattered the raw regiment from Ohio, they seized the Union batteries right and left of the road, and for just a moment victory seemed within their grasp. A fatal rent seemed to have been made in the Union line of battle.

A critical moment.

But it was only for a moment. The act of overwhelming the Lane and Conrad brigades and the capture of so many prisoners had slightly retarded the rush of Brown and Cleburne, so that Stewart's corps, which was likewise charging on the double-quick between turnpike and river, was a few minutes before them in approaching the Federal line. A withering fire from Cox's division soon made Stewart recoil. Then as Cleburne's division rushed over the Union works it received a terrific oblique fire from

The Confederates are repulsed

Cox's men which shook it from end to end. The Lane and Conrad brigades quickly faced about and were joined by Opdycke's, and a general rally about the turnpike soon expelled the Confederates and hermetically closed the temporary gap.

It was a bitter disappointment for Hood's men. Again and again they renewed the attack with bravery and pertinacity almost incredi- *and defeated.* ble. But against the storm of grape and canister and musketry in front, together with the enfilading fire of the batteries across the river, no human gallantry could stand; and by nightfall the repulse of the Confederates was complete.

Meanwhile an important cavalry battle was fought on the further side of the river. A large force of the enemy's cavalry, under Chalmers, crossed from the Lewisburg pike with the design of operating upon the Federal connections northward; but Wilson met them with a superior force, and the afternoon was consumed in an obstinate battle, which ended in driving the whole rebel cavalry to the south side of the *Chalmers defeated by* Harpeth. During the night the Union *Wilson.* army continued its retreat to Nashville, taking with it all the wagon-train, together with more than 1000 prisoners and 33 flags captured from the enemy.

When we bear in mind that the battle of Franklin began at four o'clock in the short afternoon of the last day of November, the destruction of life seems positively awful. More than 8000 men were killed and wounded, — nearly 6000 on the Confederate side, about 2300 on the Union side.[1] The losses of the Confederates bore melancholy testimony to their magnificent fighting. Especially noticeable was their loss of officers, including eleven generals. Among the dead was Patrick Cleburne, the "bravest of the brave."

Awful slaughter.

On the 1st of December, when Schofield's troops arrived at Nashville, they were joined by the main body of Andrew Smith's veterans from Missouri; and soon afterward by the Steedman division, the negro regiments, and other miscellaneous troops already enumerated, swelling the numbers of the army to about 43,000 infantry and 12,000 cavalry. On December 2 Hood's army arrived upon the scene and entrenched itself upon a range of low hills about a mile distant from the Federal lines. As

Schofield arrives at Nashville; Hood follows.

[1] I remember reading a newspaper account the day after the battle, in which the writer's phraseology unconsciously gave a delicious illustration of the purely professional point of view of a sensation-monger, e. g., "The carnage *compared favourably* with that of any battle during the war!" The italicizing is mine, of course.

his force did not exceed 38,000 men, the Confederate general could not now afford to offer battle. He hoped for reinforcements from Texas, and should Thomas attack him before their arrival, he believed that the assault upon entrenchments would meet with a bloody repulse, as so often happened. So Hood remained in his strong position and awaited the course of events.

The 2d of December was the first day in all this campaign when the Union army was strong enough to assume the aggressive. The great and decisive battle of Nashville, about to be described, was fought on the 15th and 16th. Surely the interval was not a long one when we consider the preparations that were necessary to insure a complete and final success. The material of Thomas's army was mostly excellent, but it had been hastily scraped together, and some work of organization and equipment was required. Especially important were the needs of the cavalry. Of this Thomas had a large force, with a very able commander, and he intended to make it play a great part in the coming battle. He did not contemplate a victory like Shiloh or Gettysburg, in which the enemy should simply be compelled to retire from the field. Such victories had been important in their time and place, but something more was needed now. Thomas meant

Why Thomas was not ready to attack Hood.

to make the battle at Nashville a "crowning mercy," a Waterloo which should wipe the defeated army out of existence, and for this work he counted much upon his cavalry. But Wilson's men had been toiling incessantly for six weeks, and the loss of horses had been excessive. It had been found necessary to send officers through the states of Kentucky and Tennessee, impressing horses. The barns of farmers, the spacious stables of street-car companies, even the circuses, were called upon, and handed over their animals without a murmur. The work went on briskly, and at the end of a week, December 9, the 12,000 cavalrymen were fairly mounted and equipped for battle.[1]

Meanwhile there was much excitement, not only at Washington, but at Grant's headquarters at City Point, on James river. That Lincoln and Stanton should have remembered Bragg's aggressive movements of two years before, that they should have felt nervously anxious lest the dashing Hood should contrive to elude Thomas and make a rush into Kentucky, was no more than natural. But it does seem strange that Grant, usually so imperturbable, should have had his head turned ever so little by the feeling of panic. One would suppose that his own ample experience of

[1] See General Wilson's interesting paper, in *Battles and Leaders*, iv. 467.

the vexations and misunderstandings which beset
a commander would have kept him Grant's
patient for at least a week, especially impatience.
in dealing with a man of the known character and
calibre of Thomas. But Grant's despatches from
City Point to Nashville on December 2, 5, 6,
and 8, show unusual anxiety and some irritation,
along with an imperfect comprehension of the circumstances, as in his second despatch of December 2, in which he suggested that Thomas ought to
have advanced to Franklin instead of withdrawing
Schofield to Nashville.[1] On December 9 Grant's
patience gave way, and an order was written relieving Thomas and appointing Schofield in his
place. The order was not sent, but a telegram
from Halleck informed Thomas that Grant was
much dissatisfied with his delay. The grand old
soldier calmly replied, "I feel conscious that I
have done everything in my power, and that the
troops could not have been got ready before this.
If General Grant should order me to be relieved,
I will submit without a murmur." The same evening a telegram from Grant informed him that the

[1] Nevertheless the despatch goes on to say, with Grant's customary candour, "At this distance, however, I may err as to the best method of dealing with the enemy." Grant's *Memoirs*, ii. 382. If he had been on the spot, Grant would have seen that our position at Franklin could be much more easily turned by the enemy than our position at Nashville.

order relieving him was revoked, and thus he learned of the existence of such an order without knowing its exact purport.

The harrowing ordeal, however, was not yet over. That 9th of December was the first of a series of days of freezing rain. Roads and fields were covered with a glare of ice, making cavalry operations impossible. A council of war on the 10th unanimously declared that a battle could not be prudently undertaken until the ice should melt. On the 11th the order came from Grant, "Delay no longer for weather or reinforcements." But Thomas waited for the indispensable thaw, and Grant again lost patience. At that moment General Logan happened to be at City Point, and Grant hurried him off to Nashville, with an order in his pocket directing Thomas to hand over to him the command of the army; but Grant enjoined it upon Logan not to make the order known until he should arrive upon the scene, and then, if Thomas had moved, not to deliver it at all. After Logan had started, Grant's restlessness rose to such a pitch that he decided to go to Nashville himself, and went as far as Washington, where he found the following telegram from Thomas to Halleck: "The ice having melted to-day, the enemy will be attacked to-morrow morning." Thus was

Logan's journey to Louisville and Grant's journey to Washington.

Grant saved from consummating a colossal piece of injustice. As for Logan, when he had gone as far as Louisville he heard news which assured him that he need go no further.[1]

The morning of December 15 was soft and muddy, not the best sort of day for the evolutions of either infantry or cavalry, but infinitely

[1] Grant's account of this affair in his *Memoirs*, chap. lx., shows a coldness of appreciation of Thomas which is not creditable to the writer. For instance, Grant says he was afraid that Hood might make a dash northward, and that " we might have to send troops from the East to head him off, . . . General Thomas's movements being always so deliberate and so slow, though effective in defence." Such a statement, made long after the war, demands qualification. Effectiveness in defence would hardly apply to the handling of the Union army at Nashville ; one might as well speak of Napoleon as " effective in defence " at Austerlitz. As to " slowness," I have been told that there was a deliberateness about Thomas's personal movements and his manner of speech very unlike the electric impulsiveness which was so charming in Sherman. But that is a very different thing from lack of promptness or celerity in the despatch of business, and Thomas was always prompt, while his work in that December fortnight while Grant was nagging him was really a marvel of celerity. The fact is, that ever since Shiloh there has been a grain of jealousy between the Army of the Tennessee and the Army of the Cumberland. They sometimes enjoy girding at each other, and one of the stock themes is the alleged " slowness " of the latter army and its commanders, which is simply one of the numerous commonplaces that are not true. Grant, I think, shared in this jealousy, perhaps unconsciously, and this may have affected his mental attitude toward Thomas.

On the extreme right, between the Charlotte road and the river, was stationed Wilson's fine corps of cavalry. Behind the city the river was patrolled by gunboats. Nearly the entire space occupied by the Federal army was enclosed by two small streams, Richland and Brown's creeks, rising in the Brentwood Hills, four miles south of Nashville, and flowing into the Cumberland river. On the high crest of the Brentwood range stood the humble abode of a venerable dame, after whom the road passing by was known as the Granny White pike. About midway between Granny White's house and the city the space between the forks of Richland and Brown's creeks was occupied by a low and somewhat broken line of hills, which extended northeastward as far as the Chattanooga railway. Upon this line of hills Hood's army was entrenched. *Position of Hood's army.* Cheatham's corps was on the extreme right, by the railway; the centre, commanded by Stephen Decatur Lee, of South Carolina, stretched across the Franklin pike; and on the left Stewart's corps reached to the Hillsboro road, where its left wing was sharply refused. A stone wall, running along the roadside for 1000 yards or so, was utilized as a screen for rifle-pits, and at three commanding points strong batteries were planted, while about a mile to the southwest, beyond a fork of Richland creek, two detached hills were crowned with redoubts. A further attempt was made to strengthen the Confederate left by placing a rather solid skirmish line in front of Stewart's corps, terminating in an entrenched position on Montgomery Hill, close to the Hillsboro pike, and not more than half a mile distant from Wood's salient upon Laurens Hill.

The situation boded no good to the Confederate army. These defences of its left wing were but flimsy as compared with the solid masses of Federal infantry and cavalry west of the Hillsboro pike. It was hardly prudent in Hood, under the circumstances, to accept battle. If he had been a Stonewall Jackson, he might have attempted to withdraw stealthily from his position and verify Grant's forebodings by slipping across the Cumberland river and dashing northward. But in presence of the lynx-eyed Thomas even Jackson might have proved unequal to such an exploit. Perhaps Hood might have fared better had he taken position in the first place back upon the Brentwood Hills. But in any case, with only 38,000 men against Thomas's 55,000, he could hardly look for victory. Clearly the worst thing Hood could do was to diminish the numbers which he could put into the battle, and this mistake he did commit. He kept Forrest, with the

Hood's peril.

greater part of the cavalry and three brigades of infantry, patrolling the country east of Nashville, " to drain it of persons liable to military service, animals suitable for army purposes, and subsistence supplies." [1] When the battle was fought, Forrest was too far astray to be promptly recalled, and Hood's only reliance against the powerful Union cavalry was the division of Chalmers, with which he watched the Charlotte turnpike.

Thomas's plan of battle was to make a left wheel with his whole right wing, pivoting upon Wood's salient at Laurens Hill. At the proper moment Wood might threaten the rebel works on Montgomery Hill, or perhaps attack and carry them, and press on against Stewart's angle. Meanwhile Steedman was to make a vigorous demonstration against Cheatham's right upon the Chattanooga railway, and Schofield's reserve was to play such a part as circumstances might determine.

Thomas's plan.

The early morning of December 15 was foggy, but a hot sun had burned off the vapours before nine o'clock. The movements began at daybreak. Steedman crossed Brown's creek and began a demonstration that was virtually an assault, and kept Cheatham's corps busy all day. This attack, moreover, neutralized Lee's corps and made it useless;

[1] *Campaigns of Forrest*, p. 634.

for when the alarming pressure was felt upon Stewart's left, Lee could not substantially reinforce either Stewart or Cheatham without leaving either a gap or a very thin line at the Franklin pike, and this he dared not do lest the garrison of the interior Federal line opposite should sally from its works and, charging straight down the Franklin road, pierce the rebel centre.

Lee and Cheatham neutralized.

Observe, dear reader, the brilliancy of Thomas's tactics. Here at the outset, by employing only Steedman's division and keeping his "quartermaster's forces" in their works, he eliminates Lee and Cheatham, two thirds of the rebel army, from the problem! The serious work before him now is to pulverize Stewart, and for this purpose he can use Wilson, Smith, Wood, and Schofield, nearly his whole force! This has the true Napoleonic flavour; it smacks of Austerlitz.

Superb tactics.

The grand wheel with the Federal right wing began early, but an hour or more was lost by some of Smith's infantry at first getting in the way of Wilson's cavalry. No serious harm was done, however. Wilson was presently in position on Smith's right, driving Chalmers steadily back. By noon the entire Federal right wing had wheeled past the Hardin pike

Advance of the Federal right wing.

and across Richland creek, and formed a line parallel to the Hillsboro pike, extending from the pivot on Laurens Hill southward to the detached hills that were crowned with rebel redoubts. Thomas wished to prolong this line still further, and therefore ordered out Schofield's corps, which marched behind Wood and Smith until it took position on Smith's right, facing the Hillsboro pike nearly opposite, and about a mile and a half west of Granny White's house. The van of Wilson's cavalry then pushed forward to the Granny White pike.

While these things were going on, Wood sent forward a single brigade, under Colonel Philip Sidney Post, to storm Montgomery Hill. This work was done quickly and well; the hill with its guns was soon in our hands, along with more prisoners than it was convenient to handle. *Outposts taken.*

At about two P. M. the detached redoubts were stormed by some of Smith's infantry and Hatch's division of cavalry dismounted, and their cannon were turned upon the enemy.

Next came Wood's assault in force upon Stewart's angle at the stone wall. By four P. M. all the works here had been carried, and the Confederate left wing was pushed off the ground. Darkness soon stopped the fighting, and the men slept wherever they happened to be. *Hood's left wing broken.*

Stewart's corps had been driven southward two miles, and lay across the Granny White pike. At nightfall Hood withdrew Cheatham's corps from the Nolensville road, and transferred it to his left, facing Schofield. Stewart thus became the centre, and Lee was placed on his right, with wing refused on Overton Hill. It was a stronger position than he had occupied in the morning, but his men were dispirited with the day's work, while Thomas's men, from the major-generals down to the privates, were aglow with the instinct of victory, and felt themselves invincible.

<small>Hood's new position.</small>

Strong as Hood's position was, its left wing was in danger of being turned by reason of Thomas's superior numbers, especially in his cavalry. On the morning of the 16th Thomas brought his forces close up to the enemy: Steedman on the left by the railway facing southward, Wood next, then Smith standing across the Granny White pike, then Schofield parallel to the Hillsboro pike and facing eastward, finally Wilson's cavalry threatening the enemy's flank. In order to save this flank, it was necessary that it should be sharply refused, and thus a salient was created at Shy Hill,[1] the steep summit of

<small>The salient at Shy Hill.</small>

---

[1] So called after the gallant Colonel Shy of the 37th Georgia, slain there in the decisive charge which wrecked the Confederate left.

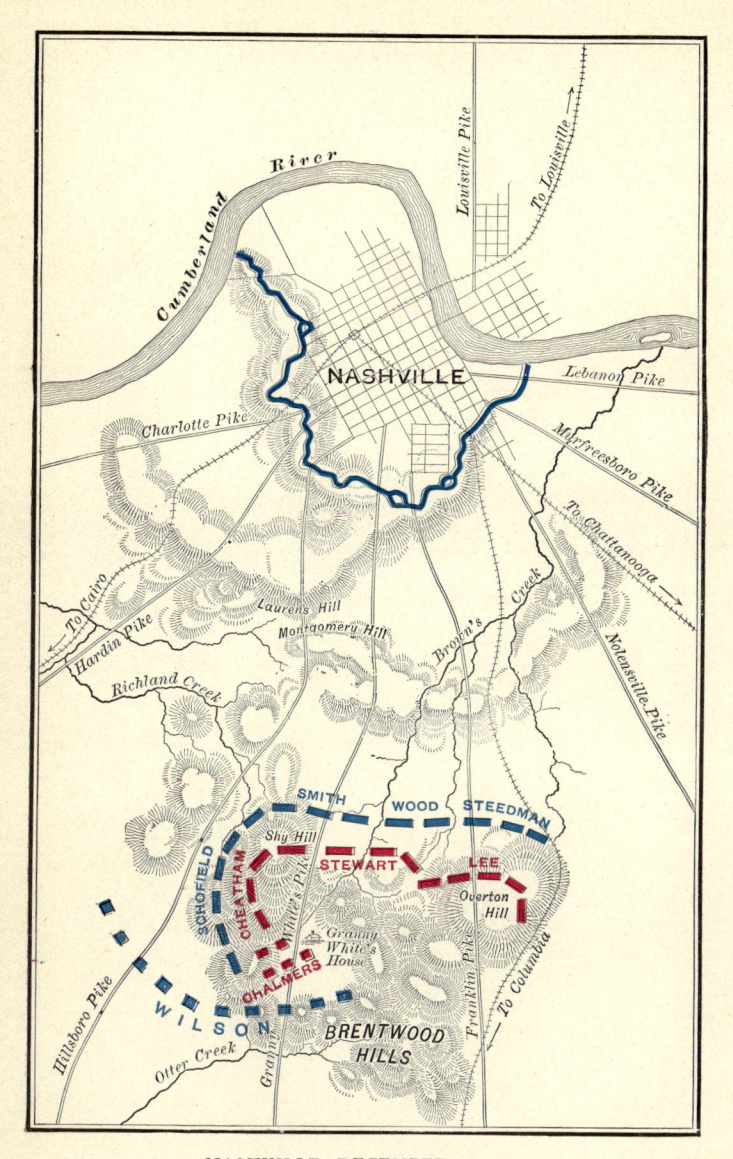

NASHVILLE, DECEMBER 16, 1864

which was fortified as well as haste would permit. Upon this salient Smith and Schofield set up a deadly cross-fire, enfilading the Confederate lines in two directions.

So much time had been consumed in moving the troops into position over the execrably soft and uneven ground that noon was past before heavy fighting began. While Schofield and Smith were hammering at the salient upon Shy Hill, an attack was made upon the Confederate right wing at Overton Hill. Colonel Post, of Wood's corps, who had acquitted himself so nobly the day before, undertook to storm the enemy's entrenchments. He was supported by Thompson's brigade of coloured troops, from Steedman's division. *The assault upon Overton Hill.* The utmost bravery was shown, by negroes as well as by white men, but the assault met with a bloody repulse. Colonel Post received an ugly wound, and was made brigadier-general on the field for his gallantry. His unsuccessful assault was not without its effect upon the result of the battle. It made Hood uneasy about his right wing, so that he took one of Cheatham's divisions — the one formerly commanded by Cleburne — and sent it to reinforce Lee's troops on Overton Hill.

At the same time the pressure of the Union cavalry upon Chalmers grew so alarming that

Hood withdrew a brigade of infantry from Cheatham in order to support Chalmers.
By these successive depletions Cheatham's line was weakened, and the angle upon Shy
Hill became so thin as to invite assault. Thereupon one of Smith's brigades scrambled up the
steep slope and with levelled bayonets drove the
defenders from their works. At the same time a
few pieces of Federal artillery, dragged up to an
eminence that commanded Shy Hill, opened fire;
while a brigade of Hatch's cavalry rushed along
the Granny White road and poured in a quick
succession of volleys from their repeating rifles.
Just then Thomas hurled forward the extreme
right division of Schofield's corps, and in a few
minutes the whole Confederate left had become a
disorderly mob running wildly for the Franklin
turnpike. This was the signal for a grand advance along the whole Federal line. Stewart and
Lee were driven back in utter confusion, and
Steedman's negroes swept victorious over the hill
which an hour before had so sternly repulsed them.
Never was rout more complete and final than that
of Hood.

Total rout of Hood's army.

The pursuit was kept up for ten days, ending
at the Tennessee river below Decatur, on the day
after Christmas. The Union loss in killed and
wounded, at the battle of Nashville, was about

3000. The total Union loss in the whole campaign of five weeks was not more than 6000. In warfare sound strategy and sound tactics are the great economizers of human life. The Confederate loss in killed and wounded cannot be estimated with accuracy; but during the battle and the pursuit Thomas reported the capture of at least 13,000 prisoners and 72 cannon. The Confederate army in the West was virtually annihilated. Nashville was the most decisive victory gained by either side in the Civil War, and one of the most brilliant.

The pursuit and the losses.

The destruction of Hood's army enabled Sherman to march northward from Savannah through the Carolinas, and the western situation was so simplified that Schofield's force was transferred from Thomas to Sherman. At the eleventh hour the Confederate government appointed Robert Lee its general-in-chief, and Lee appointed Joseph Johnston to command such forces as could be scraped together to oppose Sherman. Of these there were about 15,000 men (one third of them being the remnant of the Hood wreckage) to contend against Sherman's 90,000. At Petersburg and Richmond, Lee, with about 60,000, was confronted by Grant, with 125,000. When Sherman arrived at Raleigh,

Results of Thomas's victory.

within 120 miles of Lee, while Stoneman, seizing the railway between Lynchburg and Knoxville, cut off the possibility of retreat from Virginia into the Tennessee mountains, the Confederacy had evidently reached the last ditch. Lee's position, so long and so skilfully held, had become untenable. The only question was whether he should succumb right there, or, letting go Richmond, should unite his forces with those of Johnston. In the latter case the twain would have been crushed between the two great Union armies as between the upper and the nether millstone. Should the Confederacy's two foremost heroes be vanquished separately or together? Sheridan's victory at Five Forks cut away the latter alternative, and virtually ended the aggressive proceedings which began on the spring day in St. Louis when Grant and Sherman congratulated Lyon and Blair upon the capture of Camp Jackson.

INDEX

INDEX

Alexander, Myra, 16, 17.
Amateur generalship, 204, 207, 208.
Ammen's brigade at Shiloh, 87.
Antietam, battle of, 151.
Arkansas, the ram, 139, 140.
Arkansas Post, capture of, 205, 206.
Athens, Alabama, punishment for the sack of, 158.
Austerlitz, battle of, 98, 354.

Bailey, Theodorus, 123, 127.
Ball's Bluff, 50.
Banks, N. P., in the Port Hudson campaign, 223, 226, 231, 234, 247.
Baton Rouge, surrender of, 137.
Bayous in the Mississippi valley, 180.
Beauregard, G. T., 70-72; at Shiloh, 84-94; 134-136, 145.
Bell, Henry; 126.
Belmont, battle of, 47-51.
Big Bethel, 50.
Big Black river, battle of, 239.
Big Sunflower experiment at Vicksburg, 218-220.
Blair, Francis Preston, 1st, 8.
Blair, Francis Preston, 2d, 8-22, 202.
Blair, Francis Preston, 3d, 17.
Blair, James, 8.
Blair, Montgomery, 8, 116.
Blockade of Confederacy's coast, 108.
Bluffs on the Mississippi river, their military significance, 181.
Blunt, J. G., 197.
Booneville, skirmish at, 24.
Border states, importance of, 2.
Bowen, J. S., 229.
Bowling Green, 52.
Boyne, battle of, 41.
Bragg, Braxton, 5, 70, 71; at Shiloh, 79, 81, 88, 94, 96, 97; seizes Chattanooga, 145, 146; his invasion of Kentucky, 148-153; at Stone river, 161-177; sends reinforcements to Pemberton, 197, 198; loses a golden opportunity before Chickamauga, 265; besieges the Union army in Chattanooga, 282-292; what was he thinking of in sending Burnside into eastern Tennessee? 293-297; superseded by Johnston, 324.

Brannan, J. M., at Chickamauga, 270, 271.
Breckinridge, John C., 42; at Shiloh, 79, 94, 97; at Stone river, 162, 163, 176.
Brooklyn, the frigate, 117, 124.
Brown's Ferry, scheme conceived and executed by W. F. Smith, 287-292.
Buchanan, F., 110.
Buchanan, James, 58.
Buckner, S. B., 39, 42, 58-63.
Buell, D. C., 54, 66, 72, 75, 76, 79, 90-99, 133-147, 149-160; his alleged slowness, 144, 255, 296; punishes marauders, 158.
Burnside, A. E., supersedes McClellan, 156; 224; at Knoxville, 256, 257, 284, 293, 295-297, 314.
Butler, B. F., 115, 129-132.

Cable, G. W., 128.
Cairo, Illinois, military importance of, 41.
Caldwell, C. H. B., 122.
Cambronne, 19.
Camp Jackson, 13-20; hospitality at, 15; surrender of, 19.
Carondelet, the gunboat, 104, 105, 139.
Carthage, fight at, 25.
Cavalry raids in Tennessee, 252, 253.
Cayuga, the gunboat, 123, 124.
Chalmers, George, and the rebel cavalry at Nashville, 354, 357, 358.
Champion's Hill, battle of, 238.
Chancellorsville, battle of, 95.
Channel sawed through forest at Island No. 10, 103.
Chattanooga, importance of, 141-145; military importance of, 248; its political importance, 249.
Chattanooga, battle of, 303-315; not fought as Grant had planned it, 308; its brilliant tactics, 314, 322; its picturesqueness, 315; its great results, 316.
Cheatham, B. F., at battle of Nashville, 351, 353, 354, 356-358.
Cherub, the frigate, 115.
Chickamauga, battle of, 267-280; the fatal order at, 270; rout of the right

wing, 272; army saved by Thomas, 273-275; awful slaughter at, 279, 280.
Chickamauga valley, 260.
Cleburne, Patrick, at Stone river, 167, 168; 339; his charge at the battle of Franklin, 342; killed at Franklin, 344.
Columbus, Tennessee, fortified by Polk, 41.
Confederate defensive line, the 1st, 38, 52, 65.
Confederate defensive line, the 2d, 101; broken at Corinth, 136.
Corinth, Mississippi, its military importance, 69; evacuation of, 134.
Corse, J. M., his defence of the Allatoona, 331.
Cowpens, 249.
Cox, Jacob, at battle of Franklin, 342.
Crittenden, G. B., 39.
Crittenden, J. J., 39.
Crittenden, T. L., 39, 54; at Shiloh, 93, 94, 96; at Stone river, 163, 169, 173, 176; in the Chickamauga campaign, 265, 268, 272, 277; relieved from command, 285; his character, 286.
Cruisers, Confederate, 111.
Cumberland river, 45, 52.
Curtis, S. R., 35-37.

Davis, Charles, 136-139, 186.
Davis, Jefferson, 57, 70, 85, 131, 155, 196, 197, 267, 286, 306, 327.
Davis, J. C., at Stone river, 162, 167, 168, 171.
Dodge, G. M., 187.
Duncan, J. K., 119, 128.

Ellet, Charles, 136.
Ericsson, John, 117, 223.
Essex, the frigate, at Valparaiso, 115.
Essex, the ram, 139, 140.

Fair Oaks, battle of, 327.
Farragut, D. G., 115, 128, 186, 223, 224.
Floyd, John, 58-63.
Foote, A. H., 56, 102, 136.
Forrest, N. B., 63, 149, 198, 205, 252, 338.
Fort Donelson, 52, 56-66.
Fort Henry, 52; capture of, 56.
Fort Jackson, 117-121, 127, 129.
Fort Pemberton, 217, 218.
Fort Pillow, 46, 106; evacuation of, 136.
Fort St. Philip, 117-121.
Fort Sumter, fall of, 2.
Forts on the Mississippi river, outflanked by Grant's advance up the Tennessee, 190; importance of, in warfare, 191-194.

Fox, G. V., 116.
Franklin, battle of, position of Schofield's army at, 340; charge of Confederates, 341; a critical moment, 342; defeat of Confederates, 343; awful slaughter at, 344.
Frederick the Great, 97, 163, 286.
Fremont, J. C., 25, 26, 28-34; his edict of emancipation, 29; 45, 225.
Frost, D. M., 13-15, 19.
Fullerton, J., at Missionary Ridge, 312.

Gantt, T. T., 18, 19.
Garfield, J. A., at Chickamauga, 275-278.
Gates, Horatio, 202.
Geary, J. W., his part in the storming of Lookout Mountain, 305.
Gettysburg, battle of, 98.
Grand Gulf, evacuation of, 230.
Granger, Gordon, 274, 278; placed in command of the two corps of McCook and Crittenden, 285; at Missionary Ridge, 312.
Granny White's house at battle of Nashville, 351, 355.
Grant, U. S., 20; his early life, 43; made brigadier-general of volunteers, 44; seizes Cairo and Paducah, 45; his remark on the battle of Belmont, 51; his great victory at Fort Donelson, 58-65; made major-general of volunteers, 66; ill-treated by Halleck, 66-69; his love of whiskey, 69; at the battle of Shiloh, 71-100; in command at Corinth, 154, 155; his movements at and capture of Vicksburg, 186-247; insecurity of his position at Oxford, 194; his retreat to Grand Junction, 200; his big ditch, 212; the critical moment in his career, 230-234; appointed to command all the forces west of the Alleghanies, 285; his victory at Chattanooga, 303-315; appointed lieutenant-general with chief command of the armies of the United States, 317-319; in his first Virginia campaign outgeneralled by Lee, 320; as a manœuvrer, 321, 322; his impatience at the delay of Thomas in attacking Hood at Nashville, 346-349.
Grierson, B. H., 234.

Haines Bluff, fall of, 240.
Halleck, H. W., 34, 54; his unfairness to Grant, 66-69; 71, 133-136, 138, 140-148, 153, 156, 157, 159; made general-in-chief,147; 186-189, 195, 200, 203, 204, 206, 234; snubbed by Rosecrans, 254.
Hamilton, Schuyler, 106; at Corinth, 187.

Index

Hampton Roads, naval battle in, 116.
Hardee, W. J., at Shiloh, 79, 94; at Stone river, 162.
Harriet Lane, the sloop, 129.
Hartford, the frigate, 117, 124, 224.
Harvey, W. S., 14, 22.
Hazen, William, seizes the heights at Brown's Ferry, 290; at Missionary Ridge, 313.
Herron, F. J., 197.
Hildebrand's brigade at Shiloh, 82.
Hill, D. H., 265.
Holly Springs, capture of, 198, 199.
Hood, J. B., supersedes Johnston, 328; his early career, 328; his reputation as a fighter, 329; evacuates Atlanta, 330; assumes the offensive, 331; his plan of invading Tennessee, 332, 333; his fatal delay at Tuscumbia, 333; his northward march, 337; arrival before Nashville, 344.
Hooker, Joseph, sent with two corps to the relief of Chattanooga, 284; takes possession of Lookout valley and defeats Longstreet, 291; moves against Bragg's left at Rossville, 300; storms Lookout Mountain, 303–306; resigns and goes home, 329.
Hornet's Nest, the, at Shiloh, 84, 85, 92.
Howitzers and siege guns sent from Baton Rouge to St. Louis, 15.
Hull, Isaac, 109.
Hunter, David, 33, 225.
Hurlbut, S. A., at battle of Shiloh, 74, 83, 84, 86, 94; at Bolivar, 187; in the Vicksburg campaign, 208.

Indianola, the ram, 222.
Indians, in battle of Pea Ridge, 35.
Island No. 10, 46, 101–106.
Itasca, the gunboat, 122.

Jackson, battle of, 236.
Jackson, Andrew, 116, 127.
Jackson, Claiborne, 10–22.
Jackson, Stonewall, 264, 352.
Jefferson Barracks, 19.
Jefferson City, United States flag raised at, 23.
Johnson, Andrew, 157, 158.
Johnston, A. S., 53, 55, 56, 70, 72, 75, 76, 81, 84–86; killed at Shiloh, 84; his tactical work there, 85.
Johnston, J. E., 196, 197, 232–240, 242–245, 247; his Atlanta campaign, 324–327; a master of Fabian strategy, 325.
Johnston, W. P., 55, 88.

Katahdin, the gunboat, 123.
Kenesaw Mountain, battle of, 327.

Kentucky, importance of, in 1861, 5; her attempted attitude of neutrality, 39; defect in Bragg's strategy in, 152.
Kineo, the gunboat, 123.
King's Mountain, 249.

Lake Providence experiment at Vicksburg, 213, 214.
Lee, R. E., small progress made against him, 7; 43, 148, 151, 264; the only way to dispose of him, 323.
Lee, S. D., at battle of Nashville, 351, 354, 356–358.
Lexington, Missouri, siege of, 30–32.
Lexington, the gunboat, 86.
Lincoln, Abraham, 8, 10, 12, 22, 29, 39, 66, 68, 69, 108, 114, 151, 157, 203–207, 225, 247, 285, 295, 331.
Lindell's Meadow at St. Louis, 13.
Logan, J. A., his journey to Louisville, 348.
Longstreet, James, at Chickamauga, 267, 269, 271, 275, 282; sent by Bragg into eastern Tennessee, 293–297, 314.
Lookout Mountain, 258, 281; stormed by Hooker, 303–306.
Louisiana, the ram, 119, 127, 129.
Lovell, Mansfield, 119, 127.
Lusk, W. H., 23.
Lyon, Nathaniel, 10–28; visits Camp Jackson in disguise, 16, 17; his death, 27; great qualities, 28.

McClellan, G. B., 34, 55, 67, 147, 148; superseded by Burnside, 156; 330.
McClernand, J. A., 73, 77, 82, 83, 94, 133; in the Vicksburg campaign, 202–208; 225; dismissed the service, 244.
McCook, A. McD., 54; at Shiloh, 94, 96; at Stone river, 162, 165–169; in the Chickamauga campaign, 265–268, 272, 277; removed from command, 285; his character, 286.
McCullough, B., 25, 26, 30; death of, 36.
McPherson, James, at Shiloh, 80; in the Vicksburg campaign, 208, 217, 229, 230, 232, 235, 236, 238, 243; in the Atlanta campaign, 324–329.
Madison, George, 17.
Madison, James, Bishop of Virginia, 17.
Magoffin, B., 39, 42.
Manassas, the ram, 119, 124–127.
Marlborough's campaigns, 99.
Maryland, important strategic position of, 5.
Meade, G. G., 98, 284, 321.
Memphis, capture of, 137; as a base

from which to advance against Vicksburg, 195.
Merrimac, the ram, 117, 139.
Miller, John, at Stone river, 176.
Miller, P. T., 23.
Mill Spring, battle of, 55.
Minnesota, the frigate, 109.
Missionary Ridge, 259.
Mississippi, the sloop, 123, 124.
Mississippi river, its physical characteristics, 179-181.
Missouri, importance of, in 1861, 5, 6.
Mitchel, O. M., 54; his raid in Alabama, 143.
Mitchell, John, 119.
Monitor, a dummy at Vicksburg, 222.
Monitor, the, 139.
Montgomery, Confederate surrender at Memphis, 137.
Morgan, George, 143.
Morgan, John H., 42, 149.
Morton, Oliver, 157, 158.
Mule meat at Vicksburg, 245.
Mulligan, Colonel, his gallant defence of Lexington, 31.
Mumford, hanged by B. F. Butler for hauling down the Union flag, 129, 130.
Murfreesboro, situation of, 161.
Murphy, Colonel, commander at Holly Springs, 199.

Napoleon I., 81, 97-99, 143, 166, 233, 242, 247, 349.
Napoleon III., 132.
Nashville occupied by Buell's troops, 64.
Nashville, battle of, 1, 55; delayed by a great storm of snow and ice, 348; position of Union army, 350; position of the Confederate army, 351; result of the victory, 359, 360.
Navigation laws, 111.
Negley, J. S., at Stone river, 162, 163, 169-172, 176; at Chickamauga, 270.
Negro troops in battle of Nashville, 357, 358.
Nelson, Horatio, 110.
Nelson, W., 40, 54; at Shiloh, 85, 87, 90-96; 149.
New Madrid, 46; surrender of, 102.
New Orleans, military importance of, 112.
Nullification, 116.

Oglesby, Richard J., 46.
Oneida, the corvette, 123, 124.
Opdycke, E., 339, 341.
Ord, Edward, 154, 244.

Palmer, J. M., at Stone river, 162, 163, 171-173, 175, 176.
Palmerston, Lord, 111.

Panic at the North in summer of 1862, 151.
Paris, Count of, on the Union position at Shiloh, 72; on the hanging of Mumford, 130; on the effect of withdrawing McClellan's army from the James river, 148; on the charge of Thomas's men at Missionary Ridge, 312.
Pea Ridge, battle of, 35-37, 197.
Pemberton, J. C., supersedes Van Dorn, 155; 188, 195, 197, 198, 209, 232, 233, 235-240, 242, 245-247.
Pensacola, the sloop, 117, 123, 124.
Perkins, G. H., 128.
Perry, O. H., 109.
Perryville, battle of, 153.
Petersburg, a point from which to operate against Richmond, 148.
Phœbe, the frigate, 115.
Pickett's charge at Gettysburg, 98.
Pike, Albert, 36.
Pillow, Gideon, 47, 58-63.
Pinola, the gunboat, 122.
Pittsburg, the gunboat, 105.
Pittsburg Landing, 71-100, 133.
Polk, J. K., 40.
Polk, Leonidas, bishop and general, 40; 47, 48, 70; at Shiloh, 79, 94; 101; at Stone river, 162, 164, 173, 176; at Chickamauga, 269.
Pope, John, 31, 35, 44, 69; his capture of Island No. 10, 102-106; 133, 135, 136, 147-149, 152, 156, 190, 321.
Port Gibson, battle of, 229.
Port Hudson, fortified by Van Dorn, 140; its military value, 182, 183; its enormous strength, 184, 185.
Porter, David, 114.
Porter, D. D., 114, 116, 120-122, 128, 129, 196, 219, 221-223, 227.
Porter, Fitz John, a scapegoat for Pope, 156.
Porter, W. D., 139.
Post, P. S., storms Montgomery Hill, 355; is wounded on Overton Hill, 357.
Prairie Grove, battle of, 197.
Prentiss, Benjamin, 35, 73, 78, 81-86, 92.
Price, Sterling, 21-25, 33, 154, 336.
Pulpit Rock, 286, 306.

Queen of the West, the ram, 221, 222.

Rabbit, how to cook a, 246.
Raccoon Mountain, 258, 261, 281.
Railroads, inferior to rivers as lines of communication, 193; without them the United States could not have suppressed the Southern Confederacy, 193.
Rawlins, John, 80.

Raymond, battle of, 236.
Rebel flag hauled down at St. Louis, 20.
Renshaw, W. B., 124.
Replevin, a writ of, 18.
Reynolds, J. J., at Chickamauga, 270, 271.
Richmond, battle of, 149.
Richmond, the frigate, 117.
River fleet, importance of, 107, 108.
Rivers, their importance as lines of communication, 193.
Roanoke, the frigate, 108.
Roberts, G. W., at Stone river, 170.
Ropes, J. C., 93, 97, 148, 152, 159, 335.
Rosecrans, W. S., succeeds Pope at Corinth, 147; his battle at Iuka, 154; his victory over Van Dorn at Corinth, 155; supersedes Buell, 160; his battle at Stone river, 161-177; manœuvres Bragg out of Chattanooga, 226, 227; snubs Halleck, 254; seeds of disaster in his extension of front, 262-264; superseded by Thomas, 285.
Round Forest, the, in the battle of Stone river, 173, 174.
Rousseau, L. H., at Stone river, 162, 163, 165, 171, 172.
Rudge, Barnaby, 277.

St. Louis, a committee of safety appointed in, 12; Planters' Hotel at, 22; U. S. arsenal at, 10, 13.
Savannah, Tennessee, 71, 72, 74-77, 79, 91, 92.
Scapegoats for the disasters of 1862, 156.
Schofield, J. M., in the Atlanta campaign, 324-329; 335; crosses Duck river, 338; retreats from Franklin, 338, 339; retreats upon Nashville, 344; at battle of Nashville, 350, 353-358.
Scott, Winfield, 12, 34.
Semmes, Raphael, 109.
Seven Days' battles, the, 147.
Seward, W. H., 108.
Sheridan, Philip, at Stone river, 162, 166, 168-171; at Chickamauga, 278; at Missionary Ridge, 313.
Sherman, W. T., 20; at the battle of Shiloh, 73, 76-78, 82, 83, 92, 94, 99; on the reason why the Confederates were not pursued after Shiloh, 99; at Memphis, 187; his defeat at Chickasaw bayou, 200-202; in the Vicksburg campaign, 208-210, 219, 226, 229, 232, 234-238, 240-244, 246; goes from Mississippi to the relief of Chattanooga, 295-297; his stealthy advance toward the north end of Missionary Ridge, 298, 299; reaches the north end of Missionary Ridge and finds it occupied by the enemy, 301-303; assaults the enemy before him, 308; his defence of Grant's hammering policy, 320; his Atlanta campaign, 323-330; leaves Hood and marches to the sea-coast, 330.
Shiloh, battle of, 71-100; terrible slaughter at, 99; significance of the battle, 100.
Shy Hill, in battle of Nashville, 356-358.
Sigel, Franz, 24-26.
Sill, Joshua, 166.
Simmons, Samuel, 14, 16, 17.
Smith, A. J., moves from Missouri to reinforce Thomas, 336; his arrival at Nashville, 344; at battle of Nashville, 350, 354-358.
Smith, C. F., 46, 58, 59, 62, 67, 68, 71, 74; his charge at Fort Donelson, 62.
Smith, E. K., 143, 146, 149, 150, 152.
Smith, W. F., called "Baldy," his beautiful scheme for raising the siege of Chattanooga, 287-292.
Snake Creek Gap, where Sherman lost a golden opportunity, 325, 326.
Stanley, David, 335, 338.
Stanton, E. M., 185, 203.
Steedman, J. B., 336.
Stone, Henry, 339.
Stone river, battle of, 161-177; Confederate position at, 161, 162; Union position at, 162, 163; defect in the Union position at, 163-167; disastrous beginning, 168; the day saved by Sheridan, 169-171; and by Thomas, 172-174; Union victory, 176; terrible slaughter at, 173, 177; results of, 178.
Street car, colloquy in, 20.

Taylor, Richard, 223.
Tennessee river, 44, 52.
Thomas, G. H., 54, 55; arrival at Shiloh, 97; refuses to take command in place of Buell, 153; his high opinion of Buell, 159; at Chickamauga, 268-270, 272-278; supersedes Rosecrans, 285; captures Orchard Knob and neighbouring hills, 300; the charge of his men against Bragg's centre on Missionary Ridge, 310-313; in the Atlanta campaign, 324; sent back to Nashville to look after Hood, 331; his forces, 335-337; cause of his delay in attacking Hood at Nashville, 345; annihilates Hood's army at Nashville, 350-359; result of the victory, 359, 360; brilliancy of his tactics at Nashville, 354.

Tilghman, commandant of Fort Henry, 56.
Tiptonville, 102, 105.
Tyler, the gunboat, 86, 139.

Ulm, 247.
"Unconditional surrender," 63, 65.

Van Cleve, H. P., at Stone river, 163, 168, 171, 172, 176.
Van Dorn, E., 35, 71, 134, 138–140; left by Bragg to cover Vicksburg, 145; superseded by Pemberton, 155; 186, 234; captures Holly Springs, 198, 199; death of, 253.
Varuna, the corvette, 123, 124.
Vicksburg, fortified by Van Dorn, 138; its military importance, 182, 183; its unapproachableness, 184, 185; assaults upon, 243; surrender of, 246, 247.
Virginia, importance of, in the Civil War, 2–4.

Walke, Henry, 104.
Wallace, Lew, 5, 58–62; at battle of Shiloh, 74, 77, 79–81, 90, 94–97; 133.
Wallace, William, 74, 83; killed at Shiloh, 86.
Warren, Joseph, 27.
Webster, Daniel, 68.
Welles, Gideon, 116.
Wellington, Duke of, 191.
Westfield, the gunboat, 124.
West Virginia, beginning of, 3.
Wheeler, Joseph, 283.
Willich, at Stone river, 167.
Wilson, J. H., takes command of Thomas's cavalry, 336; his cavalry fight at Franklin, 343.
Wilson's Creek, battle of, 26–28.
Wissahickon, the gunboat, 123.
"Woman order," so called, of B. F. Butler, 131.
Wood, T. J., 54; arrival of, at Shiloh, 97; at Stone river, 163, 168, 169, 171; at Chickamauga, 270, 271; at Missionary Ridge, 313; at battle of Nashville, 350, 351, 353–358.

Yazoo Pass experiment at Vicksburg, 214–218.

Zollicoffer, F. K., 41, 53, 55.

WRITINGS OF JOHN FISKE

Historical

THE DISCOVERY OF AMERICA

With some Account of Ancient America and the Spanish Conquest. With a Steel Portrait of Mr. Fiske, many maps, facsimiles, etc. 2 vols. crown 8vo, gilt top, $4.00.

The book brings together a great deal of information hitherto accessible only in special treatises, and elucidates with care and judgment some of the most perplexing problems in the history of discovery. — *The Speaker* (London).

OLD VIRGINIA AND HER NEIGHBOURS

2 vols. crown 8vo, gilt top, $4.00.
Illustrated Edition, 2 vols. 8vo, $8.00, *net*.

History has rarely been invested with such interest and charm as in these volumes. — *The Outlook* (New York).

THE BEGINNINGS OF NEW ENGLAND

Or, the Puritan Theocracy in its Relations to Civil and Religious Liberty. Crown 8vo, $2.00. Illustrated Edition. Containing Portraits, Maps, Facsimiles, Contemporary Views, Prints, and other Historic Materials. 8vo, gilt top, $4.00, *net*.

Having in the first chapters strikingly and convincingly shown that New England's history was the birth of centuries of travail, and having prepared his readers to estimate at their true importance the events of our early colonial life, Mr. Fiske is ready to take up his task as the historian of the New England of the Puritans. — *Advertiser* (Boston).

THE DUTCH AND QUAKER COLONIES IN AMERICA

With 8 Maps. 2 vols. crown 8vo, gilt top, $4.00
Illustrated Edition, 2 vols. 8vo, $8.00, *net*.

The work is a lucid summary of the events of a changeful and important time, carefully examined by a conscientious scholar, who is master of his subject. — *Daily News* (London).

NEW FRANCE AND NEW ENGLAND

With Maps. Crown 8vo, $2.00.
Illustrated edition. *Containing about 200 Illustrations. 8vo, gilt top, $4.00, net.*

This volume presents in broad and philosophic manner the causes and events which marked the victory on this continent of the English civilization over the French.

THE AMERICAN REVOLUTION

With Plans of Battles, and a Steel Portrait of Washington. 2 vols. crown 8vo, gilt top, $4.00. Illustrated Edition. *Containing about 300 Illustrations. 2 vols. 8vo, gilt top, $8.00, net.*

Beneath his sympathetic and illuminating touch the familiar story comes out in fresh and vivid colors. — *New Orleans Times-Democrat.*

THE CRITICAL PERIOD OF AMERICAN HISTORY, 1783-1789

With Map, Notes, etc. Crown 8vo, gilt top, $2.00. Illustrated Edition. *Containing about 170 Illustrations. 8vo, gilt top, $4.00, net.*

The author combines in an unusual degree the impartiality of the trained scholar with the fervor of the interested narrator — *The Congregationalist* (Boston).

THE WAR OF INDEPENDENCE

In Riverside Library for Young People. With Maps. 16mo, 75 cents.

THE MISSISSIPPI VALLEY IN THE CIVIL WAR

With 20 Maps and Plans. 1 vol. crown 8vo, $2.00.

A HISTORY OF THE UNITED STATES FOR SCHOOLS

With Topical Analysis, Suggestive Questions, and Directions for Teachers, by F. A. Hill, and Illustrations and Maps. Crown 8vo. $1.00, net, postpaid.

Religious and Philosophical

THE DESTINY OF MAN

Viewed in the Light of His Origin. 16mo, gilt top, $1.00.

Of one thing we may be sure : that none are leading us more surely or rapidly to the full truth than men like the author of this little book, who reverently study the works of God for the lessons which He would teach his children. — *Christian Union* (New York).

THE IDEA OF GOD

As Affected by Modern Knowledge. 16mo, gilt top, $1.00.

The vigor, the earnestness, the honesty, and the freedom from cant and subtlety in his writings are exceedingly refreshing. He is a scholar, a critic, and a thinker of the first order. — *Christian Register* (Boston).

THROUGH NATURE TO GOD

16mo, gilt top, $1.00.

CONTENTS. — The Mystery of Evil; The Cosmic Roots of Love and Self-Sacrifice; The Everlasting Reality of Religion.

The little volume has a reasonableness and a persuasiveness that cannot fail to commend its arguments to all. — *Public Ledger* (Philadelphia).

LIFE EVERLASTING

16mo, gilt top, $1.00 net. Postage 7 cents.

This brief work is a contribution to the evolution of the theory of evolution on lines which are full of the deepest suggestiveness to Christian thinkers. — *The Congregationalist.*

OUTLINES OF COSMIC PHILOSOPHY

Based on the Doctrine of Evolution, with Criticisms on the Positive Philosophy. In 4 volumes, 8vo, $8.00.

You must allow me to thank you for the very great interest with which I have at last slowly read the whole of your work. . . . I never in my life read so lucid an expositor (and therefore thinker) as you are. — CHARLES DARWIN.

DARWINISM, AND OTHER ESSAYS

Crown 8vo, gilt top, $2.00.

MYTHS AND MYTH-MAKERS

Old Tales and Superstitions interpreted by Comparative Mythology. Crown 8vo, gilt top, $2.00.

THE UNSEEN WORLD

And Other Essays. Crown 8vo, gilt top, $2.00.

EXCURSIONS OF AN EVOLUTIONIST

Crown 8vo, gilt top, $2.00.

Miscellaneous

A CENTURY OF SCIENCE

And Other Essays. Crown 8vo, $2.00.

Among our thoughtful essayists there are none more brilliant than Mr. John Fiske. His pure style suits his clear thought. — *The Nation* (New York).

CIVIL GOVERNMENT IN THE UNITED STATES

Considered with some Reference to its Origins. With Questions on the Text by Frank A. Hill, and Bibliographical Notes by Mr. Fiske. Crown 8vo, $1.00, net; postpaid.

It is most admirable, alike in plan and execution, and will do a vast amount of good in teaching our people the principles and forms of our civil institutions. — MOSES COIT TYLER, *Professor of American Constitutional History and Law, Cornell University*

HOUGHTON MIFFLIN COMPANY